STRANGE THINGS DONE

MCGILL-QUEEN'S NATIVE AND NORTHERN SERIES
BRUCE G.TRIGGER, EDITOR

Strange Things Done

Murder in Yukon History

Ken S. Coates
William R. Morrison

McGill-Queen's University Press
Montreal & Kingston · London · Ithaca

© McGill-Queen's University Press 2004
ISBN 0-7735-2705-2

Legal deposit second quarter 2004
Bibliothèque nationale du Québec

Printed in Canada on acid-free paper that is 100% ancient forest free (100% post-consumer recycled), processed chlorine free.

This book has been published with the help of a grant from the Canadian Federation for the Humanities and Social Sciences, through the Aid to Scholarly Publications Programme, using funds provided by the Social Sciences and Humanities Research Council of Canada. Funding has also been received from the Research Office of the University of British Columbia and the President's Publication Fund of the University of Saskatchewan.

The authors and McGill-Queen's University Press wish to thank the editors of *Arctic* for permission to republish material included in chapter 6, and the editors of *The Western Historical Quarterly* for permission to republish material included in chapter 7.

McGill-Queen's University Press acknowledges the support of the Canada Council for the Arts for our publishing program. We also acknowledge the financial support of the Government of Canada through the Book Publishing Industry Development Program (BPIDP) for our publishing activities.

National Library of Canada Cataloguing in Publication

Coates, Kenneth, 1956-
 Strange things done: murder in Yukon history/Ken S. Coates, William R. Morrison.
 (McGill-Queen's native and northern series; 40)
 Includes bibliographical references and index.
 ISBN 0-7735-2705-2

 1. Murder – Yukon Territory – History. 2. Trials (Murder) – Yukon Territory – History. 3. Yukon Territory – History – 1895- I. Morrison, William R. (William Robert), 1942- II. Title.

 HV6535.C32Y85 2004   364.15'23'097191   C2003-906893-5

This book was typeset by Dynagram Inc. in 10.5/13.5 Palatino.

Contents

Illustrations and Maps

MAPS

Of Villains, Victims, Judges, and Hangmen: Understanding Our Fascination with Murder

What is so fascinating about murder? Why do television programs and movies dwell on it so much? Why will people who are indifferent to matters that really affect their lives – politics, the economy, and so forth – sit riveted in front of a television set for hours and months watching a spectacle such as the O.J. Simpson trial, which other than the obvious effect on the murderer and the victims, touched nothing but people's sense of decency and fairness. Bookstores carry shelves of "true crime" stories, and there can hardly be a modern psychopathic killer who does not have his own biographer. Dozens of popular writers have become rich through writing crime fiction. From Agatha Christie, whose murder mysteries had a genteel touch and who sold hundreds of millions of volumes, to Thomas Harris, creator of Hannibal Lecter, the iconic monster of our generation, books about murder have been best-sellers. Every time an execution is carried out in Huntsville, Texas, the execution capital of North America, crowds pro and con gather outside the prison walls shouting slogans. The O.J. Simpson trial, a mixture of the grotesque, the appalling, and the simply tacky, captured the attention of the world, highlighting the continued existence of racial friction in the United States and revealing some of the weaknesses of the American criminal justice system. The name of the infamous murderer Theodore Bundy is a household word in America, but how many who know it can name the

winner of a Nobel prize? We in Canada have our own sociopaths –
the egregious child killer Clifford Olson, and more recently Karla
Homolka and Paul Bernardo – whose cases tested the resistance to
nausea of the most hardened observer. In these affairs there were a
number of appalling sideshows: Olson's parole hearing gave him
an opportunity to mock his victims' families; the Toronto *Globe and
Mail*, in the name of freedom of speech and the public's right to
know, went to court to seek the release of the videotapes of Bernardo torturing his victims; and it is reported that Bernardo gets
several friendly letters a week from female admirers.

Perhaps the essential fascination with murder is that it echoes
our own mortality. The victims of killers all have one thing in common, trite as it is to point out the fact: they are all dead, and they
have not died in the manner that we would wish to die – peace-
fully and with dignity. Public rage against the brutality of murder
must be based partly on the fear and horror with which people
imagine themselves in the shoes of the victims. We want to know
how the victims got into the deadly situation. Do we make the mistakes they did? Could it happen to us? And we wonder if in certain circumstances we all might have the potential to kill. Is there a
bit of the killer in each of us?

The answer, perhaps, is yes, for most murders are not of the Ol-
son/Bernardo variety – those committed by men who truly seem to
be from another universe, so anti-human are their impulses. Most
murders are far more mundane than these high-profile cases. They
typically involve disputes between people who know each other –
spouses, friends, acquaintances – often sparked by drunkenness or
drug use. Rarely do they show ingenuity, planning, or deception,
and their details are sordid rather than fascinating. Where the interest lies in these cases is not so much in their details as in the dexter-
ity shown by the defence lawyers who attempt to make a legal silk
purse out of a sow's ear. Can a lawyer schooled in pop psychology
convince a jury that it is possible for a man to sleepwalk for three
hours, stab his wife forty times, and dispose of her body, all without
being conscious of the act? Will a jury buy the proposition that ex-
cessive consumption of junk food (the "Twinkie defence") or too
much television watching can diminish the responsibility for homicide? One never knows, but the fact that the questions arise is a de-
pressing commentary on the state of modern criminal justice.

This book is about murder, but it is also about a particular society, one isolated by distance and climate from the rest of the world, a marginal society in many ways, where acts of violence could send tremors throughout the social order. A number of representative cases have been chosen, all different in many respects and all illuminating different aspects of Yukon society, from the earliest days of penetration by outsiders to World War II. The first is the Nantuck case, one of the rare instances in which Native people committed acts of violence against whites and the only such case in the Yukon that ended in murder and execution. The Nantuck affair, which took place at the height of the gold rush, a particularly turbulent and stressful period in the region's history, reveals the racial fears that underlay Yukon society. Perhaps surprisingly, it was the only case of its type in the Yukon,[1] though this was probably largely because the whites and First Nations lived apart in the territory throughout much of its history.

The second case, that of Fournier and Labelle, shows that criminal thuggery of a very ordinary kind also existed in the Yukon. This case, which involved detective work and a pursuit across much of North America, is a classic of the "they always get their man" genre associated with the North-West Mounted Police. The Elfors case, which is examined next, is a fine example of the individual who broke the "law of the Yukon," the code of mutual trust and interdependence that made the territory habitable; and the Gogoff case, in chapter 5, is an example of the typical "other" – the man who is marginalized by society, in this case because he was foreign and mentally ill.

Alikomiak and Tatamigana, the subjects of chapter 6, illustrate the exotic in northern life. They too were "others," but this was because their culture was so strange to the colonial powers governing their land that it was as though they had come from a different planet. In chapter 7, the case of Paddy Duncan brings us into a relatively modern age, when bureaucracy and the press began to play active roles in these cases. Not coincidentally, this is the only major case in this book in which the killer was not executed; it is also an example of murder between First Nations people, and it has its own dynamics. Finally, the cases in chapter 8 bring in a variety of themes, some specific to the Yukon, others more general. The appendix deals with historical writing on the subject of murder.

This ticket was issued to permit a spectator to witness the hanging of
Peter Fournier and Edward Labelle on 20 January 1903 (National
Archives of Canada [NA], PA-205087).

The shelves of libraries groan with the weight of books on murder.
They fall into two types: "true crime" books, which are narrative accounts of cases; and academic/scientific studies of killers and cases.
In the first category, the best go beyond mayhem and gore to put the
cases in their social settings, and they try to assess their importance
as more than merely sensationalist episodes. Probably the most famous of these books in North America are Truman Capote's *In Cold
Blood* and Vincent Bugliosi's *Helter Skelter*.[2] Paul Bernardo, Canada's
own homicidal psychopath, is the subject of several books.[3] A sub-
category of this is the special pleading, of which Joyce Milgaard's
book about her falsely imprisoned son is a recent Canadian example.[4] The books in the second category are written by psychologists
and criminologists, and are generally directed at academics. But
there are some books that study murder across time and, though
containing statistics, are aimed at a general readership: Roger Lane's
excellent study, *Murder in America*, is a fine example of this type. As
well, there are innumerable scholarly articles on the subject.

This book tends to the first category more than the second, for it
is not a systematic study of murder. No attempt has been made
here to write a statistical survey of the subject – to find out what
percentage of killings ended in charges being laid or what number
of murder trials ended in acquittals (in the early days in the

North, few, if any). Rather, it is a study of cases selected to show different aspects of the social history of the Yukon. In this way it is a study of the Yukon Territory, not of murder per se. The cases themselves are, we hope, interesting, but they are not bizarre in the way such cases as the Manson murders are. In fact, they are "ordinary," in the sense that they reflect ordinary aspects of territorial life.

The current fascination with murder cases has been attributed to a modern fear of violence in society, a fear that seems irrational, given the fact that the rates of murder and other violent crimes have been falling in recent years, perhaps because the population is getting older and thus less murderous.[5] We live in a fearful age, where each outrage is presented in vivid and eventually tedious detail on the television news networks. The assertion that we identify with these cases in some way is supported by the fact that death among groups that are not close to us – prostitutes, biker gangs, drug dealers, for instance – do not generate nearly as much concern as, say, a suburban slaughter of the type that took place outside Denver, Colorado, in the spring of 1999. When high school students who could be one's own children are cut down, the middle classes sense that the bell tolls for them and for their families. Gang murders do not have the same resonance.

Public reaction to murder, therefore, is strongly influenced by class and status. When a despairing crack-addicted mother in the slums kills her children, our reaction is sadness and disgust (if we hear of the incident, which we usually do not); when a middle-class woman drowns her children in an attempt to win back her boyfriend's love, it is national front-page news, and our reaction is shock and horror. Race has traditionally played a strong part in the public reaction to murder. Historically, in the United States, murders in which the victim was white and the killer black led to outbreaks of hysteria, sometimes culminating in the mob ritual of lynching; but when the victim was black and the murderer white, the killer often escaped punishment. Although the era of lynching has passed, the "race card" is still played in the criminal justice system, most notably in the Simpson trial, though there the outcome was the reverse of what it would have been two generations earlier.

Murder, and the legal process that follows it, is a kind of theatre, a theatre of the macabre. It highlights the pathologies of our communities, and we are drawn to it because it reveals elements of our society that we find impossible to ignore: deviance, violence, anger, hatred, frustration, malevolence, greed, mental illness, cruelty. All of these are the stuff of drama. Like a theatrical production, a murder case has moments of high drama, tension, quiet and calm, stress, and release. The arrest of the suspect, the conviction, and sentencing provide a kind of relief, a confirmation that order has been restored, the cancer excised, and the fear allayed, if only temporarily. Execution has an even more cathartic effect on those who favour it. Murders and the ensuing events play with public emotions, generating not only fear and release but paranoia and the desire for revenge. To understand a society's murders is to learn a great deal about the tensions that lie beneath the surface.

For the historian, murder offers powerful tools for exploring social and public order and society's conventions. Murder reveals the authority of the state and the ultimate power that it holds over the lives of its citizens. The public fascination with the subject helps the historian, for murder is a rare event – surprisingly rare, given the complexity of human beings. But when it happens, the lives of ordinary people are exposed in a blaze of publicity, and details that normally would pass unnoticed are collected, saved, and analysed. The police and especially the courts keep careful records, which provide wonderful material for historians. When a murder occurs, and particularly a murder trial, a record is created of the social pathology of a community, often disclosing facts that would otherwise never be known. It provides a window into important aspects of a society – its social, ethnic, cultural, gender, racial, economic, and even political structure.

As historians, our interest in murder is more than merely sensationalist (though we must admit that this aspect does exist); it gives a view of the underbelly of society, of the tensions, emotions, and fears that move a particular population at a particular time and shows how the population responds to them. In this book we have chosen to study murders that occurred in Canada's Yukon Territory, partly because we are historians who study the North and partly because the Yukon was at one time a very closed society, geographically and socially, in which murders, though not particularly frequent, loomed very large.

The literary landscape of the Canadian North is full of stories of northern desperadoes, miners driven mad by cabin fever, Dangerous Dan McGrew battling for gold and a lady's affections, and claim jumpers moving in on an honest prospector's holdings. The reality is more prosaic. Or is it? A case of alleged murder in the Yukon involving two miners, George Daunt and Robert Truswell, fits the standard image almost perfectly. Both men, who had adjoining claims near Bonanza Creek, had reputations as eccentric loners. Truswell, who once hit a man in a Dawson City casino with a piece of wood, was known as Two-by-Four Bob. Add to the mix the most volatile fuel in Yukon history – claims to gold-bearing ground – and the scenario is almost perfectly sketched. Dawsonites were shocked when, on a hot summer night, Daunt allegedly shot Truswell to death near his shack. The episode is the stuff of Robert Service poetry or Jack London's short stories, and is clearly a case for Sergeant Preston of the Mounted. But there are two interesting things about this story. First, nothing exactly like this happened in the years when the Klondike goldfields were among the most famous places in the world. Second, this case occurred not in 1897 but in the summer of 2003, just as we finished writing this book. Life, it seems, does imitate fiction; as a reporter for the Whitehorse *Yukon News* commented, "People up in Dawson say gold does funny things to people."[6]

Acknowledgments

Writing the acknowledgments for a book is one of the more pleasant tasks associated with authorship, and we are happy to proclaim the fact that this work has been built with the contributions of many different people. *Strange Things Done* has had a long gestation, growing out of our interest in Yukon history, which goes back many years and has produced *Land of the Midnight Sun, The Sinking of the Princess Sophia*, and other works. Our task was aided, as it has so often been, by the exceptionally helpful archivists we encountered along the way, particularly those in the National Archives of Canada and the Yukon Archives. We have often imposed on their time and talents, and have been delighted with their input and suggestions. We draw particular attention to Douglas Whyte, with whom we have worked over the years in both Whitehorse and Ottawa, and who epitomizes the contributions of the scholar-archivists who are so central to the study of history in Canada.

At the universities where we taught over the past ten years we have been surrounded by engaging and exemplary professional colleagues and stimulated by the work of our undergraduate and graduate students. In the early 1990s we had the wonderful opportunity of working together during the formulative years of the University of Northern British Columbia, an assignment that refuelled our commitment to northern scholarship and reminded us of the important subtleties of northern life. One of us stayed at UNBC, while the other went to the University of Waikato, New Zealand, then to the University of New Brunswick in Saint John, and then to the University of Saskatchewan, each move involving the relocation of boxes of murder files relating to the Yukon Territory. While in New Zealand, the files were pressed into service for an assignment in a historical methods class, and the subsequent discussion with Kiwi students about the relevance of murder as a means of explicating historical processes proved invaluable.

If this book has taken too long to write, it is not for want of input from dozens of students and colleagues, and our students Al Grove, Bruce Shelvey, and David McCrady must be singled out for special mention. A number of colleagues, including Greg Poelzer, Mary-Ellen Kelm, Ted Binnema, and Robin Fisher at UNBC, Bill Waiser and Jim Miller at the University of Saskatchewan, and Philip Hart at the University of Waikato, provided useful insights, comments, and discussions. Bill Waiser's willingness to read an early version of the manuscript was particularly welcome, for he helped us tighten up a wandering and unfocused work. We are particularly grateful to the members of the northern Canadian history class at the University of Saskatchewan, whose careful reading of the manuscript offered further useful advice on how to strengthen the book.

The final stages of the preparation of this manuscript were aided in no small measure by the staff at the College of Arts and Science, University of Saskatchewan, particularly Barb Gillis and Sharon Ford, whose attention to the various drafts of the manuscript helped a great deal. During 2002–3, the staff in the Provost's Office, especially Amber McQuaig and Jennifer Simpson, did a wonderful job of making the final corrections and making sure that the deadlines were met. The two anonymous colleagues who read the manuscript for McGill-Queen's University Press made many helpful suggestions which we were glad to incorporate in the final draft. Thanks are also due to Stuart Daniel, a fine cartographer, and to our excellent copy editor, Carlotta Lemieux. We were also delighted to receive a publication grant from the Research Office at UNBC and from the President's Publication Fund at the University of Saskatchewan. We are grateful for their support. The initial research on the book was funded by a grant from the Social Sciences and Humanities Research Council of Canada.

In each book we have written – and we have been publishing together since 1985 – we have offered words of gratitude and thanks to our family members, and each time we mean it more. Perhaps this is because our families keep getting larger. Carin Holroyd insisted on this work being finished, even though she spent the last year wrestling with a very serious illness. Her love and her devotion to the power of ideas is inspirational. Bradley, Mark, Laura, Marlon, and Hana provided the motivation to write, in the hope that they will see in their father's work a belief in the importance of history, the value of scholarship, and the necessity of coming to terms with our past. Linda was, as always, supportive and tolerant of the academic personality, and Catherine, John, Claire, and Ruth – and now Graeme, in the next generation – are all that one could wish for in children and grandchildren.

We save our last words on this occasion for our friend and editor Aurèle Parisien of McGill-Queen's University Press. Aurèle does all the work of an academic editor with exemplary professionalism. He chides, pushes, cajoles, encourages, suggests, modifies, reorganizes and, when all else fails, threatens. He continues, for reasons we cannot quite fathom but greatly appreciate, to shepherd our work through the maze of grant agency and editorial board reviews. There is no doubt whatsoever that this work is significantly stronger for his many ministrations. But Aurèle's truest contribution lies beyond the technicalities of the editorial process, wonderfully adept at them as he is. Aurèle loves ideas, and he loves the continued use of the scholarly book as a primary means of sharing these ideas with a wide audience. A talented photographer, world-class theatre critic, and exemplary writer, he nonetheless sublimates much of his creative energy and talent to improving the work of others. Aurèle, if you were ever wondering if anyone noticed or cared, wonder no longer.

Ken S. Coates,
University of Saskatchewan

William R. Morrison,
University of Northern British Columbia

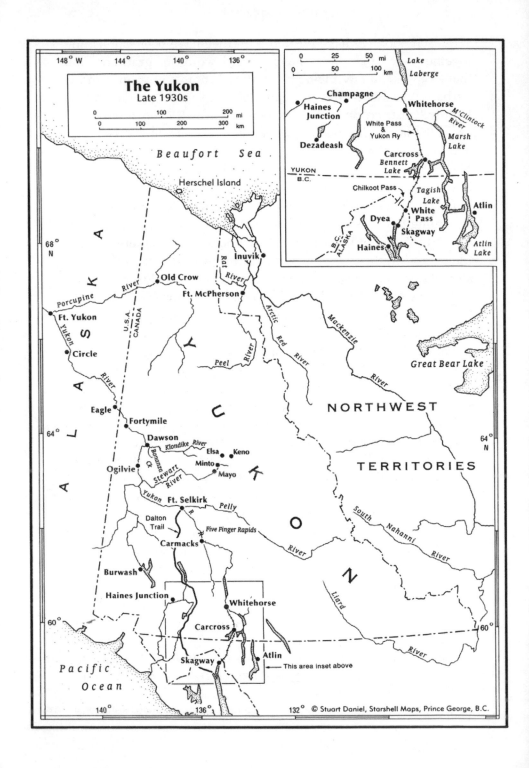

The Yukon
Late 1930s

148° W 144° 140° 136°

200 mi
100 200 300 km

Beaufort Sea

Herschel Island

Inuvik

Old Crow
Ft. McPherson

Porcupine *River*

68° N

Rat River

Ft. Yukon
Circle

Yukon River

U.S.A. CANADA

Y

Peel River

Arctic Red River

Mackenzie River

NORTHWEST

Great Bear Lake

A L A S K A

Eagle
64° **Fortymile**

Dawson *Klondike River* **Elsa** **Keno**
Bonanza Ck **Minto**
Ogilvie *Stewart River* **Mayo**

U

K

Ft. Selkirk *Pelly*
Yukon R

TERRITORIES

64° N

Dalton Trail *Five Finger Rapids*

Carmacks

O

South Nahanni River

Burwash

Haines Junction

N

Whitehorse

River

Carcross

60°
Skagway **Atlin** ← This area inset above

Liard River

60° N

Pacific Ocean

140° 136° 132° © Stuart Daniel, Starshell Maps, Prince George, B.C.

Inset (top right):

0 25 50 mi
0 50 100 km

Lake Laberge

Champagne

Haines Junction

Whitehorse

M'Clintock River

White Pass & Yukon Ry

Marsh Lake

Dezadeash

Carcross
Bennett Lake

YUKON
B.C.

Chilkoot Pass

Tagish Lake

White Pass

Dyea

Skagway

B.C. ALASKA

Haines

Atlin

Atlin Lake

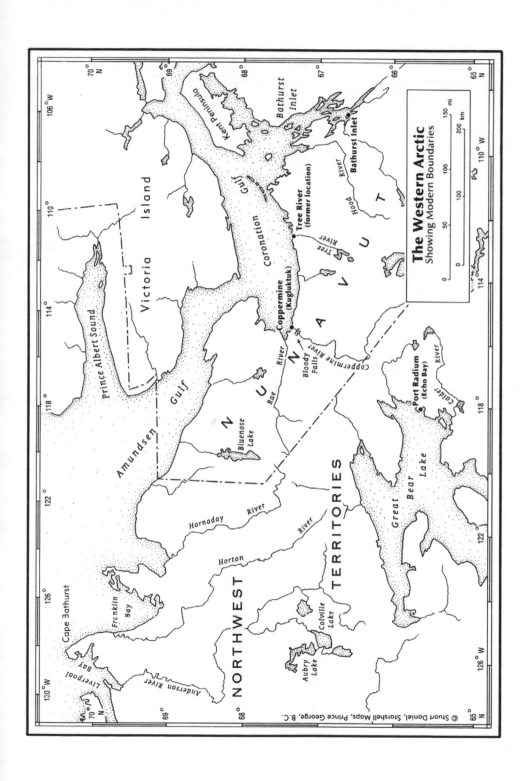

The Western Arctic
Showing Modern Boundaries

© Stuart Daniel, Starshell Maps, Prince George, B.C.

There are strange things done in the midnight sun
By the men who moil for gold
The Arctic trails have their secret tales
That make your blood run cold.

Robert Service, "The Cremation of Sam McGee"

CHAPTER ONE

The Yukon

No! There's the land. (Have you seen it?)
It's the cussedest land that I know,
From the big, dizzy mountains that screen it
To the deep, deathlike valleys below.
Some say God was tired when He made it;
Some say it's a fine land to shun;
Maybe; but there's some as would trade it
For no land on earth – and I'm one.

Robert Service, "The Spell of the Yukon"

The Yukon was and is an unusual place.[1] It was among the first parts of North America to be reached by human migration from Siberia, at least 14,000 years ago and perhaps much earlier, and First Nations people have lived continuously in the area for thousands of years. It was also one of the last parts of the continent to be settled by Europeans. The Hudson's Bay Company was the first to arrive, in the 1840s, sending a handful of traders to establish posts at Fort Selkirk and Fort Youcon (in what is now Alaska), and later at Rampart House. The first government surveyors and geologists arrived in the 1870s, at which time the area was still mostly unknown, with only a few main geographic features noted on maps. Prospecting for gold began in a small way in the late 1870s, and by 1890 there were nearly a thousand non-Native people in the Yukon.

With the discovery of gold in August 1896, the Yukon became for a time the most famous frontier district in the world. Scores of thousands of men and women set out for the instant community of Dawson City from countries as different as Canada, Japan, Britain, and New Zealand, and tens of thousands of them actually succeeded in completing the journey. On the frozen soil of the northern Yukon (created a territory in 1898) they quickly forged a unique and complex social order. The richest deposits were soon played out, and the territory fell into the hands of large mining companies, which bought up individual claims and ran them with machinery operated by wage workers. As a result, the population of the Yukon Territory fell by 90 per cent between 1898 and 1920 – from more than 40,000 to just over 4,000 people, of whom only 2,500 were non-Native. It was a tiny and isolated community, yet the society endured.

During those years, Dawson City changed from a rough frontier boomtown to a moribund company town, and the once dynamic regional society faded into near collapse. Yet the dream of prosperity lived on, and men still came north looking for another Eldorado. But it did not exist. And when the Yukon threw its heart and soul into fighting the First World War in a desperate attempt to show Canada that it too was part of the nation (it led the country in enlistments per capita, perhaps because of the number of young footloose males in the population), its society collapsed even further, though little of this affected the First Nations of the region, who had been excluded from gold rush prosperity.

A hard blow to Yukon society was struck in October 1918, when the passenger steamer *Princess Sophia* sank off the coast of Alaska, drowning all 354 passengers and crew – a significant percentage of the territory's population.[2] The Yukon limped along through the 1920s and 1930s, its tiny population sustained by dreams of future riches, along with a small tourist industry and the activities of the White Pass and Yukon Route company's railway and steamers, and by grudging support from the federal government, which kept a small administrative apparatus in place. Only with the Second World War and the decision to build the Alaska Highway was the Yukon revitalized by another invasion, this one involving thousands of soldiers and construction workers. After the war the welfare state arrived, and the Yukon was incorporated more closely into North American society.

The Yukon's image was imprinted on the consciousness of the world by the stories of Jack London and innumerable vivid newspaper accounts, but especially by the poetry of Robert Service, the "bard of the Klondike." The image was one of struggle against adversity – climate, distance, loneliness, hard work, and violence. It was an image that sold well to outsiders but did not always reflect the real face of the Yukon. It is true that there were many bad characters in Yukon society – like any frontier society, it had more than its share of thieves, professional gamblers, and thugs. It was a far more wide-open society than that found in the southern Canadian cities of the era, for gambling and prostitution were tolerated to a degree not found in Toronto or Vancouver, where they had to exist quietly on the fringes of society. In Dawson City they were always at the fore.

The confusion about the Yukon's image is partly due to false analogies with the American frontier experience. The American mining frontier has a reputation for violence and vigilantism, which, although grossly exaggerated by television and films, is essentially true. The frontier in the United States moved faster than government did, and in the typical town of the American mining frontier, local vigilante committees took on the responsibility for maintaining law and order, often after some especially horrendous series of murders. Only as the frontier phase wound down was regular authority established.

The Yukon experience was exactly the reverse: government preceded the palmy days of frontierism. Here there was no nonsense about frontier democracy.[3] The Canadian authorities took pains to make sure that the territory was heavily policed, using the North-West Mounted Police – who had proved their worth during the settling of the Prairie West – and even a portion of the regular armed forces. The NWMP were already in the Yukon when the main gold discovery was made, and they enforced the law strictly. At the same time, the territory was governed by a council appointed by the federal government, and Yukoners were not given the right to elect members to it until the gold rush had ended. The police had no objection to prostitution and gambling, feeling that these were necessary outlets in a society that was overwhelmingly male, but they were determined to preserve and demonstrate Canadian sovereignty in the region by maintaining strict public order. This is the reason why people were not permitted to carry weapons within the limits of Dawson City, and why – despite Robert Service's poetry to the contrary – no one was ever shot to death in a gold rush saloon, though drunken fist fights were, of course, endemic.

The fate that might have befallen Dawson City had the Mounted Police not ruled with an iron hand was evident in Skagway, just across the international boundary in Alaska. There was very little

Prisoners at work on the roof of the North-West Mounted Police
barracks, Dawson City, August 1901. Most prison sentences in that era
were at hard labour, and early release was seldom granted
(NA, PA-17013).

law enforcement in Skagway, just a sheriff and a few deputies, and
the town was dominated by a gangster named Soapy Smith. He
and his gang ran the town, robbing the travellers who had to run
his gauntlet on their way to the Yukon. His criminal career ended
when an upright citizen named Frank Reid confronted him with a
gun. Both were shot and died, Smith immediately, and Reid after
receiving the thanks of the community. They were buried in the
Skagway cemetery, where Smith had the posthumous last laugh;
his grave is far more popular with tourists than Reid's.

Public order prevailed in the Yukon for three reasons. First, the police were there in very large numbers. The image of the lone Mountie enforcing the law against the mob may be true in individual
cases, but on the whole there were far more lawmen in the Yukon
per capita than in other frontier communities.[4] At the height of the
rush there were more than three hundred and fifty members of the
NWMP in the Yukon, assisted by two hundred members of the Canadian army. Five hundred and fifty law officers in a community of
forty thousand is ten times the proportion for today's Canadian cit-

The "town station" of the Mounted Police in Dawson City, photographed in 1900. Dawson City was the centre of operations for the northern Yukon, and the town station was the local police station for the community (NA, PA-17152).

ies of that size. This deserves emphasis: the idea expressed by the old Texas saying "One riot, one Ranger" is completely inappropriate to the Yukon, where there were no riots, partly because there were so many law enforcement officials.

Second, the overwhelming majority of the stampeders were entrepreneurs, not bandits, and they did not want to riot; they wanted and needed order, and strongly supported the Mounted Police. There were loud complaints from miners, especially during the gold rush period, but they were directed against the incompetence and alleged corruption of government officials, and against the royalty on gold, not against the police. The miners feared being murdered or robbed, they feared the "Indian menace" (which was in fact negligible), and their ambition was to make a fortune and return south with it. Finally, the geography of the region was not kind to murderers because it made concealment difficult and escape almost impossible.

The Canadian authorities were terrified that what they perceived as American-style violence would spread into the Yukon, and they saw any assault on public order as a threat to sovereignty. They attributed their success in keeping it at bay to the virtues of the British system of governance, a boast that was largely true, since it was the strong, centralist, paternalistic way in which the Yukon was run at the time that played a large part in keeping it peaceful. *Forty Years in Canada,* the autobiography of Sir Sam Steele, who commanded the NWMP in the Yukon at the height of the gold rush, is one long paean to British paternalism and imperialism, in contrast to the alleged evils of Yankee democracy. But the authorities paid less attention to other factors that made keeping public order in the Yukon easier than it was on the American mining frontier.

One factor was the isolation. There were only a few practical routes in and out of the Yukon, unless one had the survival and bush skills to travel cross-country, which few of the miners did. The police guarded these routes and made careful lists of all those who entered and left the country, thus making it comparatively easy to find and arrest suspects. The Fournier-Labelle case shows this process at work. Then there was the climate – the long, brutally cold winters of the Klondike region (the southwestern Yukon boasts the coldest temperature ever recorded in Canada: $-63°c$, or $-80°F$, but as the locals say, "It's a dry cold"). Such a climate made social cooperation necessary and escape from the police in winter very difficult.

Another factor was that although the Yukon was large, only a small part of it – the Yukon River valley – was inhabited by non-Natives, and the mining community was a little archipelago of settlements, which was not difficult to police. In a rare example of government proactivity, the NWMP had sent a detachment of twenty to the region in 1895, so it had the tremendous advantage of being on the ground before the rush began. When the stampeders arrived, they were met by established authority and had to conform to it.

The image of gold rush violence lingers in the North partly because it serves the interests of the tourist industry and partly because of the fame of Robert Service, and in particular his two best-known poems, "The Cremation of Sam McGee" and "The Shooting of Dan McGrew." The first of these is a clever fantasy, but the second, a story of a man shot dead in a saloon, is false to the reality of Dawson City life during the gold rush. As noted above, the police rigorously enforced the prohibition on carrying fire-arms in the city, and no one was ever killed in a saloon there. Compared with American frontier mining towns in their early period, the murder rate in the Yukon was amazingly low. There were more than two hundred lynchings in the California goldfields between 1849 and 1853, but there was never a lynching in the Yukon Territory – not a threat of one, not even much loose talk of one. Given the presence of the police, such mob action was unthinkable. A study of the eastern California mining town of Bodie in the late 1870s counted thirty-one murders in six years among a population that never exceeded five thousand.[5] Twenty years later, in the 1890s, when the Yukon had a population that temporarily reached forty thousand, there were only three cases.[6]

Murder in the Yukon occurred within the First Nations population, between racial groups, and among the European population that dominated the territory after 1896. There were several murder-suicides, there were killings involving relatives and strangers, and a few that involved robbery – cases that were particularly shocking to northern society. One thing that did not occur, however, was unsolved murder. Most murders were committed in circumstances that made them easy to solve: both the killer and the victim were drunk or the case was a "crime of passion." The rare instance of planned murder turned out to be not very well planned and was easily solved, and for reasons already stated, it was not difficult to catch the killers.

The wheels of justice turned a good deal faster in 1900 than they do today. The period that elapsed between the crime and the trial (though of course it depended on how long it took the police to find the culprit and collect evidence) was not nearly as long as it is today, when a lapse of eighteen months or more is not unusual. The exceptions are the Nantuck and Henderson cases, which took place at the height of the gold rush, when a number of unique factors prolonged the period between crime and execution. Paddy Duncan's trial, for instance, took place five weeks after the crime for which he was convicted. Nor were the trials themselves long. In the Alikomiak-Tatamigana case, although a long time elapsed between the killings and the trial, the judicial process was very swift: three complete trials were conducted in two days. Paddy Duncan's trial, from the selection of the jury to the verdict and

sentencing, took place in a single day. The Gogoff trial began at
10 AM and was finished by 4 PM the same day. When the Fournier-Labelle trial went on for five full days, the judge apologized to
the jury for its length. Territorial law provided for a jury of six,
and throughout this period, only men could serve.[7]

Nor were the proceedings after the verdict prolonged. There
was nothing like the American practice today, where a byzantine
process of appeals leads to murderers living on "death row" for as
long as twenty years before their execution, permitting them to
imagine their death many times over – surely cruel and unusual
punishment by any standard. In Canada at the beginning of the
twentieth century, the process was swift. All those convicted of
murder were sentenced to death, as the law prescribed. Appeals
were promptly denied. The cases then went to the federal government to see if clemency should be extended and a sentence commuted to life imprisonment. In theory, such clemency was the
prerogative of the crown, exercised by the governor general. In
practice, the Remissions Branch of the Department of Justice made
a recommendation through the minister to the federal cabinet.
This process took place quickly, and the usual time between sentencing and hanging or commutation was only a few months.

The question of who should hang and whose sentence should
be commuted was entirely arbitrary; there were no regulations or
criteria governing the decision, so political, racial, gender, and
other considerations were bound to affect what one scholar has
called the "lottery of death." Women were very rarely executed
(twelve in Canada since 1867), and Native people were often
given the benefit of the assumption that they were not as responsible for their actions as non-Natives were. This was especially true
when they killed other Natives. From 1920 to 1957, only 62 per
cent of such cases resulted in execution; significantly, however, in
the same period, 96 per cent of Native people who killed whites
were hanged. Between Confederation and 1962, 47.4 per cent of
the 1,455 men condemned to death in Canada were hanged; the
rate for women was 21.3 per cent. Interestingly, the percentage of
executions was not, as one might think, highest in the earlier
years, declining as society became more humane in its attitudes.
In the 1870s, at which time the accused did not have a legal right
to testify and many were not represented by lawyers, the execu-

tion rate was less than 30 per cent. In the 1930s, probably because of the social turmoil of that decade, it rose to 75 per cent.[8]

The Yukon was not plagued with murder; killings took place infrequently, which is one reason why they attracted so much attention. This book is not an account of a society that lived in perpetual fear of violence; rather, it is an account of extraordinary incidents which open windows that enable us to see what society was like. There were only a few high-profile murders that attracted national attention, most notably the Alikomiak-Tatamigana case, which was exotic, and in particular the episode of the Mad Trapper of Rat River, most of which also took place just outside the Yukon and which ended in the death of the killer rather than with a trial. The killings that resulted from drunkenness, such as the Paddy Duncan case, usually did not arouse great public concern, and in fact in some instances there was a good deal of compassion for the killer and a marked public desire that the sentence be commuted. Even the cases in which there was strong public feeling against the killers, notably the Nantuck and the Fournier-Labelle cases, there was no talk of vigilantism. Yukoners had strong confidence that the police and the courts would do the right thing, and they were rarely if ever disappointed in their faith that the killers would get what they deserved. A comment about the Gogoff case from the Whitehorse *Weekly Star* makes this clear: "There are localities in which the murder of four inoffensive citizens would have been followed by summary action, but Whitehorse is not that kind of locality. Here the majesty of the law is supreme and the people have confidence that justice will be done. There is no fear on that score. The murderer will be given a fair and impartial trial and there will be no occasion for murmer [sic] at the result ... The law will determine what the consequences will be and the law will make no mistake."[9]

Certainly, there were "strange things done in the midnight sun," as Robert Service famously put it, but this was not a society obsessed with fear of murder or one in which killing was a daily event, as was supposedly the case in the American "Wild West." Most of the murders that occurred in the Yukon, like those in the rest of Canada, were simply "human tragedies."[10] Neil Boyd's study of murder at the end of the capital punishment period (the 1950s and 1960s), shows that 80 per cent of the killings were the result of social disputes of some kind, half of those being among family members; only 10 per cent involved killing for money and only 5 per cent for sex, and a final 5 per cent were committed by people who were mentally disturbed. There were too few cases in the Yukon to make a useful statistical comparison, but only one or perhaps two of the cases dealt with in this book resulted from social disputes.

Of course, not every killing results in a murder trial, and the question may be asked whether there were many deaths in the Yukon that were treated as manslaughter or were not prosecuted at all because it was felt that the killer had acted in self-defence. Such events were extraordinarily common in the United States early in the twentieth century. As Roger Lane points out,[11] in Bodie's most violent five years, of the forty men arrested for homicide, one was lynched and seven were brought to trial, but only one of these was convicted. Although we do not have the statistics for the Yukon, we confidently assert that this was not true there. The entire body of literature on the rush and the Yukon's subsequent history shows how free it was from killing (though not, of course, from assaults; there were plenty of those). It also shows that the police brought charges in cases that in other jurisdictions might never have been prosecuted (Gogoff, for instance) and that juries had no difficulty in bringing in a verdict of guilty.

The murders that took place in the Yukon provide an important means of understanding the social structure of the territory and the web of relationships that made up this interesting and important regional society. By analysing murder cases, we hope to get closer to the essence of the regional order, to understand the tensions, fears, frustrations, angers, and relationships that were woven into the social fabric of the Yukon. Such an analysis reveals aspects of northern life that are often overlooked: the mental illness, social violence, bursts of anger, the stresses brought on by climate and isolation, and the demand for protection from evildoers. The results of this analysis must be somewhat impressionistic, since the murders were so infrequent in the Yukon that it is difficult to draw firm statistical conclusions.

These murder cases do not show that Yukon society was given to brutality as a means of resolving disputes and tensions, though some of the cases were spectacularly brutal. Nor do they reveal a society in which the non-Natives lived in fear of Native violence, even though there were worries about the possibility that it might occur. What they do reveal is the many-layered relationships – of gender, ethnicity, nationality, social class, and economic position – that made up the region's social fabric.

One well-known Yukon murder is dealt with only briefly in this book (see chapter 8). This is the case of George O'Brien, who on Christmas Day 1899 shot and killed three men on the trail near Minto and threw their bodies into the Yukon River. The men were reported missing, and the bodies were discovered in the spring. O'Brien was hunted down and brought to Dawson City, where he was held in jail for over a year while the police made a case against him. He was tried and convicted on 21–22 June 1901 and hanged on 23 August. The O'Brien case is the subject of a book, M.J. Malcolm's *Murder in the Yukon: The Case against George O'Brien*, which recounts the case in great detail. Malcolm uses the device of invented conversations to move his tale along, a turgid device that we do not favour; but the book, though uncritical, gives all the facts of the case. The points we would have made in a full discussion of the O'Brien case we make instead with Fournier and Labelle in chapter 3.

Over the forty years under investigation in this book, men killed mostly with firearms. They killed their spouses, business partners, and complete strangers. They killed suddenly, without motive, or with malice aforethought. They killed as part of a planned robbery or in spontaneous rage. Some evaded capture for weeks, while others waited calmly for the police to seize them. Some went to the gallows protesting their innocence, while others confessed and apologized at the last moment. Some killers were not hanged but instead spent many years in prison. In these acts of violence lie some of the most unusual events in the history of the Yukon. If dramatic and painful events shine an unusually bright historical light on the inner workings of a culture, then the study of murder in the Yukon should provide a good opportunity to gain a better understanding of this unique northern society.

CHAPTER TWO

In the Heat of the Rush:
The Nantuck Brothers

I don't like the way those Indians act.

Billy Meehan, murder victim

The Nantuck case was the only one during the Klondike gold rush, and probably the only time in Yukon history, when First Nations people shot whites from ambush. And it is the only one dealt with in this book that caused any degree of real public alarm, as reflected in some fairly hysterical newspaper headlines. Given the marginalization of Yukon Indians during and after the gold rush, it is perhaps surprising that there were not more incidents of this sort. Part of the explanation lies in the marginalization itself. The peoples tended to live apart, the newcomers occupying a number of communities devoted to mining, in which indigenous people were not welcome. In any case, most Native people did not want to join white society. Thus, opportunities for conflict were not as frequent as one might think.

The First Nations people of what in 1898 became the Yukon Territory had lived in the region for thousands of years, probably since at least 8,000 BC. Over the millennia they had adapted to their environment, and their population in the newly formed territory had reached perhaps as much as seven or eight thousand by the time of the gold rush. These ancestors of the Athapaskan people – today's Gwich'in, Han, Tutchone, and Kaska (and Tlingit, who are from a different language group) – were hunters and gatherers, their lives governed by the seasons and the movement of game. In the north, the Gwich'in followed the Porcupine caribou during the fall migration, herding them into enclosures, or "surrounds," and killing enough animals to feed and clothe themselves. They also hunted other game, fished, and supplemented their diet with plants. In each section of the country the people adapted their lives, their seasonal movements, and their habits to make the best use of the available food resources. In the far north, the Inuit had a separate lifestyle, living mainly off the resources of the sea.

This way of life remained virtually unchanged well into the nineteenth century. European trade goods appeared in the mid-eighteenth century, brought by aboriginal middlemen from the Russians on the coast, but no Europeans came to the upper Yukon River valley until the first Hudson's Bay Company traders appeared there in the 1840s. Even then, the effect of the outsiders on the First Nations was not very great – the one exception being introduced diseases, which led to a population decline in the late nineteenth century. But as late as the Second World War, the indigenous people of the Yukon were able to maintain their way of life – hunting and gathering the produce of the land – with fairly little interference.

The reason for this was simply that what Europeans wanted from the Yukon was not the people's land but gold and other minerals, and these were concentrated in specific areas, notably the lower Klondike River valley. Even when the European population of the Yukon was at its greatest, in 1898, at the height of the Klondike gold rush, these newcomers occupied only a very small fraction of the territory. If First Nations people wanted to avoid them, it was easy to do so. During the gold rush and afterwards, they could take from the new industrial society what they wanted: some casual labour cutting cord wood for the river steamers, done in their own time, and perhaps selling meat, fish, furs, and baskets and other craft products to the miners and traders – all to produce some cash to buy goods at the trading posts. By the time the gold rush ended in 1899, sending the Yukon into a long, slow decline in population which did not reverse itself until after 1940, relations between Native and non-Native people in the territory had settled into a pattern of mutual avoidance, punctuated by periodic contact. Indigenous people were not welcome as labourers in the mines – not that such work appealed to them. Nor, for that matter, were they welcome anywhere in the wage economy. The First Nations were curiously marginalized in their own country, a situation that did not change much until the assertion of indigenous rights in the North after 1970.

The indigenous people of the Yukon were, therefore, no threat to the newcomers. But the miners, at least in the early days of the gold rush, did not know this. Moreover, thousands of them were Americans, with fresh memories of the history of relations between their government and the Natives of the western United States. The "Indian Wars," which were such a stain on the history of American westward expansion, were only just over when gold was discovered on Bonanza Creek in 1896; and the disgraceful massacre of unoffending people at Wounded Knee, the last of the major incidents in the Indian Wars, had taken place as recently as December 1890. It was to be expected, then, that many of the Klondikers would view the Natives of the Yukon with some fear, tinged with guilt. But although, on the whole, they had no reason for such fears, there was one incident that suggested the contrary. The very first murder case ever tried in the Yukon was one of four Native people accused of shooting a white man, an episode that alarmed the miners and seemed to confirm their fears.

In the spring of 1898, the great wave of Klondikers broke over the Yukon River valley. All through the summer and fall of 1897, after news of the great discovery of the previous year reached the south, thousands of men and women had come to the West Coast ports and travelled to Skagway and Dyea, climbing throughout the winter over the White and Chilkoot Passes, building boats on the shore of Lake Bennett, and waiting for the spring breakup that would permit them to float downriver to the goldfields. Two of these men were Christian Fox and William Meehan, experienced northerners who had lived in Juneau, Alaska, before heading to the Klondike.

They had got an early start that year and were travelling on the ice of the Yukon River. But towards the end of April they broke through, soaking their equipment, and were forced to stop and build a boat. We owe it to them to pause and consider what "forced to stop and build a boat" means in the context of that time and region. They had to chop down a suitable number of trees, cut them into boards with a two-handled saw, shape them, get a supply of nails, then hammer the boards into the shape of a scow, caulk the seams with pine resin or whatever they could find, and

The Nantuck brothers under arrest at Tagish. Frank, the youngest, is in the middle. The original caption reads "Indians at Tagish Post that shot Meehan and Fox on the McClintock R" (NA, PA-13424).

hope that the boat would not sink before they got to Dawson City. There was a lot of work involved in that simple phrase.

At the end of April 1898 they were camped near the mouth of the M'Clintock River, and on 2 May two Tagish men, Joe and Frank Nantuck, approached them and asked for something to eat. There were four Nantuck brothers: Frank, Joe, Dawson, and Jim. Their ages are not recorded, not even in the court records, which might seem surprising, but the omission was common in the trials of that era. A photograph taken after their arrest shows the four of them standing side by side under the watchful eye of an armed member of the North-West Mounted Police. Two of the brothers could be in their late twenties or early thirties (the judge thought that Jim, the oldest, was about twenty, but he looks older in this photo). One looks about eighteen, and the other – Frank, the youngest – no more than fifteen.

When Joe and Frank came into the camp, Fox and Meehan fed them, and over the next week the Nantuck brothers set up camp nearby and visited the two miners in a friendly fashion on several occasions. The Nantucks gave no cause for alarm, although at the end of the week, when their brother Jim arrived with two boys and three women, they fired some shots from their rifle, making Fox and Meehan somewhat uneasy, Meehan saying to his partner, "I don't like the way those Indians act."

On the morning of 10 May the two prospectors rose before dawn and caulked their new boat. The Nantuck party arrived, and Frank asked how much they would charge for a passage downriver. Fox said that he could come for free, but soon all the Nantucks left, and when they didn't return, Fox and Meehan set off in their boat about an hour before noon. They had been on the river less than half an hour when, without warning, shots were fired at them from the bank. Fox was hit, a bullet tearing through his body and knocking him over in the boat. Bleeding badly, he yelled, "Goodbye, Billy, old boy, I guess they have fixed me." More shots rang out, one hitting Meehan and fatally wounding him. Later, Fox, who survived the attack, described what happened next:

I was lying on the sacks against the side of the boat ... and I saw Joe standing with his gun like this ... and all the boys went into the brush, and I says to myself "Now they have shot us for our outfit, and are hurrying down to the next bend in the river to catch the boat ... My only show is to get to the opposite side of the river and try to make for a white habitation" ... I took the paddle in my hand and tried to paddle the boat but I was too weak, so I ... used it as a pry ... The boat ran up to a nice little level place where it was grassy and as I stepped out I stepped over the leg of my partner as he was stretched out over the boat with his head back and his mouth open and I saw that he was dead, and I said "Good by Billy, old boy, I can do nothing for you here."[1]

Creeping through the woods, afraid that the Nantucks would find and kill him, he reached a miners' camp, where his wounds were dressed and the police sent for.

The next day, Corporal H.E. Rudd of the NWMP arrived, talked to Fox, and immediately arrested Jim Nantuck, who was still in the vicinity of the crime. The other three brothers were arrested later by a "scout" (a special constable), who was left behind while Rudd searched for the body. Jim Nantuck told him (through a police interpreter) that his brothers had probably buried it, but after a search that lasted on and off for more than ten days, he changed

Members of the North-West Mounted Police pose in front of the detachment building at Tagish. It was to this building that the Nantuck brothers were brought after their arrest. No date is given, but the photograph is from the gold rush era (NA, C-000461).

his story and led the police to the corpse. It was found in the river near the scene of the crime, weighted with a pickaxe. A coroner's inquest held on 28 May revealed that there were three bullet holes in the body. A valise with Fox and Meehan's names on it was found in the Nantucks' possession, along with some food belonging to the two men and some other articles.

During this time the Nantucks, having been advised of their rights, made a number of statements to the police. Jim Nantuck admitted putting the body in the river, and Frank later said that "the biggest of the four prisoners here [in court], Jim, was boss of the outfit ... that he had arranged the positions that they were to take up before the firing commenced. He said that he, Frank, was very nervous; was trembling; the gun was shaking in his hand and he said to Jim 'I shake a lot' and Jim said 'Don't shake; you have got to do what I tell you.'"

The four were tried in sequence in this first murder trial in the Yukon. A Dawson lawyer, Henry Claude Lisle, "an advocate of many years' experience," was appointed defence council, and two interpreters were sworn in as well. On 28 July 1898, Dawson, Joe, and Jim Nantuck were arraigned before Justice Thomas H. McGuire and asked to enter a plea. According to Judge McGuire, the legal process was "very carefully and fully explained by the interpreters." Asked if they had any statement to make, the Nantucks said that they and the whites were "good friends," but that "two white men a year or so ago had killed two Indians." Joe admitted that he and Dawson had fired at Meehan intending to kill him, so a plea of guilty was entered. Jim Nantuck denied firing a shot, and a plea of not guilty was entered for him.

The trial began the same day at 2 PM. Six witnesses were called for the crown, including Frank Nantuck, who testified against his brothers. No witnesses were called for the defence, though Lisle did cross-question the prosecution witnesses and argued at the end that Joe had not fired a shot and thus was not guilty. The jury did not accept this argument, and after thirty minutes' deliberation found all three guilty. The next morning Frank was tried and found guilty, though in his case the jury recommended clemency because of his age and because he had cooperated with the police. On the afternoon of 29 July the four brothers were brought before the court and sentenced to hang on 1 November.

It was at this point that events began to go somewhat off the rails from the point of view of the authorities. The length of time between conviction and execution was long by the standards of the day (though amazingly short by modern standards – modern U.S. standards, that is, where a man was executed in Texas recently after spending nineteen years in jail). In the rest of the cases covered in this book the period was about three months, but in the Nantuck case there were no hangings for more than a year, not until 4 August 1899, when Dawson and Jim Nantuck went to the gallows. Frank and Joe had both died in jail within five days of each other – of tuberculosis – in February of that year.

The delay in execution was partly because of a serious flaw in the way the trial was conducted, though there were other reasons too – this being the territory's first murder trial and the only one in which First Nations people had killed whites. The Nantuck case is unique in Yukon history not only because of its racial nature but also because it is the only one (apart from the Alikomiak-Tatamigana murders, which, though tried in the Yukon, did not occur there) that has been extensively studied by outsiders. No fewer than three scholarly articles have been published on the Nantuck case, two from a legal and one from an anthropological perspective.[2]

The public alarm associated with the Nantuck case was undoubtedly a result of the racial factor and because of the unsettled, frontier nature of the Yukon at that time. The anthropologist Julie Cruikshank quotes headlines from the *Klondike Nugget* illustrating what she calls the "interpretive genre" of the day: "Indians Shoot White Men to Rob Them of their Supplies" (16 June 1898), "Deliberately Tried to Kill Their Benefactors for Their Outfits" (27 July), "The Treacherous Instincts of the Aborigines Will Get Their Necks Stretched with Hemp" (27 July). More significantly, she quotes a report in the *Nugget* on 3 August reflecting public unhappiness with the fact that the Nantucks refused to explain their actions or show remorse. They seemed alien from "normal" society, treacherous and insensitive. Nor would they conform to the stereotype of "noble savages":

The questions put to the murderers … showed them to be wholly deficient in the most ordinary morals. Their cunning, also, was of a low order. They could plot to destroy the two men in the boat and steal their goods but appeared to be stolidly indifferent to the results of the admissions they were making, though it was repeatedly impressed on them. Questioned about their knowledge of God or a future state everyone was surprised to find that they knew nothing about either one. Even the "Great Spirit" and the "Happy Hunting Grounds" of the North American Indians were unknown to them.

At a remove of a century, the cultural naiveté expressed by the newspaper reporter is painful to read; the business about "happy hunting grounds" makes one cringe, but it was standard for the time and for many decades afterwards. Even Judge McGuire, when commenting on Frank Nantuck's age in his summation to the jury, described him as an entirely different species: "It has been suggested that he is only 15 or 16 years of age, but it is hard to arrive at the age of indians [*sic*] by trying to compare them with white boys of the same age. He further observed that the Nantucks might be 'of a very low order of humanity,' but that did not excuse their actions."

A perfect example of the gulf between the two cultures comes from Frank Nantuck's testimony at his brothers' trial. As a crown witness, he had to be sworn in, but the usual "so help me God" formula was of no use in this case. The attempt to get him to promise to tell the truth produced the following exchange, which is worth quoting in full as an example of cultural incomprehension:

Q (By the Court) Ask him if he is a Christian.

A (Through the interpreters) No sir, he knows nothing of a Supreme being.

Q Has he any knowledge of God?

A That is what I asked him.

Q Has he any fixed and clear belief in religion at all?

A He says, he has seen the missionaries but never heard them.

Q Has he any religion of his own at all, or has he any fixed and clear belief in a future state of rewards and punishments, or does he know anything about being punished or rewarded after he dies for the good things he did while he was alive?

A He says, when he is dead he is dead – that is all I can get out of him.

Q Does he know anything about anything that will happen to him after he is dead, or does he just think that when he is dead that is the end of everything for him, just the same as a cow or moose or any other animal?

A He has no idea: I asked him if his father was alive and he said "No.", that he was dead, and I asked him where he thought he was and he said "He is dead; that's all."

Q Has he any knowledge of God at all or any idea about a future state of rewards and punishments?

A No sir.

Q Or any clear belief in religion of any kind?

A No sir.

Q Will you say to him that we want him to tell us the truth and not to tell us anything that is not the truth; that he may be punished if he tells us anything that is not the truth; that we are going to ask him some questions and that he must tell us just the truth; ask him if he will agree to do that.

MR WADE: My lord, I think I can make it clear to him – by asking him a question in English.

Q (By Mr Wade) Frank, you speak a little English; you have been studying English for some Moons and you read English a little; Now you want to tell the judge what is true and not to tell a lie.

THE INTERPRETER: He says he will tell the truth.

Q Frank, you said to Corporal Rudd that you would rather be killed than not tell the truth.

(The witness nods his head)

Q (By the Court) I want the interpreter, if he can reach his intelligence, to see if he has anything corresponding to our form of making an oath. I see that I am allowed by the statute to accept the testimony of parties making a solemn affirmation or such form as approved by the Court; now the only form by which I can reach his intelligence is this: "Frank, you know what it is to tell the truth?"

A Yes.

Q Now will you promise to tell the truth, the whole truth and nothing but the truth; now when you are asked some questions concerning this shooting will you promise to do that; solemnly affirm and declare that you will tell the truth, the whole truth and nothing but the truth?

A He says, yes.

THE COURT: Now you can ask him questions.[3]

Cruikshank's exploration of the case has gone beyond a depiction of common racism to expose an entirely different level of cultural misunderstanding. For along with the official account of the case, there was an entirely different and much more long-lasting account – that told by the First Nations of the region. Although the case caused a sensation in the miners' society, it was soon forgotten in the whirlwind of the gold rush, though it was later cited in histories of the Mounted Police as an example of how the force made the Yukon safe for miners. Julie Cruikshank quotes to this effect from a 1927 history of the police[4] and pointedly describes standard accounts, which, she says, "begin with self-righteous indignation, continue by denigrating the accused, and conclude by wallowing in tristesse about the enormity of the white man's burden."

Among the First Nations, the Nantuck case not only remained alive but had "enormous repercussions," according to Cruikshank, and became a part of First Nations oral history that persists to this day. This oral tradition suggests a very different version of the case, particularly the motive for the killing. The Nantucks had given the clue at their trial when they told McGuire that their actions had something to do with the death of some Native people at the hands of two white men a year before. McGuire ignored their words, though he included them in his written account of the case sent to the minister of justice. But the words meant something, and two First Nations elders ninety years later explained their meaning.

According to Mrs Kitty Smith, sometime before the shooting of Meehan, an old lady from Marsh Lake had found or was given a can containing a white powder which she thought was baking powder but was probably arsenic, used in the process of refining gold. She used it to bake bread and carefully fed it to a dog first before giving some to an old man and a boy. The dog did not show symptoms in time; the man and the boy both died. Angela Sidney, who was born in 1902 not far from the site of the events, gave a slightly different but essentially the same version of the story.

The point of the story and how it relates to the killing of Meehan lies in the fact that members of the same clan as the people who had been poisoned – the Crow clan – had a responsibility to avenge their death, in accordance with tradition. The usual procedure was negotiation for compensation, which was a payment of a suitable amount of goods; or, failing that, the death of a "social equivalent" of the victim. The accounts of the Yukon elders, as related to Cruikshank, suggested that "the two prospectors ... were chosen as representing the 'clan' of the white people responsible for the incident, that the prospectors were chosen as social equivalents of the deceased. The visits made by the Native men to the prospectors' camp may have been intended to give the men 'responsible' for the deaths their opportunity to open negotiations."

If true, this explanation shows how alien the value systems of European and First Nations residents of the Yukon truly were. The Nantuck brothers would have expected that the miners would open negotiations with them, and when they did not, would feel perfectly justified in killing them. From the white perspective, the story about some Indians who were accidentally poisoned was completely irrelevant to the shooting of Meehan, just some Indian nonsense hardly deserving mention.

However, another account of the poisoning exists, and it comes from the same source, Mrs Kitty Smith, who told Julie Cruikshank that some said that one or more Native people found the fatal can at an abandoned camp and that their deaths were accidental: "Somebody found that can, some white-man place. An old lady found it – an old lady just like me."[5] It would interesting, but idle, to speculate why Cruikshank cites both versions in her book, while in her article she gives only the one that exculpates the Nantuck brothers, in that they were doing their duty by enacting revenge. The other version seems to have just as good a chance of being true. After all, why would miners gratuitously poison Native people when there was no advantage and considerable risk in doing so? The version of accidental poisoning completely invalidates the Nantucks' defence and thus much of the point of Cruikshank's article.

Of course, even if the court had known of the poisoning story and believed the version more favourable to the defence, this would probably have made no difference to the outcome, since no court of that era would ever have accepted that kind of culture-based explanation as an excuse. Still another version of this story was given by Frank Nantuck at his brothers' trial when he said that they had plotted to kill the two white men because "white-men had killed two of their friends; that they found one of their bodies and the other they never did find ... one about a year [previously] and the other was about 2 years."

There are two reasons why so much time elapsed between sentence and execution in the Nantuck case. Both are elaborated in Alan Grove's article on the case.[6] The first was another murder case that took place seven months before the Nantuck affair, though the trial took place after it. Edward Henderson was an American miner heading for Dawson City with two companions, Tomberg Peterson, a Dane, and George Gale. When news of the great gold discovery reached the outside in the spring of 1897, the three men were close enough to the Klondike to get to the Yukon River valley before freeze-up that year. Henderson was plagued by a bladder condition that required him to urinate every ten or fifteen minutes, day and night, forcing him to sleep close to a tin can. His condition, which was described as "catarrh of the stomach" and involved discharge of blood as well as urine, caused him to suffer, as he said at his trial, "the tortures of the damned." He got very little sleep and was in constant pain.

One night in the autumn of 1897,[7] when the three men were camped near Marsh Lake, two in one tent and one in the other, the can of urine was upset onto Peterson's blanket. A fight ensued, in the course of which Henderson shot Peterson. He was tried on 9 August 1898 and sentenced to hang on 1 November, the same day as that fixed for the Nantucks' execution. The two cases became tangled as a result of the public reaction to them and because of the delays in carrying out the sentences.

One of the oddest things about the Henderson case was the length of time between his arrest, which occurred right after the crime, and the trial. Ten months was far longer than any of the other cases and calls for an explanation. Grove's explanation is that the authorities wanted to "appease the American miners … Once the Nantucks were convicted, it was politically safe to prosecute Henderson." But this does not explain why Henderson's trial was delayed so many months, unless the suggestion is that the authorities were waiting until some Native people committed a crime that could be tried first, which hardly seems likely. (How would anyone have known in advance that the Nantucks would carry out a murder?) In any case, the history of the Yukon shows that the miners, Americans and others, were strongly in favour of law and order and were glad to see murderers tried and hanged, regardless of race or nationality. If the Mounted Police had wanted to cater to the Americans, they could simply have charged Henderson with manslaughter, which, given the facts of the case, was a reasonable charge. Yet it is difficult to think of a more plausible explanation for the long delay, unless the severity of winter had something to do with it – but even then, they could have tried him well before August.

The second cause for delay was that the date of execution set for the Nantucks and Henderson was 1 November. Virtually on the eve of the hanging, someone – a Roman Catholic priest, it was rumoured – reminded the local authorities that this was All Saints' Day, a federal holiday, and one particularly dear to Quebecers. The French/English issue, which so bedevilled Canada in that era and subsequently, had echoes in the Yukon. French-speaking miners had held meetings in Dawson City in the summer of 1898 to protest the mining laws, and the handful of francophone civil servants in the Yukon had complained that they were being discriminated against. It was partly for this reason that the federal government appointed a Quebecer, Calixte A. Dugas, a Montreal police magistrate, to replace the retiring McGuire in the fall of 1898. McGuire, who had served on the Supreme Court of the North-West Territories from 1886 to 1898, had been in the Yukon only six months when he left for Prince Albert. After a flurry of legal manoeuvrings, Judge Dugas postponed the executions for four months, until 9 March 1899.

The third and most important cause for the delay of the executions was that there was a serious procedural flaw in the trial of the Nantucks. The facts surrounding this flaw are as follows. First, the Yukon was, at the time Meehan was killed, a district of the North-West Territories, and Judge McGuire held his position as a judge of the Supreme Court of the North-West Territories. The Nantucks were arraigned and tried in this court on 28–9 July. However, on 13 June, the Yukon Territorial Act had come into effect, making the Yukon a territory, as it is today, and notice of the act arrived in Dawson City on 9 August. As of 13 June, McGuire had been judge of the territorial court of the Yukon Territory, this court having been established along with the territory. Consequently, the trial of the Nantucks had taken place in the wrong court, under authority that had lapsed. In Henderson's case, the trial had begun the day before news of the change reached Dawson City and it was stopped. The indictment and charge were then amended to reflect the new title of the court, and the trial proceeded. The Nantucks, though, were not retried.

The federal government puzzled over the problem. The minister of justice, David Mills, a Liberal member of parliament who had lost his seat in the 1896 election and been appointed to the Senate, asked for advice and was told by a consultant that there was certainly a defect in the trial procedure and that the proceedings were null and void under law. His deputy minister, however, told him that he was "not aware of any reason" why the executions of the Nantuck brothers should not proceed. Mills then advised the governor general that clemency was not called for.

Why did this happen? Why were the Nantucks not retried when it was clear that there had been a defect in their trial, one that today would unquestionably lead to a retrial? Alan Grove puts it down to "political ambition, money, and racism," and calls the Nantucks' case a "judicial homicide." His argument is that Mills had a promise from Prime Minister Wilfrid Laurier that he would get the next vacancy on the Supreme Court and that the embarrassment of botching this case might have denied him the prize. Edmund Newcombe, the deputy minister, also feared embarrassment, since he was responsible for the fiasco that had resulted in the lapse of jurisdiction. The two men (both of whom were later appointed to the Supreme Court, Mills in 1902 and, Newcombe in 1924) thus conspired to send the Nantucks to the gallows.

This is a very strong charge, and there is no convincing evidence to show that the two officials sacrificed the convicted men to their own ambitions, since one can only guess at what motivated them. People who look for conspiracies can generally find one; it depends very much on one's outlook. Another explanation, which is just as plausible and fits a less dark view of officialdom, is that Newcombe and Mills decided that the Nantucks were guilty, that a second trial would come to the same conclusion as the first and at great cost (officials worried a great deal about expenditures in those days), and perhaps that the public in the Yukon would resent another postponement. This is callous, and a cavalier attitude towards justice, but it is far from judicial homicide.

While the Nantucks' case was at the Department of Justice awaiting a recommendation for or against clemency, (no one seemed to care enough to write about Henderson, though his lawyer did appeal, unsuccessfully, for a new trial), petitions and letters arrived from private citizens, most notably from William Carpenter Bompas, Anglican bishop of the region, who appealed through the Mounted Police to the government to show clemency to the four brothers. He did not comment on the Henderson case; he was notably less interested in the whites than in his First Nations charges. Bompas was one of the notable missionary figures of the Victorian Church of England. Born in London, he had taken holy orders in 1859 and volunteered for missionary work in northern Canada in 1865. He spent the next forty-one years in the North and was made bishop of Athabasca in 1874, of Mackenzie River in 1884, and of Selkirk (now Yukon) in 1891. Having spent almost all his career on the northern frontier preaching the gospel to First Nations people, he was unprepared for the gold rush and unsympathetic to the newcomers, doing his best to keep his people away from them.

Bompas's letter of 1 August asking for "compassionate clemency" for the Nantuck brothers was based mostly on practical grounds. Clemency, he wrote, "would tend to cement the cordial feelings at present maintained between the Indians of all this neighbourhood and the Canadian government, and the miners and their respect for the Queen." Although this is confused thinking – since the First Nations would have favoured clemency, while the miners wanted the Nantucks to hang, so both groups' feelings could not be satisfied – it is clear that Bompas wanted the sentences commuted. But he then went on to say that if there had to be a hanging, "it should occur near the coast where it might be overawing the coast Indians," because, if it was carried out locally, "it might possibly be resented by our Indians as a poor return for peaceable behaviour." Another letter, signed by all the Protestant clergy of the region, contained the same message, suggesting that the "boys" be punished and then placed at a mission, where they would be "taught the duties of citizenship."

None of this had much effect on the government, though Frank Nantuck, the youngest of the brothers, had his sentence commuted to life imprisonment on account of his age and the fact that he had cooperated with the prosecution. This did him no good, since he died within months of the trial, as did his brother Joe. On 4 August 1899, Henderson and the two surviving Nantuck brothers, Dawson and Jim, were hanged at Dawson City in front of the usual crowd of witnesses. Henderson had expected to die before his execution but survived to mount the gallows. The three were hanged together. According to newspaper accounts, the execution was partially botched. As the three men fell, Dawson Nantuck's left hand broke free of its restraints, and he clutched at his neck, making gurgling noises. The hangman had to raise his body and then drop it in order to break his neck and end his suffering.

This was not a promising start to the administration of justice in the Yukon as far as dealing with capital crimes was concerned. The entire episode was full of irregularities, whether caused by racism, incompetence, or politics it is difficult to say. Certainly, the newness of the territory and the general confusion of the gold rush had something to do with it. On the whole it was an embarrassment to the Canadian justice system.

CHAPTER THREE

They Always Get Their Man: Fournier and Labelle

It seems impossible that any human being made in the
image of God could be guilty of such a crime.

Mr Justice Craig, sentencing Fournier

The Fournier-Labelle case was one of thuggery with a northern twist, perpetrated by two brutal men with criminal pasts. Fournier and Labelle were the kind of men whom the North-West Mounted Police liked to describe as the "scum of the coastal cities" of the United States, the kind of riff-raff that the American system supposedly spawned – except that these two were Canadians. They were the kind of men whose activities the NWMP had been set up to suppress – whisky traders and the group of wolf hunters who had massacred defenceless Assiniboines on the prairies thirty years before. This case had murder, treachery, brutality, and even a pursuit across the western United States. It was the stuff of legend, and it stimulated at least one "true crime" account some years after the event.

One of the Canadian Heritage Moments, the vignettes shown in movies and on television about aspects of Canadian history, focuses on Sam Steele, commander of the NWMP detachment in the Yukon at the height of the gold rush. The redoubtable Steele, resplendent in red serge, is shown, unflinching in the face of a loaded handgun pointed in his face, staring down an unsavoury American. "We don't allow handguns in Canada," says the phlegmatic NWMP officer, and his equally formidable colleague clamps his hand on the gambler's shoulder and escorts him back to Alaska. It has often been written that the Mounties "saved" the

Klondike for Canada; their firm (albeit somewhat flexible) hand is typically credited with maintaining order on the northern frontier.

While it can be argued that the NWMP "made" the Klondike experience, it is also true that the Yukon made the Mounties. In the late nineteenth century, the NWMP had a solid reputation but an uncertain future. The police had proved their worth in the 1870s, when their skilful handling of indigenous affairs had aided the comparatively peaceful settlement of the Canadian plains. They stumbled a bit during the lead-up to the Métis rebellion of 1885 and had to be bailed out by a Canadian military expedition. After the 1885 contretemps, the NWMP fell back into a less dramatic role in the West, aiding the tens of thousands of settlers who entered the region, and providing a full range of government and legal services for them. But after 1885, the Mounties' work was rarely exciting and only occasionally attracted much attention. They rested on the memory of their 1874 march to the western prairies, in which the police waved the flag and pronounced the establishment of Canadian sovereignty in an area threatened by American whisky traders and other ne'er-do-wells; and they took pride in tales of confrontations between First Nations leaders (especially Sitting Bull) and leading NWMP officers, such as James Walsh and Sam Steele.

When the police were dispatched into the far Northwest in 1894, with Inspector Charles Constantine sent to investigate complaints about American incursions into the Yukon River basin, the force was looking for a new role. Since the western plains were settling down, the government's interest in maintaining an expensive national police force was declining, and there were rumours that the NWMP was about to be disbanded. The Yukon offered the police another opportunity to prove their worth, and they jumped at it. Constantine recommended that a permanent police station be opened in the Northwest, and he was sent back to the Forty Mile region in 1895 with twenty men to accomplish this. He moved quickly to stabilize governmental affairs in the area, eliminating the once powerful miners' meetings, which had filled the power vacuum in the area with American-style direct democracy. The police also strongly enforced the Canadian boundary, making it clear that there were different laws operating in the Yukon, especially compared with the unruly and disorderly Alaskan frontier.

The Klondike gold rush once more brought the NWMP into national prominence and, even more importantly, it made them storybook international figures. They benefited from the good fortune of being on site when the gold strike was made in August 1896, and were able to establish administrative order while working almost exclusively with men and women who were already in the North. By the time the full rush hit the northwest in 1897–98, the NWMP had erected a series of police posts along the main transportation routes, especially along the Lake Bennett – Whitehorse – Dawson City corridor. They had taken their place atop the Chilkoot and White Passes, where they checked incoming miners for criminal records, handguns, and other signs of undesirability, and turned many men back. The police showed considerable latitude, as well, for they let dozens of prostitutes through to Dawson City and then largely turned a blind eye on their sexual commerce, believing that to do otherwise would create tensions and conflict.

The police also stepped well outside their legal authority by refusing entry to any stampeder who was not carrying a year's worth of food and supplies. This rule, established on the spot by local NWMP officers, recognized the shortage of foodstuff in the Northwest and the difficulties that would be involved in rushing additional supplies into the remote region. Undoubtedly, the decision (widely applauded at the time and in subsequent years) prevented massive shortages among the often ill-prepared miners. It also created an enormous market for supplies in Skagway and Dyea and helped fuel business activity in Seattle, Vancouver, and Victoria, the main departure points for the Klondike. It is not difficult to imagine the hardship and conflict that would have befallen the region had the police not acted in this way. Their willingness to take the law into their own hands displayed both the initiative for which they are justly praised and their responsiveness to local circumstances.

The Yukon made the North-West Mounted Police famous. Stories of their activities and descriptions of their impressive presence filled thousands of newspaper columns and became fodder for many novels and poems. The police, of course, revelled in the attention, which they did much to promote. But even they could not have anticipated the longevity of the Klondike legend. The police story lasted for decades, becoming a staple in Hollywood movies and, in the 1950s, being celebrated in the famous "Sergeant Preston of the Mounted" television series. If the Yukon is, in international terms, the most famous event in Canadian history, the Mounties are among the most important elements in that global reputation.

The status of the Mounties did not spring solely from the control they exerted on the Klondike trail or from their dramatic red serge coats or their stern but helpful demeanour. It also arose because they stopped crime and managed, through a variety of creative and professional means, to keep the criminal element in the Yukon at bay. But try as they might, they could not stop all crime.

When faced with a significant breach of the law, when their authority and ability were truly tested, the Mounties found themselves on very public display. The prospect of widespread violence was ever-present, especially in the eyes of the NWMP and the Canadian government. So, too, was the deeply ingrained fear among the miners that every twist in the river hid a desperado and that every stranger along the trail might be a criminal. Within months of establishing the police post on the pass above Sheep Camp, thus regulating the movement of stampeders in and out of the Yukon Territory, the NWMP had a formidable reputation to uphold, one based on its ability to maintain order and respond swiftly and decisively to criminal acts. Such was the case in the summer of 1902, when the Mounties faced perhaps the most difficult detective challenge of their northern experience.

All societies worry about murder, and all societies respond rapidly to the realization that there is a murderer in their midst. But in late-Victorian and early-Edwardian Canada, and certainly in the Yukon, the public attitude towards murder was harsh enough to satisfy the severest moralist. No one in the Yukon romanticized murder or murderers. In a frontier society with a turbulent ever-changing population, people feared anonymous violence. Death at the hands of a stranger, the theft of the proceeds of a gold strike, the violence (as the American experience showed so clearly) that was always possible on a mining frontier – it was to prevent such crimes that the Mounted Police exerted their authoritarian influence over the Yukon.

It is important to remember that the police established their dominance over the Klondike gold rush with the virtually unanimous support of the mining population. This was no mob of unruly miners desperate to enjoy the fruits of libertarian excess.

From the beginning and throughout the gold rush, the stampeders depended on the police and the Canadian government to protect them, their mining claims, and their personal property, and they enjoyed the benefits of a remarkably safe frontier.

The Fournier-Labelle case[1] tapped into the deepest fears of Yukoners. It concerned a murder based on greed, carried out in the most brutal manner imaginable, without mercy, in secret, and by stealth and cowardice. Moreover – and it was this that so appalled the public – it was carefully though clumsily planned. This can be said of only one other murder described in this book: the O'Brien case, discussed later (and there the victims were simply in the wrong place at the wrong time, whereas Fournier and Labelle carefully selected the time and place). In fact, Fournier-Labelle may well be the only case of totally premeditated murder in the history of the Yukon. Solving the case, in the sense of establishing its facts and identifying the murderers, was easy enough, but apprehending them was a different matter and required the use of police resources that were amazingly sophisticated and might surprise those who believe that police work in this era was crude and direct.

In the summer of 1902, three French Canadian men arrived in the Yukon to find their fortune. By that time, the gold rush had been over for three or four years, and there were no more fortunes to be made, at least not by men whose only assets were their physical strength and a little money. The gold creeks were now falling under the control of the "concessionaires," capitalists with money to invest in the technology – the hydraulic equipment and dredges that were now necessary to extract small amounts of gold from the creeks at a profit. That three French Canadians were venturing into the far Northwest was not in itself surprising. While national mythology has it that French Canadians rarely ventured outside Quebec and a few small settlements in Ontario and Manitoba, the reality is that they were in the Yukon in substantial numbers even before the Klondike gold rush. Interestingly, as the Mounted Police were to discover later, there was something of a French Canadian "circuit" in the western mining camps – small groups of French speakers in town after town, providing a measure of cultural familiarity among the overwhelmingly anglophone western and northern mining frontier.

The men were Léon Bouthillette, Guy Joseph Beaudoin, and Alphonse Constantine (whose name was also spelled Constantin in the records). Bouthillette, aged forty-two that year, was a carpenter from St-Francis, Beauce County; Beaudoin was from St-Evariste, in the same county, and was twenty-three years old, just out of college; and Constantine was a forty-one-year-old farmer from Saskatchewan (which had not yet become a province). The first two were newcomers to the North, while Constantine had come to the Yukon in 1898 and was returning after a visit to his home. Bouthillette's wife had recently died, leaving him with five children who, given his age, were probably teenagers and younger, though the accounts make no mention of them. He spoke very little English.

The three men, who had not known each other previously, met in Vancouver in early June 1902 and decided to travel to Dawson City together, probably because they were all French-speaking. On 14 June they arrived in Whitehorse by train, where they met two other men, both French-speaking, who offered to take them down the Yukon River to Dawson City by small boat, thus saving them money on the steamboat fare. Their new friends proposed to take them to Dawson for five dollars each, while the steamboat fare was forty dollars. Since Bouthillette apparently was carrying $1,100 in cash (though evidence given later contradicted this), and the other two also had money, this was an unnecessary economy, which proved to be fatal.

On 14 July, a body was discovered in the Yukon River forty kilometres upstream from Dawson. When the police were notified, they went to the scene and found the body still in the mud and sand of the river, two metres from the bank. Brought to the morgue in the Dawson City police barracks, it was examined by Dr MacArthur, the Yukon's medical health officer, as well as by the NWMP's Corporal Piper, who had seen it in the river, and others. It was determined that the body was that of a man in his forties who had been shot three times from behind, once in the back and twice in the head.[2] The Daily Klondike Nugget, reporting these events, expressed confidence in the Yukon's "excellent police service," saying that the task of solving the case seemed hopeless and "a broad field for fine detective work is now open."[3]

Fine detective work was indeed needed, for catching the killers involved a careful investigation and a dramatic hunt across Canada and the United States. The unofficial slogan for the Mounted Police (one which they profess to hate) has long been "They always get their man," a testament to their persistence, professionalism, and excellent track record. The 1902 pursuit, played out in the newspapers of the nation, only solidified an already impressive reputation. The case became more urgent twelve days later, when on 1 August a second body was brought to Dawson City (the third body was not found until June 1903). A log rafter named Paul Forrest had been carried by the current into a backwater near the community of Ogilvie, where he saw a body caught in roots and debris by the bank. Forrest pulled it from the river and notified the police detachment at Ogilvie, and they sent word to Dawson. A first examination of the body showed a piece of cord tied around the left wrist and another around the left ankle. It was badly mutilated – the whole upper part of the face was missing – though for what reason was not immediately apparent.

The identity of the first victim was soon established, for there was a set of keys in the pocket with a metal tag bearing the names B. Bouthillette and E. Broughton. The police at first thought that these were two people and sent a constable to the Marconi Saloon on First Avenue, a place "much frequented by Frenchmen," where they discovered that E. Broughton was East Broughton, a town in Beauce County, Quebec. One man in the saloon, Joe Plant (Plante?) knew a B. Bouthillette, but the man had died four years earlier. He did have a son, however, who had been living in St-Francis, and whose name was Léon Bouthillette. Plante, who was distantly related to the family, informed the police that Léon Bouthillette had planned to come to Dawson that year, but he did not know whether or not his relative had arrived. He also gave the police the names of Father J.O.D. Naud, a priest at East Broughton, and Theodore Paulin of St-Francis, who would be able to tell the police whether Bouthillette had in fact left for the North.

The police then telegraphed the two Quebec addresses and also contacted the detachment at Whitehorse, which kept track of those passing through the town and made a point of registering all private boats and passengers leaving the community for Dawson. The answer soon came from Quebec that Bouthillette had left that province on 4 June, and the Whitehorse detachment reported that on 18 June he had left the town in boat 3744, accompanied by Guy Beaudoin, Alphonse Constantine, Peter Forrest, and Louis Ladouceur. On 19 June, at 1:30 in the morning, boat 3744 was found abandoned near the bluff at Klondike City, across the Klondike River from Dawson City. The hunt was then on for the other men who had travelled in the boat, especially for Forrest and Ladouceur. The police suspected, and it was later confirmed, that Forrest and Ladouceur were false names. These two men were in fact the murderers Peter Fournier and Edward Labelle.

Although Fournier and Labelle have gone down in history as a pair of murderers, it was not an equal partnership. Both were natives of Quebec. Fournier was a drifter, unemployed, a passive character, not very intelligent – all in all, a rather minor actor in the drama. Labelle on the other hand was quick and resourceful and was, moreover, an experienced criminal. He was the leader, Fournier the follower. Nor was Labelle simply a drifter. His family was not poor: his mother owned property in Montreal. More important, his sister's husband, J.E. Émile Léonard, was a barrister and a member of parliament for a Quebec constituency,[4] a fact that gave the police and the Department of Justice some uneasiness throughout the trial and sentencing process.

Labelle was more than a petty criminal. According to a biography published in the Vancouver *Daily World*,[5] he had had a career as the leader of a gang of drug smugglers operating out of Victoria, with a distribution network that stretched across Canada into the eastern United States. His "passages with the law" were "too numerous to be recorded," but the reporter did recount one example of his "quick wit and cool nerve" which, if true, shows that Labelle was not simply a stupid thug. In fact, his drug-smuggling activity showed that he was ingenious, and it is surprising that he ended his criminal activities with a murder plot as clumsy as the one that brought him to the gallows. It is hard to square the clever and daring organization of his drug career with the crude brutality of the murder plot of 1902; the two crimes sound as if they were those of two entirely different men.

In the summer of 1888, twelve years before his last crime, Labelle was a young man who made his living bringing opium into Canada through Victoria and shipping it to the American Midwest. In June of that year he and a partner shipped $50,000 worth of the drug from Victoria to Cartwright, a little Ontario village on the banks of the St Clair River, a few kilometres from Sarnia; $50,000 was a substantial sum in that day, when the average wage of industrial workers in the United States was about $400 a year, so the shipment was worth, very roughly, about $5 million in modern day purchasing power.

Edward Labelle (upper) was the one who planned the
murders of the three prospectors. Peter Fournier (lower)
was a follower, but he went to the gallows with his
partner (NA, PA-205087).

Labelle, who was working as a grocery clerk in Port Huron, Michigan, took delivery of the opium at the Cartwright railway station, but the police had been tipped off. Three American detectives from Chicago – McKale, the "great Chicago officer," and Hussey and Ling, two other noted detectives – were following him and saw him take the shipment from the station, put it in a wagon, and drive off towards a nearby Native reserve, where he was staying in a cabin. The detectives believed that Labelle knew he was being watched and therefore would not dare to try and take the opium across the border. Moreover, the weather was bad and getting worse, so the policemen went to bed.

By 10 PM the storm had become so bad that the lights of Port Huron could not be seen from the Canadian side, and it was at this moment that Labelle took the opium and set out across the river, a trip that took him over four hours. Twice he nearly capsized and once was almost run down by a passing steamer. Eventually he reached the American side, and in the morning he shipped his cargo from the village of Smith's Creek to its destination, Indianapolis.

The police followed his trail, and the shipping agent who had sent the parcel and had been suspicious of it told them where it had been sent to. When Labelle took delivery of the parcel at the Indianapolis express office, he was arrested and taken to the customs house, where the parcel was searched. He also had in his possession some incriminating documents – three letters which named his partners and outlined some of this operations – and his first action after being arrested was to eat the letters.

Labelle spent forty days in jail in Indianapolis while the police questioned him and tried to get him to turn state's evidence. Eventually he "decided on a bold move" and told the police he would help them in return for a light sentence or other favours. His plan was to escape back over the international boundary, and the first step was to get the American authorities to bring him closer to it. He named two residents of Port Huron as his partners (it turned out that they knew nothing of his drug dealings) and demanded in return to be taken to Port Huron to identify them and disclose the details of his operations. The authorities agreed and sent him to Port Huron on a special train, guarded by a U.S. marshal.

Once in Port Huron, however, Labelle refused to talk, so on the morning of 20 July 1888 the authorities in disgust prepared to take him to Detroit. He had luck on his side, for some legal technicality delayed the train until nightfall, when it pulled out of Port Huron carrying Labelle in handcuffs and no fewer than twelve government agents. Eight kilometres or so out of Port Huron, Labelle asked for a drink of water and was told to get it himself. He walked to the end of the car, suddenly opened the door, and jumped from the train, which was travelling at about sixty kilometres an hour. The newspaper account gave the dramatic climax of the story:

Crashing against and breaking a fence around a cattle yard in his fall, he found himself at the crossing in the village of Hoptin Works. He arose, stunned and bleeding, heard the sharp whistle of bullets, for the train had stopped and the officers were coming in pursuit. He fell again from weakness, but again staggered up and saw what he did not before, that a horse and carriage had stopped at the crossing to avoid the train, which was now backing toward him. The only occupant was a little boy, and to spring in, push him out, and start at a mad gallop for the river, holding the reins bound together by the steel bracelets, was the work of a minute. A terrible drive of seven miles, and Marysville, on the river bank, was reached. It was yet early and a ferry boy who had just come in from the river, was hauling his boat up on the bank. Springing forth from the buggy, and threatening the unfortunate urchin with a common pipe, which, fortunate[ly] for him, made a very satisfactory substitute for a re-volver, Labelle compelled him to land him on Canadian soil.

At the reservation a friend relieved him of the handcuffs, and after writing from Sarnia to thank his former guardians for their kindness, and advising them of his safe arrival in the Dominion, he bade his adieus to Sarnia and returned to Victoria, where he remained for some time, and then returned to the province of Quebec. When the rush to the Yukon set in, he drifted north, with the result of which all readers are aware: He robbed and murdered.[6]

The account does not say why the American authorities did not apply to have Labelle arrested in Canada and extradited. Perhaps he lay low in Victoria or changed his name, or went back to Quebec and lived there quietly. Whatever the reason, he seems to have stayed out of trouble, or at least out of the hands of the police, for the next fourteen years. In 1898 he was living with relatives in Ste-Rose, and in that year he left for the Yukon.

The murder plot of 1902 was as simple as can be imagined, and as stupid: Labelle suggested to Fournier that they could make money by offering to take some passengers in a boat from White-horse to Dawson City and murdering them on the way. However, this required some preparation. It must be emphasized that the murder was entirely premeditated and carefully planned. It was this fact, more than the number of victims or the crude brutality of the deed, that caused such horror and revulsion in the Yukon.

At the end of the first week of June 1902, Labelle and Fournier, who had been living in Dawson City, left for Whitehorse on the steamer *Clifford Sifton*, giving false names on the passenger list and stating that they were going "outside" for the summer. They arrived in Whitehorse on 11 June and began to prepare for the rob-bery and murder. They bought a small boat from a Whitehorse boat builder, a rifle, and some other supplies. They then spent time at the Whitehorse train station, talking to passengers bound for Dawson City, and they arranged with a man named Mack and another man to take them to Dawson at 8 AM on the morning of 17 June. But when Mack and the other man arrived at the White-horse dock, they found that the boat had left with three other pas-sengers the previous evening.

The stupidity of these proceedings is difficult to understand – at the trial, the prosecution was able to produce the boat builder, who identified the accused as his customers, and the two would-be passengers, who identified the accused as the men who had of-fered them passage and then left without them. Witnesses to their trip back to Dawson City were also produced. The only conceiv-able explanation of such self-incriminating behaviour is that La-belle and Fournier were extremely foolhardy or simply that they lacked common sense. On reflection, Labelle's 1888 adventure shows daring rather than intelligence. Certainly, there was no in-telligence shown in the planning of the 1902 crime, though Labelle did exhibit a good deal of desperate cunning after his arrest.

As noted above, the boat was registered by the police, as the rules required, and was given the number 3744, and the names of the passengers were recorded as Bouthillette, Beaudoin, Constan-tin [sic], Forrest, and Ladouceur. The party was seen at a number of places on its trip down the river. At Selkirk the men came ashore and visited a roadhouse operated by a Mrs Nelson, who had known Labelle when he lived at Eldorado Creek in 1901. At the risk of being repetitious, the question must again be raised: What were Labelle and Fournier thinking of? They were laying a trail a child could follow – the challenge to the police lay not in identifying the murderers but in catching them. Did the two men think that the bodies would not be discovered, that the police would not look in the list of boats registered in Whitehorse and would not conduct inquiries down the length of the Klondike River to find anyone who had met the five men? Fournier even pawned a watch belonging to one of the victims, an action tantamount to suicide. It seems incredible that men would concoct such a clumsy plot, one that was bound to lead them into the hands of the executioner.

Concoct it they did, however, and a few days after leaving Whitehorse they carried it out. The murder took place on an unnamed island near the place where the Stewart River flows into the Yukon. Later, when Labelle and Fournier were under arrest, they both made statements accusing the other of carrying out the murders, so the exact truth will never be known – though given the fact that the idea was Labelle's and that Fournier was weak and alcoholic, it was probably Labelle who did the actual killing. The police believed that Labelle shot Beaudoin and Constantine, and that Fournier shot Bouthillette; they came to this conclusion because two of the men were killed by rifle fire and the third with a revolver, presumably at the same time. In either case, the three travellers were shot and killed, probably as they came out of their tents in the morning. Their bodies were then weighted with stones tied to their arms and legs, and thrown into the river.

The amount of money taken from the three men, according to Fournier's later testimony, totalled $161. Fournier and Labelle divided their victims' money and possessions, and went on in the boat to Dawson. They lived there for some time, doing a good deal of drinking – Fournier seems to have been constantly drunk – pawning or selling the stolen goods. At one point they took a trip to Eagle, Alaska, where they picked up a man named Guilboult and murdered him in the same way. They came back to Dawson City, and when the first of the three victims was found, Labelle fled to the United States, while Fournier continued to hang around Dawson City.

LEON BOUTHILLETTE (3rd Man
Murdered. This man was shot by
FOURNIER with .44 Cal. Revolver
and was the first body found
near Indian River)

ALPHONSE CONSTANTINE
(First Man Shot with Rifle)
by La Belle)

Guy BEAUDOIN (2nd Man Shot
with Rifle)

Alphonse Constantine, Léon Bouthillette, and Guy Beaudoin,
victims of Fournier and Labelle (NA, PA-205086)

By the end of July the police at Dawson City were fairly sure
that Fournier and Labelle were the murderers. Fournier was put
under police surveillance, while W.H. Welsh, a police detective,
was given the task of tracking down Labelle. Welsh's pursuit and
arrest of Labelle is the stuff of police legend, a tale that would be
recounted endlessly in the bars and cabins of the Klondike as de-
finitive proof that the Mounties "always get their man." Although
it took over a month and covered several U.S. states, Labelle made
it easier, since he made little real attempt to cover his tracks or
conceal his identity – he continued to wear a gold pin in his lapel

showing a miner's pick and shovel, by which several people were able to identify him to Welsh. He also stayed exclusively within the large French Canadian community in the towns and work camps of the American West, including those in California. Perhaps he thought the police would not go to the trouble of following him so far south.

Welsh left Dawson for Whitehorse on the evening of 26 July, arriving on the morning of the thirty-first, having, conducted interviews with police officers at the various detachments along the way. In Whitehorse he examined the hotel registers, and he did the same at Skagway on 1 and 2 August, as well as visiting "all French prostitutes." [7] Arriving in Vancouver on 6 August, Welsh visited the chief of police and asked him to recommend a local detective to assist him. With this detective, whose name was Wiley, he visited "French resorts,[8] French hotels and other hotels, R.R. ticket offices." He found the hotels where the three victims had stayed, and cut their names out of the registers as evidence.

He then went to Seattle and spent two weeks in that city and the region digging up information on Labelle. He talked to hundreds of people, among them "at least 200 French prostitutes" (Is it possible there were that many French-speaking prostitutes in Seattle?). "On the 17th," he reported, "Mr. Rook arrived, and as I was getting a great deal of information about Ed Labelle, and a great many people seemed to know him, and that he had been in Seattle four or five weeks before, I was certain that it would not be long before we had him." Rook was the man in Whitehorse who had sold the boat and outfit to Labelle and Fournier, and the police paid him to accompany Welsh in the hunt for Labelle, since he would be able to identify the fugitive. Welsh described Rook's role in the hunt:

I started Mr. Rook out with Louis Beaupre. Mr. Rook visited almost all of the towns, logging camps, coal mines, and any other places where there were large gangs of French Canadians working, in company with this man, and was in and out of Seattle until we left there on the evening of the 27th. I took up my quarters at the Hotel Northern and kept in touch with Rook and his men, and used all Frenchmen that knew Ed Labelle that I thought would do us any good. I wired Chicago, Missoula, and Butte, kept in touch with you at home and with Mr. White in Ottawa.[9] ... Met Joseph Dalpe who I knew in Dawson ... He told me that he had met Ed Labelle about the 1st of August in Seattle and had a drink with him and a short conversation, and that Labelle had told him that he was going East. He thought that I ought to know him. Labelle told him that he did not have money to go home and did not know exactly where he would go. He gave me a description of his clothing and told me that he had a Gold Pan with a pick and shovel crossing on the lapel of his coat.

Welsh then went to Spokane, where he found that a French Canadian with the telltale lapel pin had been there but had gone farther east. Welsh went on to Missoula and Butte, and found that Labelle had been there for about ten days, leaving a week previously. In all these towns he received total cooperation from the local authorities. In Butte, for example, the police chief had assigned a detective, Barney McGillick, to the case, and by the time Welsh arrived, McGillick had traced Labelle's movements in town. "I accompanied him," Welsh reported, "to different French resorts and in Chapleau's place No 29 East Mercury Street found a French boy who had served Labelle or a man with a gold pan and pick and shovel on the lapel of his coat with drinks in company with a prostitute."

The task of tracking down Labelle was really a matter of persistence. Welsh's account of what happened next shows the sort of work that was involved:

I visited the prostitute and she said that his name was Labelle but did not know where he had gone. I visited many other prostitutes [Labelle apparently preferred his countrywomen] and in a saloon met a man who said that he thought Ed Labelle had shipped to work on the railroad with some other Frenchmen from the St. Paul employment office. We went to the employment office and all the information that we could obtain there was that on the 26th August he had shipped 14 men to Ogden to Hanson's employment office, but he did not have their names ... We visited the R.R. Office and got the names of the conductors who left Butte on that day and found that the conductor lived in Pocatella [Pocatello] and was on the end of the line ... arriv[ed] in Pocatella at 1:30 a.m. on the 31st. The conductor that was on the train that we were travelling on was kind enough to take Mr. Rook and myself to the house of the conductor ... Woke him up and gave him a description of the man we were looking for, but he could remember nothing about him ... Left there at 3 a.m. for Ogden ... Was introduced ... to detective Fitzpatrick of the Southern Pacific Railway Company who stayed with me while I was in Ogden and gave me every assistance possible. He showed me where Hanson's employment office was but told me to be careful that the Employment offices were shipping men backwards and forwards over their line at cheap rates, taking advantage of the construction of the Railroad and pretending that they were shipping their men to work, when the men were really tourists, so I watched my opportunity at Hanson's employment office, when he was away got hold of his clerk a young man and got him to give me the telegrams from Butte and also the book with the list of the men he had shipped out that week on the railroad.

After further adventures of this sort, Welsh and Rook ended up at a work camp outside Wadsworth, Nevada, just east of the California state line, where three hundred men were at work. Rook, posing as a timekeeper, began to visit the tents.

He came to a tent and in taking the names came to a man who gave his name as L. Stone. Mr. Rook took a good look at him and asked him a second time what his name was. Mr. Rook and myself had a signal arranged that when he got the right man he would put his hat on the back of his head. I was at the foot of the hill watching Mr. Rook. He came out of the tent with his hat on the back of his head. I hurried to him while the Constable was tying the horses and motioned to the Constable to hurry up. I met Mr. Rook and he said "He is in that tent, I am certain it is him." I immediately went into the tent. There were several other men in the tent with him. As soon as I saw him I recognised his face as a familiar one that I had seen in Dawson. I walked up to him and stuck out my hand to shake hands with him addressing him saying "How do you do." He reached to take hold of my hand and I grabbed a hand and put on a hand cuff. He was sitting on the side of a bunk with his suspenders hanging down. I asked him what he gave the name of L. Stone for, that his name was Ed Labelle and I knew him well …

He acknowledged that his name was Ed Labelle and we immediately picked up his clothing and rushed him out of the tent to the waggon and drove to Wadsworth about as fast as the horses could go. Just as we got into the waggon to leave a tall man stepped up to the waggon and said "Frenchy what are they doing with you." We were gone before "Frenchy" had a chance to answer him.

As soon as we got into Wadsworth we drove towards the jail, went to the hotel and into our room and kept to ourselves. We then took Labelle before a Justice of the Peace and I informed what he was arrested for, told him [Labelle] that I had no right to take him out of the state of Nevada, that he had a right to a lawyer and that he could hold me for several weeks until I got extradition papers to take him out, but that if he wanted to return to Dawson without causing me any trouble that I would dictate an agreement that he could sign and we would start that night. If not, that I would take him to Reno, place him in Jail ... He finally agreed to sign the papers, which he did ... I made arrangements for a special engine to get out of there in case there was any trouble, as I had heard of trouble happening in Nevada before, being very familiar with the State.

Now alone with Labelle, Welsh told him that Fournier had been arrested and asked if he had anything to say. He does not seem to have given him the usual caution – that anything he said might be used in evidence against him. Instead, Welsh told Labelle that Fournier had told a story and that if Labelle did not contradict it, the police would naturally have to believe it. Labelle replied that Fournier was "a very bad man, and that Fournier had some influence over him that he could not understand, while he was in his company." This was the gist of his defence, which he elaborated later in statements made to the police and at his trial.

Welsh took Labelle back to the Yukon via Sacramento and Portland, in chains and leg irons, which he had made in Reno for the purpose. They left Wadsworth on 1 September and were in Whitehorse on the seventh. During this part of the trip Welsh did give Labelle the usual warning, after which Labelle made a number of statements to him which were later used as evidence in court. They left on a steamer for Dawson on the eleventh and on the way north stopped at Selkirk, where Mrs Nelson, owner of the local hotel, identified Labelle as a man who had stopped with a party at her establishment on 22 June. They finally arrived at Dawson City on the 14 September.

The cost of this chase was considerable, almost $10,000. Some of these expenses were for travel and lodging, not only for Welsh but also for those whom he had hired in the United States to assist him. Nearly $400 was spent on photographs of Labelle, and a similar sum on telegrams, for Welsh had sent his superiors reports on every step of the chase. The cost was so out of the ordinary that the police appealed to the Department of Justice for financial assistance, an appeal that was rejected.

For someone who had planned such a crude and stupid crime, Labelle, after his arrest, showed a good deal of cunning in trying to

"On Murderer's Island. Yukon River. Sept 02. "The finding of the Tell Tale Bullet."

Three men, two wearing police hats, pose at the scene of the crime. The original caption reads "On Murderer's Island Yukon River – Sept. 1902 (The Finding of the Tell Tale Bullet)" (NA, PA-205090).

defend himself, making the best of what was essentially a hopeless case. While under arrest in Nevada, he wrote a number of letters to his family in Quebec, outlining what was to become his main defence – that Fournier had committed the murders and that he himself had gone along with them out of fear of Fournier. These letters were given to Welsh for mailing, and Welsh had them copied before sending them, something that Labelle presumably expected. Fournier, not surprisingly, made the same argument as Labelle, only in reverse, claiming that Labelle had killed all three men. Labelle admitted that he had travelled to Whitehorse under a false name but said that he had done so at Fournier's request, since Fournier had told him that he feared trouble because of some small crime. He admitted changing his name again in Whitehorse because he had been on a drunk and was ashamed. He admitted buying the boat and the rifle but denied that there was a plot to murder the men. His account of the actual killing, given as testimony at his trial, put all the blame on Fournier:

Fournier told him to take his rifle and take a look around the island because during the night he thought he had heard something moving on
the island, probably game; that he went off and was gone about fifteen
minutes when he heard five revolver shots; that he feared there had been
trouble and feared to return to the camp; when he did return to the camp
he found Fournier stirring up a fire and carrying goods to the boat, the
three men missing. Asking Fournier what had happened to them he replied that he had killed them and thrown their bodies in the river; every
trace of the crime, he said, had been removed from the ground, and he
had been absent at the furthest an hour and a half. Without much further
talk, or any, they entered the boat together and proceeded on their way to
Dawson ... His excuse for not reporting the matter is that he was under
dread not only of Fournier but of the circumstances of his having been
found in Fournier's company.

The disappearance of Guilboult he explained in much the same
way. Fournier's story was the reverse, except that he admitted
that there was a murder plot from the beginning:

He ... admitted ... that Labelle had asked him to join him in an adventure
in which they should entrap and waylay men coming into the Yukon and
murder them on the down river trip for their money. He says he did not
believe Labelle had the pluck or gall to carry out this scheme but he
joined him in it ... his story of the murder being that as the men rose in
the morning to go out Labelle shot them with his rifle and that he helped
to put the remains in the river, and he stood by and saw it done and gave
no warning to the men. He admits his guilt; his only excuse is that he did
not actually commit the fatal deed.

On 25 September a preliminary hearing was held for Labelle before the Dawson police magistrate. Twenty-one witnesses for the
prosecution were present and a number for the defence, and public interest in the case was so great that the courtroom was full to
capacity with standing spectators. The case for the prosecution
was outlined, a number of witnesses called, and after a day and a
half, Labelle was committed to trial.

Labelle and Fournier were tried separately for the murder of
Bouthillette. Labelle's trial began first, on Monday, 27 October. He
was defended by K.C. Hagel and Auguste Noel. The prosecutor
was Fred T. Congdon, a local lawyer who was well connected to

the Liberal Party and became commissioner of the Yukon Territory, 1903–4, and the territory's member of parliament, 1908–11.[10] It was rumoured that Labelle's brother-in-law Émile Léonard, the Quebec MP, would come north to act in his defence, but this did not occur. Léonard did, however, take an active interest in the case, corresponding often with the defence lawyers and later with the government.

The case had aroused tremendous interest in the territory, and by the time the trial began, Fournier's account of the events had already been published in the press. As Labelle's lawyers later pointed out in appealing for a new trial, it was probably impossible to find six men for a jury in the Yukon who did not know about the case and had not already formed an opinion on it. (As territorial law dictated, the jury was made up of six men rather than the usual twelve.) Because the accused and several of the witnesses were French Canadian, an interpreter was provided, but proceedings were carried out in English. However, two members of the jury were French-speaking.

The trial lasted five full days, from Monday to Friday, a long trial by the standards of the time – made long by the detailed circumstantial evidence on which the prosecution based its case. There was a good deal of cross-examination of the crown's witnesses. Then Labelle testified on his own behalf, saying that Fournier had committed the crimes, and he too was cross-examined at length. The jury was permitted to ask a number of questions of the witnesses. The transcript of the trial ran to 375 legal-sized (35 cm) pages of single-spaced typing. The transcript does not include the opening or closing statements of either the prosecution or the defence, though it does include the judge's closing remarks and some of the written evidence, in particular translations of the letters Labelle wrote to his family after his arrest, as well as the account of events he wrote for Welsh.

Labelle's letters and statement, the first written from Wadsworth and the last penned on the steamer heading north to the Yukon, were quite long, amounting to twenty legal pages, single spaced. As well as putting forward the defence that Fournier did the killing, they played what might be called the linguistic card. In a letter from Seattle on dated 6 September, Labelle wrote: "Dear father, see monsieur Le Judge Aldericque Ouimet with Emile [the MP] and ask them if I have the privilege of having a French

Canadian jury; that they will see that things are arranged ... I can see myself in a court of justice not understanding half of the questions that will be asked me and I on my side unable to explain myself as I could in my proper tongue." He swore that he was innocent: "My heart breaks in seeing the pain you must endure, but I cannot help myself. Now, I am awaiting your help. Truly if I were guilty dear parents I would avow frankly that it would be useless to go to that expense for me, but I swear to you that my innocence will be proven."

Athough the case against Labelle was circumstantial, it was very strong. The jury would probably have convicted him no matter what the judge said, but His Lordship's address, given at the end of the trial, nailed Labelle's coffin shut. Justice James A. Craig began by thanking the jury for listening with patience to the "long and wearisome" trial. (One wonders what he would have said about a criminal trial that lasted a year.) He then gave a speech praising the work of the police, and, in particular, he spoke to the question of the propriety of the police in intercepting and reading the letters Labelle had sent to his family:

Before proceeding to a short review of the evidence in this case, I must compliment the officers of the Crown for the way in which they have done their work in this case. In our civilized society of today, where many of the criminal class are the cleverest men in the community, where crime is systematized and perfected, we demand the assistance of skilled experts in tracing and bringing to justice those felons. Modern society would be wholly unsafe, life would be wholly unsafe today were it not for the detective force engaged in all civilized countries; your properties and your lives would be wholly at the mercy of the criminal classes, skilled, as they are, in all the devices of crime, were it not for the able detective forces employed in civilized communities. In the pursuit of crime these detectives have to resort to various artifices ... [The one in this case] is not a new one. That has frequently been adopted by detectives, commented upon by judges in the highest courts of this land and in England and approved of.

The judge then spoke to Labelle's explanation that he had changed his name because Fournier had asked him to:

This man [Fournier] proposes to an innocent man that he shall take him out of the country and pay his expenses, and the innocent man concurs. He goes further than that. He consents to change his name; the prisoner's folly is that while up to this time he is a perfectly innocent, moral individual, he changes his name. For what reason? Men do not give up their own name for trifles. What reason? – because you must consider the reason given. The reason is that because this worthless, good-for-nothing Fournier is going out of the country, tells Labelle that he wants to escape from the country because he suggests that probably he may have committed a robbery, and to aid him in the escape, the prisoner says "I will change my name." Now, take that statement itself and analyze it and see what it means. Is there sense, is there reason for it? That is for you to say. And can the changing of that name be of any aid to Fournier even if he had committed the crime? What aid would the changing of an innocent man's name, travelling on the same vessel, be to Fournier? What sense would there be in that?

After more along these lines, the judge got to the central point of Labelle's story – that Fournier had killed the three men while Labelle was elsewhere on the island and that he had waited an hour and a half before returning to see what had happened. We cannot, of course, hear the tone of the judge's voice, but reading his words it is reasonable to suppose that they must have been heavily laden with sarcasm.

He comes on the scene of the murder after being absent an hour or an hour and a half and he finds Fournier carrying blankets to the boat. He also sees him after that standing over the fire stirring up the ashes in the fire, and everything, every trace of the crime removed, not a scrap or tittle of evidence to indicate a struggle – the death struggle of the three men – that had gone on at that spot. In an hour and a half at the outside Fournier commits these murders, drags the men to the river, weights them with stones and clears up the remains, lights a fire, burns the clothes, and is so considerate of the feelings of his partner, Labelle, that he leaves no traces of the crime behind – the man that he intended to associate with and communicate with – the whole of the crime – the man into whose hands he was giving his life, the man upon whose secrecy he was depending for his safety, the man who had to be in the boat with him … was so considerate of the feelings of this man that he destroyed every trace of the crime before he arrived on the scene; everything was clean. The story covers everything that can offend the most fastidious, and all traces of the crime were cleaned up. Now, gentlemen, it is for you to say whether that story is a reasonable one.

The judge went on to comment on the question of circumstantial evidence, then returned to the question of Labelle's name change. He then spoke to the fact that Labelle had continued to associate with Fournier after the crime and that Guilboult had perhaps been killed in similar circumstances:

He goes about Dawson with this man, and I do not think I can impress too strongly upon your minds the fact that Labelle who now claims to be innocent knew that Fournier had committed this crime and was one of the bloodiest murderers that ever perpetrated a crime anywhere under the sun. We thought we had reached the climax of crime in the O'Brien case but it fades into insignificance compared with this case. O'Brien gave the men some shew for their lives, but this man who committed this crime shot their comrades down – men who had been their comrades for a week ... Knowing this man to be a heinous murderer he consorted with him, travelled with him, aided him in every way in the disposing of all the articles. Is that consistent with innocence? Is that consistent with the state of mind which he wishes you to think he had at that time? ... I could quite understand a weak man, frightened and under terror of Fournier and under terror of the circumstances, doing all that, if he were innocent ... but can you understand a man who had been compromised once and had been brought into peril of his life and character by the act of his comrade, who had been brought within the shadow of the gallows by his comrade's act, again in another small boat, with guns again, going down to Circle City with that same man ... can you understand it as being reasonable that this man would again venture out upon a journey with this murderer on a trip in a small boat?

There was more along these lines, as Judge Craig spoke sarcastically about Labelle's trip to Circle City with Fournier – how Guilboult had disappeared while Labelle was temporarily sick, how "for a short time [he] was in the bush with some American who sprang up from the earth somewhere down the river" while another murder was perhaps being committed.

Then the judge reminded the jury that Labelle was "entitled to the benefit of every reasonable doubt." But before concluding, he raised as an afterthought yet another point of Labelle's testimony which he found unbelievable, a minor point but another indication that he considered Labelle a liar. Nothing that the judge said was untrue or even particularly unfair by contemporary standards, but it certainly reinforced the prosecution's case. In fact, it sounded like a summation for the prosecution. Labelle and his lawyers must have heard it with sinking hearts. The remarks concluded at 7:30 PM.

The jury then retired, and "after having been out for some considerable time" (about two hours), returned to ask for some clarification about the law on circumstantial evidence. Judge Craig read some passages from "Roscoe's Nisi Prius Evidence" to the effect that "circumstances are in many cases of greater force and more to be depended upon than the testimony of living witnesses inasmuch as witnesses may either be mistaken themselves or wickedly intend to deceive others, whereas circumstances and presumptions naturally and necessarily arising out of a given fact cannot lie." The jury again retired and at 10:30 PM returned with a verdict of guilty. The judge then asked Labelle if he had anything to say and, when Labelle said that he did not, pronounced a sentence of death, the execution to take place on 10 January 1903.

Fournier's trial took place shortly thereafter, the proceedings taking only seven hours. He testified in his own defence, the gist of his story being that all the police evidence was true, except that Labelle had done the actual shooting:

Landing on the island, we had supper and went to bed. Bouthillette was at our feet. Labelle was next to the door of the tent. Between 4 and 5 o'clock, Labelle awakened me with a stick of wood and went away. In fifteen minutes, Constantine got up and went out. I heard a shot and Labelle came back and said Constantine had shot a rabbit. He stood at the door. Beaudoin went out and another shot was heard. Soon Bouthillette put his head out and Labelle shot him.

This may have been true, or nearer the truth than Labelle's story, but it made little difference. The jury retired and after three minutes returned with a verdict of guilty. Judge Craig, in passing sentence, observed, "It seems impossible that any human being made in the image of God could be guilty of such a crime," and he pointed out that Fournier, who admitted that he knew of the murder plot – the stick of wood was a prearranged signal – was as guilty as if he had fired the actual shots. Fournier, when asked if he had anything to say, replied, "What's right is right. I thank you very much judge, for what you have given me. I have always been a little man, and will take my medicine like a little man." The sentence was death.

The rest was mostly pro forma. The lawyers launched an appeal based on alleged irregularities in the trial. For instance, Fournier had been brought from jail to sit in court while Labelle was testifying on his own behalf, and apparently he had made comments and gestures that might have influenced the jury. As well, it was alleged that Labelle's statement to Welsh made in the United States was coerced and that his request to be tried in French had been denied. Labelle's lawyers also objected to the fact that the supposed murder of Guilboult (whose body had not yet been found), had been mentioned by the judge, though the matter had first been raised by Labelle himself in statements to the police.

The appeal was rejected. Labelle's lawyer, writing to Léonard on the question of an appeal, noted that it was really impossible to find an untainted jury in the Yukon: "I cannot however dismiss from my mind the fact that great prejudice existed against both the accused persons especially on account of our isolated position in this Territory where every circumstance connected with the crime is read by every man in the Territory and where as in this case the statement of Fournier was published in advance and was read by everyone and was followed by unjustifiably strong expressions in the public press touching the same, the whole making a fair and unprejudiced trial almost impossible under the circumstances."

From a modern perspective it would be hard to deny that this was true, but it should be emphasized that the procedure in this trial and the tone and substance of the judge's remarks were entirely consistent with the way criminal trials were conducted in the Yukon and North-West Territories in this era. There was nothing unusual about Craig's tone or attitude, no matter how biased it may seem to the modern reader.

The last act of this drama was the execution of the two convicted murderers which, after a postponement, took place on 20 January 1903. Both Judge Craig and the Department of Justice had strongly recommended against commutation. Émile Léonard got up a petition for clemency, which was signed by a number of Montreal residents who had known Labelle, but such things had little effect on the justice system, and this petition was no exception. The police expressed some apprehension that Léonard might be able to bring political influence to bear to save Labelle, but this did not happen.

Just before 8 AM, on the morning of 20 January, Fournier and Labelle were brought to the gallows. As was the practice at that time, the execution was a semi-public event. It took place in a compound behind the police barracks, a space that held a hundred people. One hundred passes were issued, and all were taken up. The newspaper accounts do not mention the point, but at other executions held in Dawson, first comers were permitted to stand on the gallows, and this was probably the case with this execution. The newspapers reported the executions in detail:

Edward Labelle and Peter Fournier were duly executed this morning at 7:54, in the presence of about one hundred people. A priest had been with Labelle since 3 o'clock, and to the holy father he confessed and received absolution. The priest accompanied him to the scaffold.

Both of the condemned men died game. Fournier said to Labelle in the guardroom, while they were strapped: "Labelle, you look fine."

The hangman pulled the straps somewhat too tight, whereupon he diverted his attentions to him, observing: "You might as well break me in two while you're at it."

To Welsh, the detective, he was vindictive. "You, Welsh," he said, "I promise you for the balance of your life, you sleep uneasy; you mind that."

Fournier, of the two was the more unconcerned. On the trap he looked around and through the crowd with careless glance. He would not accept a priest. At the last moment, with the black cap on his head, he kissed the cross and said, "I am sorry."

Labelle spoke for a few moments in alternate French and English. He said: "If I have any enemy I hope they may forgive me, as I for my part, forgive them. I hope that all may meet in the better world. I deserve what I am getting to-day for my sin. That is all I've got to say."

The sheriff then turned to Fournier, asking if he had anything to say. He replied: "No, sir."

When the hangman placed the noose on Fournier he stretched the neck so as to make a good fit. There was even then no tremor, no weakening.

Labelle showed a slight trembling of the knees, and prayed constantly, kissing the cross twice.

When the trap sprung there was no movement except that Fournier drew up his legs.

The bodies were cut down in sixteen minutes, rough coffined and buried in the jail yard in quick time [*sic*, quicklime?].[11]

One footnote was the appearance of an account of the case in *International Detective Magazine* sometime around 1940, which was the year a typed transcript of the account was copied by the RCMP and put into the Department of Justice file on Labelle. The account was written in an incredibly purple style, and although it is perhaps unkind to make fun of it, the first paragraph can be quoted as an example of the cheap detective fiction of that day:

A small, flat-bottom boat swept swiftly along with the seething, foam-flecked, murky waters of the Yukon River on the afternoon of July 16th, 1902. One of the occupants, a burly, tanned individual sat near the stern of the little craft, his eyes glued to the treacherous current ahead, his hoary hand firmly grasping the tiller. Another man, his eyes shielded from the glaring sun by a soft felt hat, lay prone on the bottom of the boat, a sack of potatoes beneath his head ... It had been several days since they had left Skagway on their perilous voyage full to [*sic*] terrors and hardships. They had successfully crossed the Chilkoot Pass [in fact, they took the train across the White Pass] which had claimed the lives of many bold and venturesome gold-seekers and which had been the Waterloo for those of less stout hearts, causing them to abandon their well laid schemes and return to civilization.

And on and on for fourteen legal-size pages full of adjectives. One wonders what the writer meant by a "hoary hand." Of particular interest is the writer's account of the execution. Since the story was probably taken from newspaper accounts, it is curious that the writer chose to give a totally false version of the conduct of the condemned men:

And so on the morning of January 20th, 1903, Labelle and Fournier stood side by side on the gallows and laughed and joked contemptuously while a small crowd of spectators and officials shivered in the fifty below weather of that gray dawn. Suddenly the trap was sprung. A deep throated laugh of derision from Fournier was cut short. The pair plunged into eternity. The murder of three members of the ill-fated Bouthillet party had been avenged. The mystery of the river of blood in the Klondike had been solved.

One suspects that Welsh did not heed Fournier's admonition to "sleep uneasy." The police had a duty and they had, as expected, carried it out with dispatch and professionalism. A heinous crime had been avenged, as demanded by Yukoners and Canadians at large, and the execution in Dawson City was accepted as a fitting end to a sorry tale. The case of Fournier and Labelle demonstrated a truism of frontier life – that evil men did lurk among the thousands of responsible, dependable travellers who moved through the Yukon in the Klondike era. Everyone knew they were there, despite the best efforts of the police to turn them back at the border and, in the mythology of the day, to limit their northward migration to Alaska. And everyone knew that some of the most dangerous of the desperadoes, like Fournier and Labelle, were practically invisible, identifiable in most instances only after they had completed their acts of treachery and brutality.

The North-West Mounted Police worked in a world of high expectations and responded remarkably well to the challenges they faced. They stared down, in good Sam Steele fashion, many of the ne'er-do-wells who attempted to make it across the border into the Yukon. Their willingness to bend the law in the interests of peace and the maintenance of order found many admirers in the Northwest, who cheered when the police rode petty criminals out of town on the infamous "blue ticket." But the northern miners were also realists. They knew that criminals passed among them, and that evil things could happen in the vast loneliness of the Canadian Subarctic. When murders occurred, as in 1902, the public did not rush to condemn the police for their inability to provide complete protection from evil. Rather, they urged on the NWMP, counting on the Mounties' record of success and integrity to lead them to the offender and bring the criminals to justice. The level of confidence expressed in the police proved to be an effective incentive to the Mounties, for they acted as though their future credibility rested on the prosecution of every major case. The determination with which Welsh tracked down Fournier became a glowing example of the Mounties' credo. They did "always get their man" – in the North, at least.

CHAPTER FOUR

Breaking the Faith:
The Elfors Case

There remains nothing to do save the formality
of his trial and execution.

Whitehorse *Weekly Star*, reporting the arrest of Elfors

The Elfors case[1] was one in which a man went against the code that governed the relations between strangers in this remote and potentially dangerous land. Ned Elfors broke what the poet Robert Service called "the law of the Yukon," thus striking at the stability of the whole community. His act was more than a robbery and murder. It was an assault on the system of trust that underlay the Yukon's entire social structure. Yukoners feared nothing more than insecurity. They lived in a land of isolation, danger, and extremes – of darkness and cold in winter, of light in summer – a land of dramatic mountains and thundering rivers. The Yukon was, in many respects, an island. Despite its physical attachment to the North American continent, it had only seasonal access to the rest of the world. For five months of the year the gold-bearing part of the territory was virtually inaccessible, and until the construction of the telegraph line to the Yukon in 1901, the region was starved for news of the rest of the world. During the gold rush, with thousands of prospectors in the North, with supplies at a premium, and with virtually no opportunity to bring emergency goods into the area, Yukoners were well aware of their exposure to the elements and to the perils of northern life.

A profound sense of vulnerability pervades the early descriptions of non-Native activity in the Yukon. Nineteenth-century fur traders such as Robert Campbell and John Bell wrote extensively about their loneliness and their fear of being forgotten by the outside world. That Campbell and his Hudson's Bay Company colleagues routinely lost canoe-loads of supplies (and the lives of boatmen) in the vicious rapids of the Liard River only heightened their level of anxiety and their sense of abandonment. The early gold miners shared these sentiments, though they conveyed a mixed message about their situation. On one hand there were those who spoke eloquently of the "community" of prospectors in the North and the cooperative spirit that ran through the place. Others gave a more ominous message, like that in the poems of Robert Service (whose message was very mixed). They spoke of isolation, intense loneliness, "cabin fever," and the fear of starvation, cold, wolves, floods, or any of the other disasters that might hit the Yukon.

There is a romantic image of life in the Yukon in the early years of the twentieth century, one of mateship, mutual support, and a common struggle against the elements – and much of this was true. But realism suggests a more varied image. The Yukon was a tough place to live. Only a few people in Dawson City and even fewer in Whitehorse lived in comparative comfort; the grandiose government house erected in the post-gold-rush years offered a deliberate if misleading statement about the livability of the North. There were many reasons why people usually stayed only a few years – if that long – in the Yukon Territory. The first was the isolation of the place. Although there was a regular sleigh service from Dawson City to the railhead at Whitehorse, it was a long, cold, and expensive journey, and few took it willingly. As a result, the northern Yukon was effectively cut off from the outside world for much of the year, so that the last river boat's passage south from Dawson City each October was a melancholy event. Half a year would pass before the sternwheelers again moved along the Yukon River and its tributaries. Whitehorse was, of course, quickly and comfortably accessible to the outside via both a steamship and a railroad service, but it was a small transportation village of a few hundred people. The centre of population was far to the north.

Add to the isolation the small, temporary nature of most homes, hastily constructed on permafrost out of green logs and notorious for leaning drunkenly after a few years and for letting the bitterness of winter seep through the walls. Imported food was expensive, even with the railway and sternwheelers in operation, and it was unobtainable fresh in the winter, forcing residents to adopt the most rudimentary of diets, dominated by bannock and canned goods, and supplemented by local products, including moose and caribou meat, berries, and fresh or frozen fish.

There were episodes of hunger in the Yukon's history, especially away from the main centres, and anyone caught ill prepared in the subarctic wilderness paid bitterly for the poor planning. One of the most famous Yukoners of the post-gold-rush age was, the quiet and stolid Isaac O. Stringer. (The O did not stand for anything. Like Harry S. Truman, Stringer just liked the sound of the initial.) He was famous not for his years of missionary work but for a single episode when he was caught without food in the northern Yukon and became, in the title of his biography, *The Bishop Who Ate His Boots*. The thought of the clergyman chewing on his shoes makes for a compelling image, and it attracted some nice donations to the Anglican Church (though what he did, in fact, was boil the boots and drink the broth). Nevertheless, the story captured one of the truisms of the North. It was – and is – a dangerous place.

Yukoners, though a tough-minded and independent folk, were not reckless and as a rule placed a high premium on reducing risk. They stockpiled food in the ubiquitous caches that stood outside almost all cabins, and they assembled piles of firewood for heating their cabins in winter. Supplies were ordered months ahead of time, and annual expenditures were carefully planned to ensure that sufficient money was set aside to cover the necessities of life. Communities organized themselves for mutual self-help, principally through volunteer fire brigades.

The Yukon Order of Pioneers, an organization of longtime Yukoners, provided a measure of collective security against poverty or ill health. Initially, one had to have been in the Yukon before the gold rush to qualify, but this was later amended to require twenty years' residency. Much later still, and only after a lengthy court challenge in the 1980s, women were allowed to join. Yukon society combined, in a curious but strong fashion, fierce individualism and communal values. These became institutionalized in the "law of the Yukon," which made it an offence to ignore the suffering of another and mandated – by community pressure rather than law – that cabins and food be available to travellers in need. It was unthinkable to refuse help to a stranger, and at a more recent date it was made illegal to pass a stopped car on the road without offering assistance.

Yukoners developed effective strategies, outside and around the law, for coping with potential troublemakers. Before the gold rush, miners' meetings regularly expelled malcontents and troublemakers from their midst. In an unintended copy of the Inuit system of social control, the miners got rid of people when they appeared to be about to make trouble, rather than after they had thrown the first punch. The northern version of "The dog is entitled to its first bite" might well have read "The dog is not even entitled to its first snarl." When the North-West Mounted Police arrived in 1894, they introduced the rule of Canadian law, but they also quickly discovered the value of the miners' system, even as they suppressed it. They introduced an informal mechanism described as the "blue ticket," by which would-be troublemakers were moved out of the territory (and into Alaska, where the NWMP thought they would likely be more at home); they were ordered to leave immediately or face arrest and almost certain conviction, followed by a sentence and hard labour. In this manner, which was totally illegal, the police were able to control Yukon society and lessen the degree of vulnerability.

Collectively, Yukoners urgently sought to control the level of uncertainty and, through any means required, to provide such protection as they could against all measure of threats, human or climatic. As a consequence, they enjoyed a fairly high level of security, particularly given their position on the distant fringes of North American society and the extreme conditions in which they lived. Yukoners lived in the knowledge that they were well supervised by the police, could call on their countrymen for support, and shared a common concern about the vagaries of climate and geography.

This meant, however, that they were intensely unforgiving of those who broke the territorial code. The collectivist impulse, the strong sense of interdependence, and the fear generated by isolation meant that Yukoners responded with fury to those who dared to challenge the central tenets of their society. The Yukon worked, they believed, only if there was deep trust. If neighbours and travellers could not be relied upon, the system would surely break down into the kind of stereotypic American-style anarchy which they had all come to fear. The case of Ned Elfors, which involved a violation of the Yukon's code through a brutal murder, provided just such a test of the spirit of the Yukon.

Ned Elfors was born Nestor Elgfors in Bjorneborg, Finland (then part of Russia), on 5 August 1853. In most of the Yukon murder cases very little was known of the murderer's early life, and in Elfors's case nothing at all was known except the place and date of his birth, which appear in the coroner's report issued after he was hanged. Little interest was paid to the early lives of these accused killers unless, as in the Gogoff case, there was the suggestion of hereditary or long-standing insanity, which would have been a defence against a murder charge. Whether the murderers had been abused as children or whether there were other factors that led them to become killers was of no interest to the authorities, since such things had no validity as a legal defence in that era.

Elfors appeared in the record in the fall of 1907, when he met David Bergman and Emil Anderson in Seattle, where the three agreed to travel together to the Yukon. Anderson, who was in his early twenties, and Bergman, an older man, were both Scandinavians. When the northern navigation season opened, the men went to Skagway. Elfors had hardly any money, while the other two had about $300 each. Apparently they walked from Skagway to Whitehorse to save money on the train fare – a formidable accomplishment. At Whitehorse, they bought a small boat for the trip to Dawson City, leaving in late May or early June 1908. On 8 June the three men were camped on the bank of the Yukon River, about twenty kilometres downstream from Selkirk. The nearest inhabitants were some men working at a wood camp, about ten kilometres away.

Elfors, Bergman, and Anderson were following a familiar Yukon pattern. They had apparently not known one an other before they headed north. Succeeding in the Yukon required partnership   it was almost impossible to succeed alone – and prospectors and travellers routinely formed, dissolved, and reformed partnerships.[2] In doing so, they implicitly accepted the "spirit of the Yukon" and clearly realized that they needed to trust and cooperate with one another in order to reach the Klondike. Since the early 1870s, when the first outsiders arrived to look for gold, Yukoners had come together in mutually beneficial alliances and then, for reasons of personality, personal choice, or disagreement about gold-mining plans, had separated, only to form a partnership with someone else. The three men moving towards Dawson City had assimilated, through physical necessity, the central concept of Yukon life. And in trusting each other – a decision that would cost two of them their lives – they had likewise adopted the trust in their fellow men that was basic to survival and social order in the Northwest.

During the five or six days when the three had been on the river, Elfors had suggested several times that they should go out on a hunt. At 4 AM on 8 June, Elfors and Bergman left Anderson asleep in a tent and went out to look for game. After a time, Elfors returned, awakened Anderson, and told him that they had shot a bear and that Bergman was skinning it. So Anderson, followed by Elfors, went to join Bergman. Elfors had a rifle slung on his back and also a pistol in his pocket. Suddenly, without warning, he shot Anderson with the pistol, the bullet entering Anderson's neck under the ear and coming out through his cheek, taking away part of his cheekbone. Anderson turned and grappled with Elfors, who shouted that it was an accident.

Believing this to be true, Anderson let Elfors go, whereupon Elfors grabbed his rifle and aimed it at the bleeding man. Anderson turned and ran, losing his boots as he went, and did not stop until he reached Selkirk, twenty kilometres away, bleeding all the way, his feet torn to pieces. In Selkirk he was given medical treatment, and the Mounted Police were alerted. Two days later the police found Elfors asleep in his tent behind a woodpile, his beard shaven off and two loaded rifles by his side. Several days after Elfors's arrest, Bergman's body was found, covered with brush and earth, about seventy-five kilometres from where Anderson had been shot. Bergman had five bullets in his head, some of which had first gone through his arms, a fact that suggested he had been holding up his arms to ward off the shots.

Elfors, under arrest in Dawson City, and apparently believing that his victim's body would not be found, claimed that on the morning of the shootings he had seen Bergman on the shore of the river negotiating with four men in a boat to go downriver with them, and that this was the last he had seen of him. He said that he had shot Anderson in self-defence when Anderson attacked him without provocation. For a number of reasons, including the fact that Elfors had Bergman's money in his pocket and that his account of the supposed struggle with Anderson did not square with the nature of Anderson's wounds, it is clear that Elfors's story was a clumsy fairy tale and that he was guilty of murder and attempted murder.

At his arraignment, which took place on 27 June, Elfors had pleaded guilty, but since his lawyer was for some reason not present, the judge refused the plea and sent for the lawyer. After consultation between lawyer and client, Elfors said that he had pleaded guilty only because he thought there was no use in defending himself, since he was "poor and had no friends." A plea of not guilty was then entered.

Elfors's trial took place on 6 and 7 July 1908 before Judge James Craig. The crown prosecutor was J.B. Pattullo; counsel for the defence was George Black, the territory's most prominent Conservative politician. Pattullo was the older brother of Duff Pattullo, the future premier of British Columbia. The two brothers had come to the Yukon during the gold rush to make their fortune, one as a lawyer, the other as a public servant. James B. Pattullo's appointment in 1903 as crown prosector had been a Liberal patronage appointment, and he was made a KC in 1908. In 1914, since the Yukon continued to decline, he moved his practice to Vancouver.[3]

George Black, Pattullo's opponent, had a long career ahead of him, much of it greased by the strong hand of Conservative patronage politics. A young Yukon lawyer at the time Sir Robert Borden and the Conservatives won in Ottawa in 1911, Black was made commissioner of the Yukon. The Borden election victory was marked by a remarkable sight, well described by Laura Berton[4] – the Liberals heading out of town, pushed from the generous sinecures granted by their party, while a band of carpetbagging Conservatives headed into the Yukon to take up their patronage appointments.

George Black had been in the Yukon since the gold rush and was rewarded for sticking with the party during the dark years of the Laurier administration. His was the pick of the government appointments, and it gave him a role and status in the Yukon that he never relinquished. He subsequently was MP for Yukon from 1921 to 1949, except for the years 1935–40, when during his illness his wife Martha held his seat (the second woman in Canada elected to Parliament). He was speaker of the house during the administration of R.B. Bennett, 1930–35, and died in 1965 at the age of ninety-two. The Elfors trial, however, was not his finest hour. Since Elfors had no money, Black must have been working *pro bono*, and the defence he mounted could not have taken up much of his time to prepare; it took only a few hours to give.

The trial lasted two days, an average length in that era, but they were not long days. Proceedings began at 10 AM and ended about 4 PM, with an hour off for lunch. Eighteen witnesses were called for the prosecution and none for the defence. At the beginning of the trial, Black challenged F.R. Chute, a juryman who had already been sworn in, for cause. He asked Chute if he had formed an opinion on the case, and Chute replied that he had; that he thought the accused was guilty. Pattullo asked him if he thought that after he had heard the evidence he could come to a different conclusion, and Chute replied that he believed he could. The judge then asked two of the other jurors (or "triers") to decide upon this evidence whether they believed that Chute was a "fair man to put on the jury," and they decided that he was. Clearly, the principle of "innocent until proven guilty" did not apply. The use of triers seems antique; it derives from English tradition and is still part of the Canadian criminal justice system, though it has died out in the United States.[5]

As far as the newspapers were concerned, of course, Elfors was guilty, and the Whitehorse *Weekly Star* had no hesitation in saying so. Two weeks after the killing, under the headline "Murder Most Foul," the paper had noted that the Mounted Police had been sent to investigate the incident "where Ned Elfors shot and killed David Bergman," and it concluded that "there remains nothing to do save the formality of his trial and execution." The Yukon press, which in the glory days of the Klondike had been an intense, frenzied, and highly partisan fourth estate, did not pull punches on murder trials. In the tightly knit and shrinking community of Dawson City, and the even smaller settlements that dotted the post-Klondike Yukon, opinions were formed quickly and were soon widely held. Rarely, if ever, did these opinions offer much room for doubt.

A second juror, F.W.G.C. Clark, was challenged on the grounds that he had read press reports stating that Elfors was guilty. Judge

Craig, showing signs of impatience, instructed the two jurors deciding Clark's fitness as follows:

Now, the system which prevails in some countries other than our own is that the most ignorant men are chosen for jurymen, that men who would read the papers are excluded. I hope we will never come to that pass. What we want is jurymen who recognize the solemnity of their oath and the responsibility of their office ... It is almost impossible for a man in these modern days to avoid reading the papers. If you exclude all men of that class you exclude the intelligent jurymen ... But the question is after reading the papers is the mind so biased that if a man is proven innocent by the evidence, if the evidence leads to innocence, is Mr. Clark so biased against him that he would find him guilty anyhow, or, on the other hand, will he give a fair verdict?

Black chimed in to say, "The evidence must shew, not his innocence, but his guilt." The judge retorted, "He must be able to find a verdict upon the evidence; if the evidence points to innocence then he must find him innocent; unless the evidence points to guilt you cannot find him guilty." The two jurors split on the question, and Clark was excluded.

To the modern reader used to our current system, which is much more protective of the rights of the accused, all this may sound as if the deck was stacked against Elfors, which by our standards it was. But it may be of some comfort to remember that the evidence against Elfors was overwhelming. The testimony of Anderson alone would have been enough to convict him, apart from the flimsiness of Elfors's story and the amount of material evidence. An acquittal would have been astonishing, and clearly no one expected it, not even the accused.

There is another interesting twist to this case – the part the judge played in the trial. In most of the trials dealt with in this book, the judge made it perfectly clear that he thought the defendant was guilty and that the jury would be shirking their duty if they did not convict. Here, however, the judge was to go beyond this position, not only restating the case for the prosecution but demolishing the defence's case with both logic and sarcasm.

As with other cases of this sort, the Elfors affair served to reinforce Yukoners' confidence in their justice system. They realized

that murders would always occur, that it was part of the nature of
some men to kill, and that circumstances would sometimes lead to
killing. What they wanted from the justice system was not that it
should prevent murder – there was no talk of "root causes" and
"contributing factors" in those days – but that murder be punished, that killers be caught, tried, and hanged as expeditiously as
possible. Although the papers usually said that an execution
served as a warning to evildoers, no one expected that hangings
would end murders, though perhaps they might prevent a few.
What hangings did was to bring a kind of balance into play, in
which the death of the murderer settled the account of his deed.
This restored some harmony to society.

Along with this desire for balance was the fundamental insecurity of subarctic life and the northerners' continual awareness of
their acute vulnerability. Together these make the Yukoners' demand for retributive justice more readily understood. Northern
society needed to rest on assumptions of trust and collective reli-
ability, and Elfors's behaviour struck at the heart of the region's
desire for security and hence had to be dealt with swiftly and
firmly.

The Elfors case is a good example of the official response to this
demand. The case was handled so quickly and, from the point of
view of the public, so satisfactorily, that the *Star* even printed a
kind of self-congratulatory scorecard showing how well it had
been dealt with. In the first place, Black had very little to work
with in defending his client. He cross-examined all the prosecution's witnesses at length, but it was hard going, and he was reduced to asking questions such as whether the alleged bullet holes
in a hat might not have been poked through it with a pencil or the
point of an umbrella – questions which presumably made little
impression on the jurors. By the time Black made his summation
to the jury he must have been desperate, for his speech was wild
enough to provoke the judge into a strong retort. Unfortunately,
the trial transcripts of these cases do not record the summations
for the prosecution and defence, nor do the newspapers, but this
one was so over the top that Judge Craig summarized it in his report to the Department of Justice.

Craig's report to the government shows that he was concerned
not only with making sure that Elfors was convicted but also with

making sure that the integrity of the jury system, as he saw it, was not compromised by a verdict based on what he called a "ridiculous" argument put forward by the defence lawyer. According to Craig, Black discussed and analysed the evidence for ten or fifteen minutes and then spent over an hour admitting Elfors's guilt, "asking the jury to let him go free because Elfors had been destined by God Almighty to kill Bergman and it was not Elfors' fault if Bergman's life was shortened." Black went on to cite other disasters that had taken human life: railway accidents, theatre fires, the Quebec bridge disaster, "drawing an analogy between the position of these corporations in relation to their sacrifice of life and the position of the accused in connection with the crime charged."

Apparently Craig, despite his earlier statement of faith in the intelligence of jurors who read newspapers, did not believe it strongly enough to have faith that these jurors would see the absurdity of Black's argument. "I commented upon this address," he reported, "because very gross miscarriages of justice have taken place in this Territory within the past two years by jury verdicts and by jurors yielding to just such ridiculous arguments as were advanced in this case."

As an instance I might cite a late trial for receiving gold dust to the amount of $40,000 stolen from the Post-office in Dawson, where the jury by their verdict gave effect to the plea that because the Bank of Commerce had received part of the stolen gold dust and had not been indicted along with the accused, therefore the accused should be allowed to go; and this ridiculous plea actually prevailed with the jury, as one of them afterwards confessed to the judge and asked to be stricken off the rolls of jurors because of his mental imbecility in yielding to such a plea … Many cases I might cite of a like nature where justice has been defeated by silly jurors. I thought it my duty in this case to deal rather more severely than I would otherwise do, with the extraordinary argument of the counsel.

The judge was clearly worried about the cosy and occasionally quixotic behaviour of northern juries. Ever since the Klondike gold rush, an anti-establishment ethos had run through the territory, fuelled by the patronage scandals of the early twentieth century and the libertarian spirit of the mining frontier. Save for the North-West Mounted Police, who had a special place in the hearts and minds of Yukoners, major institutions such as government agencies and banks were often held in contempt. The antagonism ran both ways, for officials from William Ogilvie, the first commissioner, through to Judge Craig had often made disparaging comments about the unruly, ill-kempt, and ill-mannered mobs in the Klondike. The American tinge that coloured the Yukon added further to the authorities' distrust of the mining population (though only British subjects were eligible to serve on Yukon juries) and fostered sharp class and status divisions, especially in Dawson City. Craig's comments about the jury fitted the prevailing attitude of the authorities towards the working men who toiled in the Yukon.

Craig's charge to the jury, which must have taken him at least half an hour to deliver, is as close as a command to convict for murder as one is likely to find in the history of Canadian jurisprudence in the twentieth century. To get the full flavour of this remarkable diatribe it would be necessary to quote all 2,600 words, but some excerpts will give the idea. One must picture the scene: the wooden Dawson courthouse, built in 1901 (which still can be visited today, for it is preserved as part of the old government buildings), in its subarctic, shabby Victorian grandeur, crowded with spectators, as it always was during murder trials, and the jury, their minds no doubt already made up, nodding as the judge confirmed their belief that the accused was guilty. In the dock sat Elfors. Since his English was good, he was able to catch the meaning as the judge erased any possible doubt, if such existed, in the minds of the jury. The defence lawyer's face must have been red with anger, and perhaps with embarrassment. That the judge was a Liberal and George Black a "lost in the wilderness" Tory added a touch of partisanship to the proceedings. The crown prosecutor night perhaps have wondered what he was being paid for, since the judge was doing the work for him in putting the case for conviction so neatly to the jury.

Craig began by sweeping away any idea that the case was complicated or that much deep thinking was involved in reaching a verdict. "Fortunately for you and me," he told the jurymen, "the case is a very concrete one, the facts simple and easily understood." "What are we trying," he asked rhetorically, "just in a plain, common-sense way, as reasonable, common-sense men;

coming out of the clouds and coming down to ordinary every-day reason, what are we trying? We are trying whether the man in the dock killed Bergman or not."

He then paid the crown prosecutor a compliment: "The case for the Crown was presented, I think, with admirable fairness. I might go further and say with leniency. The address of the Crown counsel was eminently fair and eminently reasonable. He put the facts before you just as they occurred, as the witnesses in the box swore to them." There was no suggestion in Craig's remarks that the facts were other than as the witnesses had described. He went on to summarize the facts, repeating the prosecution's case and dismissing any idea that there might be a different interpretation of events. He was clear on the motive; it was robbery, and in case any juryman might think that no one would take a human life for such a small sum, he made the point clear: "It may seem very extraordinary to you that ordinary rational human beings would commit a crime of this nature for a paltry $400; yet we know that the history of the Yukon River reveals many similar crimes. Those of you who have lived in the Yukon for any length of time know, and the records of this court tell us the tale of more brutal crimes than this committed for very much less money ... Men are so strangely constituted that they will deprive their fellowmen of life for a few paltry gold dollars."

Craig, of course, exaggerated mightily. There had been few murders in the Yukon – far fewer than most observers expected – and most were crimes of passion and anger, not callous attempts at brutal robbery (though the O'Brien and Labelle-Fournier cases may have been in the judge's mind). That he stated the case so strongly suggests that he understood, and perhaps shared, the community's fear that criminals stalked the subarctic forests. His argument made it clear that he had no intention of tolerating for one second this portrait of the vulnerability of travellers in the Yukon valley.

He then demolished Elfors's story that he had seen the victim leaving with some other men in a boat:

Is that a reasonable story? Why should Bergman desire to leave his own party? What reason is suggested for Bergman leaving his own party to go in a boat with four other men? Have you heard any suggested? If that was the body of David Bergman which was lying in the woods a mile or a mile and a half back then it could not have been David Bergman that Elfors saw negotiating with these men for a trip down the river. If you are satisfied that that man who was killed was David Bergman, the man who came over the trail with Elfors and Anderson, it could not have been David Bergman that this man said he saw negotiating that morning to go down the river. If David Bergman was lying in the woods a mile and a half away covered with brush and earth then it could not have been David Bergman who stood on the shore of the river at the same time. Then what do you say as to the story of Elfors? He told that story before he knew of the discovery of the body. This story was told to Smith on the 13th, 14th, and 15th of the month and the body was not here until the 20th. It was discovered sometime about the 17th.

The main witness against Elfors was Anderson, whom Elfors claimed had attacked him. Craig took special care to deal with Anderson's credibility:

Apart from all the surrounding circumstances did the story strike you as being a truthful story? If you come to that conclusion then the balance of the matter is very simple, it seems to me. Then what is there in the story itself to make you think it was a fair and reasonable story? Take the condition of the man himself. What are the conditions? He arrives near Selkirk and he met Mr. Swinehart in a state of intense excitement, Swinehart says, which excitement lasted until he met Mrs. Stillman and Mrs. McLachlan who dressed his wounds. He came there covered with blood, bleeding from a wound inflicted [from] the rear, his feet torn. Now what would that indicate to you as reasonable men? Would it indicate that this man ran away from a great terror which was following him, or that he came there with a made-up story? Which do you think is the true solution of this appearance which the man presented when he arrived at Selkirk? Then you have the evidence of the constable who says he is an accustomed trailer [tracker], who has trailed with the Indians; he saw the jumps which this man took as if the man, in the very spot where the thing occurred, were in hurried flight from the place. You have Anderson's story of the encounter between himself and Elfors. You are also entitled to take, because the Crown gives it in evidences, the story which Elfors gave of the same encounter. Which of these stories appeals to you as the

one having the most truth about it, the story which Anderson tells or the
story which Elfors tells? ... Which one will you believe?

He then dealt with the actual shooting of Bergman and with
Elfors's story that the two had gone hunting, leaving Anderson
asleep:

Elfors says – "I was out with Bergman hunting and we killed a bear ...
He says himself that he went out first alone with Bergman, and the
Crown suggests to you very reasonably – why didn't they all go hunting
together? Why should Elfors have invited Bergman to go alone first and
afterwards invite Anderson to go alone? Elfors and Bergman went out
alone together and Elfors alone returned. What happened on that memorable journey which Elfors and Bergman took on that morning? Did he or
did he not shoot that man and are the bullets which were found in the
dead man's head those which Elfors fired into him? Is that what occurred? You have a right to draw any inference from the facts which the
evidence seems to warrant in that connection. Then it is shewn that one
of the wounds inflicted on Bergman was similar to the wound inflicted
on Anderson, that is, a shot fired from the rear, passing through the
cheek ... Does that lead to any conclusion in your minds, the similarity of
these wounds which were found, one we know found on the person of a
living man and the other on the body of a dead man?

Black had raised the objection that the evidence against his client was circumstantial, that there was no witness to the actual killing. Craig made short work of that:

Now, it has been said that the evidence is circumstantial, and the Crown
very truly tells you that circumstantial evidence is perhaps the best evidence. Very many eminent jurists have said that circumstantial evidence
is far better than the evidence of direct eye-witnesses because once having got the facts or the circumstances securely proven it is easy to draw a
deduction from them. Circumstances, after all, in most murder cases are
the main facts which lead to conclusions. So that having the circumstances proven, if you believe the evidence which the Crown puts in, if
you believe those circumstances, if you believe that it is David Bergman's
body, if you believe that the bullets were in his head, if you believe

Anderson was shot in the back of the neck, if you believe that he came to Selkirk all wounded and frightened as he was, and then what conclusion do you draw from these things; that is circumstantial evidence ... And when you hear the bugaboo raised that a man should not be convicted on circumstantial evidence, it is not sound because that is what circumstantial evidence is, proven facts and deductions from them.

Judge Craig scoffed at the attempt of the defence counsel to bring in outside arguments to show that Bergman's death was an accident of fate, something for which Elfors could not be held responsible:

The argument of the defence is, I do not hesitate to say, a most extraordinary one. I have not heard in a British court of justice an argument of just that kind addressed to a jury. The argument boiled down is this[,] that because there are railway accidents you must let this man go. Men have been killed in railway accidents, men have been slaughtered by trust companies, wrong is done in high places, therefore you must violate your oath. Because the train ran off the track and somebody was killed today, you jurymen, sworn to find a verdict according to the evidence, must allow Elfors to go free ... I ask you to use your reason upon the evidence in this case. You are trying Elfors ... and you are not trying God Almighty regarding Cain's escape.

At length Craig brought his devastating speech to a close, with one final exhortation to the jurymen to do their duty and avoid being influenced by pity or squeamishness:

You have a duty to see that that man does not go to the gallows innocent; but you have a like duty to see that he does not escape if he is guilty. You stand to protect the public and you stand to protect that man ... As to the reasonable doubt, it must not be a fear, it must not be a shirking of your duty, it must not be paltering with truth or trying to escape from bringing in a verdict which your reason and your conscience compels you to because you do not want to see a man hanged. That is not reasonable doubt. Reasonable doubt is a doubt which your reason leads you to have, based on the evidence. If you doubt that this evidence does not lead in the one direction then you have a right to give that reasonable doubt full weight and give the man the benefit of it; but if your reason leads you to the other conclusion your duty is to bring in a verdict according to the evidence. You will now retire and consider your verdict.

The jury was out for all of ten minutes and returned with a verdict of guilty. A short exchange took place between Elfors and the judge, in which Elfors made a pitiful and ineffectual attempt to defend himself. The judge ignored him, and passed the mandatory sentence upon him:

THE COURT (to the prisoner) – Have you anything to say why the sentence of the court should not be pronounced against you?
THE PRISONER – I would like to speak to Anderson
THE COURT – Anything you want to say you can say to me now as to why sentence should not be pronounced against you.
THE PRISONER – Anderson has not been talking right.
THE COURT – It is always a painful duty to sentence a man when found guilty of a capital offence. But I must say that the jury could have come to no other conclusion upon the evidence than they have come to. All that could have been done on your behalf was done for you; everything that could have been said for you was said for you and the Crown presented the case with great fairness to the jury. I suppose no words that I could say would be of any avail or have any meaning to you. You committed a most brutal crime. It is hard to understand how a man in human form could be guilty of such an act; but we know there are such men. We know it too well in this Territory. I will not harrow the feelings you have by any further comment on that matter. The only duty remaining to me is to pronounce sentence on you, and the sentence of this court is that you be taken back to the place whence you came and thence to the place of execution on the 6th of October and there hanged by the neck until you are dead; and may God have mercy on your soul.

No serious consideration was given at any level to commuting Elfors's sentence, and no friends or relatives petitioned the government on his behalf. Nor is there any indication that George Black appealed or took any steps to secure a commutation. The judge in his report to the government recommended against clemency, and the Remissions Branch concurred, noting in a memo to the minister of justice that the judge believed that "the speedy arrest and punishment of this man will ... have a very beneficial effect upon the great number of rather rough characters who are passing down the Yukon in spring time in just the same way as the unfortunate victim." Court sentences often have the dual goal of punishing the convicted and warning the potentially criminally minded. The entire handling of this case, which was followed intently by local residents and no doubt was the subject of many fireside conversations in the coming weeks, sent a powerful message about the North's distaste for bushwhackers and, less directly, their intense fear of being alone in the subarctic wilderness.

On 6 October 1908, Elfors was brought to the gallows in Dawson City. Standing in front of the noose, he was asked by the sheriff to confess:

SHERIFF: Elfors I want to have a few words with you. You are about to pass over the Great Divide, and this is the last opportunity you will have to enlighten the public and clear the public mind of who is the guilty party that killed that poor man on the 8th of June last below Selkirk. You have been accused and been tried and found guilty, but you have not yet confessed. If you are an honourable man, you want to do your duty before you face your maker, you have a duty to perform, a duty that you owe to yourself, to the jury, to the Judge, to everyone connected with your trial. Who killed Dave Bergman on the 8th of June last?
ELFORS: I killed him yes sir.
SHERIFF: You killed him?
ELFORS: Yes sir.
SHERIFF: Who shot Anderson on the same day the 8th of June last?
ELFORS: There was been [sic] a fight, that is all there is to it; there was been a fight.

Either at the same time or a little before, Elfors signed a short note, written in pencil, probably by the sheriff: "I Nestor Elfors accept the sentence of death imposed upon me in punishment of my crime – I pardon everybody as I hope to received pardon from my God that I am going to meet at this hour." Understandably, given the situation, the signature is noticeably shaky. The confession was crucial, for it provided confirmation that the decision of judge and jury had not been in error and that the community at large was justified in taking Elfors's life.

At the end of the trial, the Whitehorse *Weekly Star* concluded with satisfaction that the episode showed the speed and efficiency of British justice, compared with "other places" – the United States – where things ran less smoothly. This comparison was often made by the authorities in the Yukon. The Mounted Police, in particular, liked to point out how peaceful the Yukon was compared with the lawlessness of American frontier towns. Under the headline "How Criminals Are Dealt With in the Yukon," the *Star* observed:

The following is a record of which all Yukoners should be proud as, while no undue haste was employed and while three long months were given the condemned man for appeal, it is an exemplification of the manner in which law should be carried out. If the same course was pursued in the majority of other places where the courts are "monkeyed" with for months and years in connection with murder cases – premeditated and cold blooded – a more wholesome respect would be entertained for the law. The matter referred to is the record – a sort of diary – of the Elfors murder case and is as follows:
June 8 – Murder committed
June 10 – Elfors, the murderer, captured
June 11 – Preliminary examination begun
June 17 – Body of David Bergman, the victim, found
June 22 – Coroner's inquest concluded, verdict that deceased had come to his death by gunshot wounds inflicted by Ned Elfors
June 26 – Preliminary concluded
June 27 – Elfors arraigned and trial fixed
July 6 – Trial begun
July 7 – Trial concluded, verdict of guilty and sentenced to be hanged October 6.[6]

Yukoners found much to be satisfied with in the handling of the Elfors case. The criminal was quickly apprehended, charged, tried, and executed. Virtually no Yukoners and very few travellers, other than the victims, had more than a passing acquaintance with Ned Elfors. He was not a Yukoner and had no local friends to support him, and no one who knew him came forward to offer help or give so much as a character reference. Like so many of those associated with the northern frontier, Elfors was not from the North and had been unlikely to stay in the North. If he had not been a murderer, he would, like tens of thousands before him, have passed swiftly through the territory leaving scant record of his northern journey.

Elfors had committed what was, in the eyes of Yukoners, a dual crime. Most obviously, he had killed a fellow traveller and had done so in a callous, brutal, and unforgivable fashion. But he had also broken the "law of the Yukon," the unwritten but clearly understood agreement that northerners could count on and trust their neighbours. Without such a "law," anarchy would prevail. And whatever attraction a libertarian frontier might have in more gentle, southern climates, it had no place whatsoever in the isolated, lonely, and vast wilderness of the Northwest. In a world where theft of food could easily mean starvation, where the unexpected use of a cabin's woodpile could carry tragically frozen results, and where the refusal to provide assistance to someone in need could be the seal of death, Yukoners needed to know that they could trust the people with them and, indeed, could count on others who were travelling and working in the North.

Elfors's vicious attack was proof that, on occasion, the "law of the Yukon" could break down and that some small number of northerner travellers and workers did not share the commitment to the stability of the northland. The swift reaction of the courts, the cheers that erupted when the guilty verdict was issued, the death sentence that was imposed, and the execution that was carried out – all made it clear that Yukoners would tolerate absolutely no break in the fundamental assumptions that underlay their society.

CHAPTER FIVE

The Foreign Madman: Alexander Gogoff

In my opinion, he is perfectly rational.

Judge Charles Macaulay to the Department of Justice,
recommending against clemency for Alexander Gogoff

Alexander Gogoff[1] was an outsider, one of many who drifted in and out of the Yukon over the years. He was an outsider for two reasons. First, he was a "foreigner," which in those days meant someone who was not British or Canadian, or even American (Americans were simply "Americans," in their own category). A "foreigner" was someone who did not speak much English and was therefore a person of little importance in the territory. Second, Gogoff was odd, eccentric to the point of mental illness – to what degree it is impossible to determine, since he was examined only by amateurs in the field of mental disorders. He came many thousands of kilometres to seek his fortune in the Northwest (from where, no one was exactly sure) only to die on a Yukon gallows for killings that made little sense to his contemporaries. Like some dangerous and exotic import that posed danger and destruction to society, he had to be exterminated without too much soul-searching.

Yukoners love to talk about the "colourful 5 per cent," the eclectic and raffish group of oddballs who have long been a distinctive feature of northern life: "marginal" individuals, often strange ducks but, unlike Gogoff, generally harmless and thus tolerated. All frontiers have traditionally served as a safety valve for society, providing people like these with an opportunity to reinvent themselves, to escape their past and build a new future in a new land, or just to decay in some quiet corner. So it has been in the North, where the openness of the frontier combined with the mystique of Klondike gold created an almost mystical belief in the redemptive capacity of the region.

This meant, in practical terms, that long after the large dredging companies had shouldered aside the individual miner in favour of huge machines that scoured the creek bottoms for the last few flakes of gold, the Yukon continued to attract travellers, prospectors, and dreamers. Each spring, coastal steamers and the White Pass and Yukon Railway brought north the latest instalment of would-be stampeders, each believing that the magic of the Yukon could touch him as it had George Carmack, Skookum Jim, and Tagish (Dawson) Charlie. Each fall, the same railway and ships carried out the disheartened and chastened, their dreams of wealth and adventure dashed on the realities of northern prospecting.

The Yukon came to rely on this steady stream of young men (and the tiny handful of women) who came north every year. A few – the number declining with each passing year – came back year after year, happy to work the long northern summers on the riverboats, the railway, and the dredges. Northern work paid well by southern Canadian standards, and companies were anxious to find strong backs and willing workers who would put up with the long hours and hard-driving schedules of the Subarctic's intense summer work season. The White Pass and Yukon Route company used seasonal migrants to staff the riverboats that formed the backbone of the northern transportation system. Most of the ships' captains earned sizable incomes during the summer months and then fled south to spend the winter in Vancouver, Vancouver Island, or Seattle. Unskilled workers received higher pay in the North, but few could afford the luxury of a winter at leisure; they combined northern seasonal employment with winter work in the big cities to the south.

But the core of returning workers met only part of the demand. The railway and riverboat company needed a steady supply of temporary workers to help with the maintenance of the railbed, to bring the riverboats in and out of the water, to cut wood along the rivers, and to keep the North's transportation system going through the all-important summer season. The region was moribund during the winter months, most of the key community leaders, like the ships' captains, fleeing for warmer climates. But each spring they returned, eager to capitalize on the commercial opportunities that flourished for a few months.

The system worked well enough to keep the sparsely populated territory's economy going. And although the goldfields held little magic by 1905, the need for workers ensured that very few of the migrants found themselves destitute. At worst, they had to work, and work hard, for a few months to cover their living costs and to raise enough money to buy their return passage south. Add to this the fluidity of the North and the fact that people could escape their past by heading to the Yukon, and the elements for an ever-changing impermanent society were well established. This was indeed the nature of non-Native society in the Yukon from the end of the Klondike gold rush through to the Second World War – dominated by young, mobile men, whose commitment to the North rarely lasted more than a season.

Societies in flux attract all kinds of people. They also generally lack the social order and community institutions that provide stability and incorporate newcomers into the regional order. In the Yukon, this situation created a potentially volatile mix, especially as many of the people entering the North lacked social skills and failed to fit in. Little thought has been given to yet another dimension of this society – the fact that many of those entering the North came from non-English-speaking countries and did not have the language ability and cultural knowledge to fit in easily with the overwhelmingly British nature of the non-aboriginal population.

Much has been made of the Klondike gold rush being a global event, and from the earliest times chroniclers remarked on the polyglot society that formed on the banks of the Yukon River. But too much, it seems, has been made of this social complexity. The vast majority of the stampeders came from the western United States and Canada – though, admittedly, some of them had earlier arrived from distant countries. The 1901 Yukon census, for example, reveals a wide diversity of backgrounds (based on place of birth, though some had been raised in North America): 66 Austrians, 3 from Brazil and Peru, 1 Costa Rican, 9 Greeks, 7 Hungarians, 6 Icelanders, and 2 Romanians, 7 Spaniards, 61 Japanese, 5 Chinese, and 2 Turks. However, of the 27,200 people reported in this census, over 17,000 came from Canada (including First Nations people), the United States, or Great Britain. The origin of 6,400 was "unknown." The Yukon and Alaska were English-speaking territories, and the French Canadians who made their way into the region found few who spoke their language. Those from other countries – Japan, China, Russia, Poland, and the like – must have found life very lonely, with few fellow speakers in the entire North and with almost no one understanding their culture or social expectations.

In the fast-moving ever-changing society of a Yukon summer, some people were bound to be outsiders. Many stood apart because of language or cultural differences (and construction workers, riverboat hands, and others of their ilk were not widely known for cultural sensitivity and inclusiveness). Others, the colourful 5 per cent, were isolated by their peculiar personalities, which might be manifested by aggressiveness, social withdrawal, odd habits, quirkiness, or hygiene. With some of the foreigners, cultural differences were confused with craziness, and the inability to speak English was often equated with lack of intelligence. One of those stigmatized in this way was Alexander Gogoff.

Gogoff was born in Russia in 1886 or 1887, in Velly Dzay in the Caucasian province of Jersky. (His foreignness was emphasized by the wide variations in the spelling of his place of origin. One witness said that the village was named Tsai, which he placed some sixty kilometres from the town of Christiansky, in the province of Tersky or Torsky.) At the time of his crime, Gogoff was "six feet tall" and of "strong, athletic build." His native language was Ossetian, and he apparently spoke Russian as well, though not a great deal of English. Little else is known about him, for neither the courts nor the newspapers were particularly interested in his early life. His name was spelled in several ways. The papers wrote it "Gagoff," though the spelling used here is the one given in the criminal records. The few facts known about him come from a deposition made by a cousin after his conviction. Originally, like thousands of other ephemeral figures of the Klondike, he was part of the scenery and not important enough to attract much attention.

Gogoff arrived in Canada in 1911 and lived and worked with a cousin clearing land in the Vancouver area. In 1914 he went to the Yukon with the "Mischenko party," which consisted of about forty Russian-speaking men who travelled to Whitehorse, built

Part of the route of the White Pass and Yukon Railway
through the coastal mountains, south of the section
where Alexander Gogoff shot four railway workers
(NA, PA-149828)

boats, and went down the Yukon to prospect. Like most such men, they found little or no gold, and like many of their compatriots, some opted to stay on for a time, perhaps realizing that the North's prospects, however thin, were better than their opportunities farther south.

H.G. McPherson, a druggist on Front Street in Whitehorse, befriended Gogoff and later testified:

He used to come around in front of the store and look in and I rather took pity on him; he seemed a nice quiet boy and he knew very few words of English at that time. I would say "Hello" and he would say "Hello." I called him "Alec." He called me "Mack," and by degrees Alec used to come into my store, when he would get through work he would come into my store along probably half an hour after dinner, just hanging around the store; he was very quiet; I used to think he was a very nice, quiet boy, a good Russian, but unfortunately he could not speak the English language, and he was lonesome.

Gogoff spent the winter of 1914-15 in and around Whitehorse, and in the spring of 1915 he worked for several weeks as a section hand for the White Pass and Yukon Railway. During this period "he was under police surveillance for a few days because his actions were such as to excite doubts about his sanity,"[2] (though later the police seem to have had no doubt that he was perfectly sane). In May he quit his job and went south, returning in September to complete the working season.

Gogoff had found work, as many did in this era, on one of the most remarkable railways in Canada. The White Pass and Yukon Railway was one of the few lines built in Canada without a government subsidy, something of a marvel in the halcyon days of railway promotion. Initial planning on a railway from tidewater along the Alaska panhandle into the Yukon interior actually predated the Klondike gold rush, and promoters were lining up cash and developing plans in the belief that the construction of a rail link would stimulate rapid economic expansion.

To the promoters' delight, the discovery of gold and the subsequent stampede proved the wisdom of their planning. As the Klondike rush enveloped the region, work began on the construction of a railway from Skagway, at the head of Lynn Canal, to Whitehorse, the head of navigation on the Yukon River. The timing was fortuitous in many ways. The railway project provided work for hundreds of would-be stampeders who arrived in the North too poor to buy the supplies necessary to last the winter; and the construction along the White Pass soon provided an alternative to the time-consuming and arduous back-pack trail up the Chilkoot Pass. By 1900, the narrow-gauge White Pass and Yukon Railway was finished, marking a major turning point in the history of the region.

The White Pass and Yukon Route company (wpyr) subsequently came to dominate the post-gold-rush Yukon. The company had huge investments in the region and expanded them to

Constable York guarding two enemy aliens on the tracks of the
White Pass and Yukon Railway, probably early 1915. Tom
Bokovich is on the left and an unidentified German on the right.
Bokovich was shot by Alex Gogoff near this spot a few months
after this picture was taken (Glenbow Archives [GA] NA-1663-22).

include a fleet of riverboats, which soon had a virtual monopoly
on the upper Yukon River (extending as far as central Alaska and
competing successfully with transportation companies that
sought to bring in supplies via the Bering Strait and the lower
Yukon River). The WPYR also expanded into other areas, purchasing much of the prime land in Skagway and Whitehorse, and developing a lake steamer service to Atlin, British Columbia, site of a
small echo-boom in 1898.

Early in the twentieth century, the WPYR, anxious to maintain its
traffic in the post-rush era, began to capitalize on the mystique of
the Klondike, actively promoting summer tourism, a forerunner
of the current boom in Northwest Coast cruise ship and vacation
travel. The company continued to be innovative: in the 1960s it

pioneered a ship, road, and rail containerized shipping system that was subsequently emulated worldwide. Economic conditions in the Yukon and competition from a new highway forced the railway to close in 1981, but the most scenic part of it was subsequently reopened as a summer tourist attraction.

The company hired dozens of men such as Gogoff every year as it raced through the short summer season to make up for a winter's worth of wear and tear on the railway line and the equipment. The core of the crews, like those on the riverboats, came back each summer. The grunt labour – men in dire need of money, with strong backs and a willingness to work hard through the season – came from the pool of transients that flowed through the Yukon each year. Representing the diversity of Yukon society and the impermanence of the non-Native population, these crews enabled the railway company to repair the line, fix the bridges, and otherwise keep the trains running. Most of the workers were based in Skagway and worked on the steep and difficult line from tidewater to the summit at the Alaska – British Columbia border. There were only a few other main stations, a food stop at Lake Bennett, a maintenance yard at Carcross (at the narrows between Lake Bennett and Nares and Tagish Lakes), and the terminus at Whitehorse, where the trains met up with the WPYR sternwheelers.

At 1 PM on Thursday, 30 September 1915, a railway section crew was relaxing and eating lunch beside the track about four kilometres south of Whitehorse. The crew consisted of five men: Pat Kinslow (the foreman), aged fifty-five; George Lane, fifty-four; Tom Bokovich, forty-four; Henry Cook, sixty; and Arthur Wilkinson, age not given. Kinslow had come to the Yukon in 1898, Lane was English, Bokovich was an Austrian who had been interned in the Yukon as an enemy alien in 1914 but had been permitted to work, and Cook apparently was German. Of these men, only Wilkinson escaped to tell the story:

We had finished with our lunch and some of us were sitting and others sitting around the handcar where we had eaten. I heard someone say "Here comes Alex." I looked around and Gagoff was coming down the hill from the opposite side of the track. He walked toward us and just as he stepped on the track he fired. Realizing that he was shooting to kill, we all started to run and he continued shooting. I concealed myself in the brush below the track as quickly as possible and did not see the others fall ... I do not know how many shots were fired but there were several.³

Wilkinson survived because he ran back towards Whitehorse, while Gogoff chased the others, who had run in the opposite direction. Kinslow was shot in the heart and died instantly, Bokovich in the head. Lane was shot in the leg, and while he was tying a handkerchief around it to stop the bleeding, Gogoff came back to him and shot him in the head. Cook was badly wounded and died in hospital that night.

After killing the men, Gogoff took their handcar and returned to Whitehorse, stopping just outside town at the home of Frank E. Leslie, who was in charge of the railway roundhouse and lived near it. Leslie later testified that he had seen Gogoff about 10:30 that morning, heading south along the tracks, and had asked him what he was doing, and Gogoff had replied, "I am going hunting." When Gogoff returned that afternoon, Leslie was asleep. His wife woke him, said Leslie, telling him that "Alec the Russian section man was outside the door and wanted a drink of water, and that I was to go out, that he was either crazy or shot himself." Leslie gave Gogoff a pitcher of water and asked him what the matter was. Gogoff told him that he had shot three men who had "come at him like dogs." He asked about a man named Fighting Mike, one Mike Sinnett, against whom he had a particular grievance but who had not been there that day.

Leslie's testimony provided as much of a motive for the crime as was ever discovered. Since the evidence of the murder was clear enough, the authorities were not particularly interested in the motive and did not try to delve into the reasons why Gogoff had killed the men beyond the fact that he had a grudge against them. Leslie testified that he had known Gogoff for several months and had always thought he was insane or mentally weak: "He came after me for about five days [in June 1915] and was continuously in my company ... and walked around with me and everlastingly asking me to buy him a gun. The reason I didn't buy him a gun was because I thought he was going to commit suicide; he told me about his troubles on the section ... He said the men had been teasing him and making life unbearable for him ... I would think his mind was about the mind of a child of about six years old."⁴

Such comments, of course, were not untypical in North Americans' descriptions of foreigners, whose lack of English-language skills were often equated with limited intelligence. Further, Leslie's observations about the torment that Gogoff endured, while scarcely a justification for multiple homicide, revealed something about the social difficulties, isolation, and hardship endured by foreigners in the Northwest.

Gogoff left Leslie's house, got back on the handcar, and went into town, while Leslie phoned the railway station with the news of what Gogoff had told him. Leaving the handcar, Gogoff walked down Front Street in Whitehorse, carrying the rifle and holding the cartridges between the fingers of his hand. A man named Brenton Hyatt or Hyett, a baggage handler for the railway, who had been in the depot when Leslie phoned in the news, came out and met Gogoff going into McPherson's drug store. Rather bravely in the circumstances, Hyatt put his hand on the rifle (a 30-30 carbine) and asked Gogoff to give it to him. But as McPherson the druggist testified, Gogoff

came into the store, and over the cigar counter, the front part of the store, he reached his right hand which was absolutely free of cartridges, and said "Good bye Mack." I said "Alec, where are you going, what is the matter?" He said "You know I kill three men; I go to gaol [jail]." I came around from behind the counter and stood in front of him and I said "Alec, you are joking, you didn't kill three men." He said "I kill three men ... I kill Tom and George and Pat; I shoot another man; I am sorry I shot him; he no hurt me." I said "What did you shoot them for, Alec?" He said "They say Alec no good; I show them Alec good man." With that he beat his breast three times as if he was considering his power.

Gogoff refused to give up the gun and went into the White Pass Hotel, where he was apparently staying. Hyatt followed him, heard him ask for his bill and say, "I shoot three men, I go to jail." Hyalt again asked for the rifle, saying, "That is a pretty nice gun." But Gogoff "kind of drew off," and Hyalt didn't force him. Gogoff then went back into the drug store, where McPherson also asked for the rifle, saying, "Alec, leave that gun with me; you know I am a good friend of yours." Gogoff then gave him the rifle and left the store. A few minutes later he passed the store again with three letters in his hand, heading for the post office. McPherson hailed him and offered to mail the letters for him and took down his mother's address, promising to write to her. Two or three minutes passed, and Constable Fletcher of the Royal North-West Mounted Police (as the force was now called) appeared and arrested Gogoff, who offered no resistance.

The public reaction to the killing was one of horror, the *Weekly Star* saying that Whitehorse had "experienced the greatest shock of her existence." But there was no panic, nor was there any talk of vigilantism. Given the history of the Yukon and the strong hand of the police, such talk was unnecessary, even unthinkable. The newspaper made this point clear in an editorial commenting on the burial of the victims, which took place on 3 October: "Whitehorse survived the shock and ... performed her duty to the dead as became a law-abiding community, and 'rope' was never mentioned except in connection with the ordinary course of justice." The main reason why there was no great outcry was that the public had perfect confidence that Gogoff would be speedily tried, convicted, and hanged. There was no need for the public to bay for blood when the outcome of the affair was predictable, no need for "victims' statements" from the relatives of Gogoff's targets when his fate was certain.

Gogoff, whom the Whitehorse newspaper called the "murderer of four men" – no dancing around with the word "alleged" in 1915 – was speedily arraigned in front of the Whitehorse magistrate. His trial took place three weeks after the killing. Gogoff was not represented by a lawyer but did have two interpreters present. On the nineteenth he was brought before the judge, Mr Justice Charles D. Macaulay, and pleaded guilty to the charge of murdering Henry Cook. Cook had made a statement in front of witnesses before he died, and presumably this made his case easier to prove. Macaulay told Gogoff to change his plea to not guilty, and the trial began the next day.

In many ways murder cases, especially in the North, were much less complicated early in this century than they are now. Trials were shorter and the technicalities of evidence fewer, and so were the ways in which a convicted person could have his sentence reversed or reduced. There was not much agonizing by the courts about the motive for the killing: murderers were assumed to be either evil or crazy. Those who killed for greed, fear, hatred, or lust were evil; the rest were crazy.

Very likely, if a survey were taken today, the majority of the population would hold the same views. The difference is that at the beginning of the century nearly everyone held them, and so did the authorities. Whatever else one might say about this simple philosophy, it was easy to understand and live with. Most murderers were evil and deserved to die, unless there was some reason why they should be shown mercy; the rest were insane and deserved to be locked up, for society's protection and their own.

For determining insanity, there was no consideration of emotional distress, diminished capacity, or any of the defences that are used in court today. The standard was the nineteenth-century McNaughton rule: to be insane under the law, a person had to be unaware that what he (or she) was doing was wrong. Such a rule, if imposed today, would mean that a good many people now judged mentally ill would not be so judged. For instance, hearing voices in your head from space aliens that urged you to kill your mother would not be sufficient for a defence based on insanity if a jury believed that you knew that what the voices were telling you to do was wrong. The fact that you did not have the will to resist their message was no excuse. This meant in practice that men went to the gallows who today would never see the inside of a penitentiary because they would be sent to an institution and treated for mental illness. Alexander Gogoff was such a man, and his case shows how difficult it was to mount a defence based on insanity, especially when the courts were not sympathetic to the whole idea of insanity as a motive for murder.

Gogoff's trial, including sentencing, took less than five hours, beginning at 10 AM and ending at 4 PM, with a break for lunch. One reason it was so short was that Gogoff again pled guilty and refused to change his plea. On hearing this, Judge Macaulay dismissed the jury panel and told Gogoff that despite his plea, witnesses would be heard, and it would be decided whether his plea was justified. This was done, and at the conclusion Macaulay pronounced that the plea of guilty was fully justified, and he sentenced Gogoff to be hanged on 10 March.

After the sentence was passed, Gogoff asked a number of questions through his interpreter, some of which were so naïve that one wonders if he really knew what was going on. Certainly, he had little idea of how the prison system worked. He asked if he could write letters and have his friends visit him, and the judge told him that there was no difficulty with that. Then he asked if he could have a razor to shave himself, if he could be hanged in Vancouver rather than in Whitehorse, and if he could be shot instead of hanged. The judge replied that he had nothing to do with prison regulations but he thought that Gogoff would not be permitted to have a razor. As for the other requests, Gogoff had "transgressed the law and he must abide by the law."

It was after the trial that matters became less cut and dried. Gogoff had a number of relatives in Canada, and after his conviction they tried to have him declared not guilty by reason of insanity. Judge Macaulay was unsympathetic to this idea, and in his report to the Department of Justice he took pains to debunk it. He dismissed Frank Leslie's contention that Gogoff was insane, saying that Leslie had no basis for his belief except that Gogoff had been excited after the murder and that, in Leslie's opinion, he had cruel eyes and was mentally undeveloped. Everyone else, said the judge, thought the there was nothing wrong with Gogoff, including the druggist McPherson, who knew him as well as anyone and thought he was sane. Macaulay concluded:

From the appearance of the prisoner in the dock during the trial ... he appeared to me to be very sane ... In my opinion, he is perfectly rational. He had a grievance, or some supposed grievance, against some of the section men, and he expressed regret for having shot one of the men, whom he mistook for the man he called "Fighting Mike." As for the others he had no regret at all, but seems to feel that he has avenged himself. In my opinion, this was a cold-blooded, premeditated murder. There is nothing that I have seen in the evidence or in the conduct of the prisoner that would justify me in making any recommendation for executive clemency.

Soon after the trial ended, Gogoff's relatives – Layon, his brother in Vancouver, and Akim, his cousin, also in Vancouver – hired J.A. Russell, a Vancouver lawyer, to represent the interests of the condemned man. Another brother, Tom Gogoff, working in Douglas, Alaska, also participated in this part of the case. It appears that the first these men had heard of the affair was from

Gogoff himself, who wrote to them after the trial. They wrote back on 11 November, asking him a number of questions about things the lawyer wished to know: "Is it a fact that you had trouble with these men, if so what was the nature of the trouble? Did they prevent you from getting work? ... Did they ever threaten to kill you and were you afraid that if you did not shoot them they would kill you? Were you perfectly clear in your mind? ... Did you know what you were doing?"

But Gogoff was no help. His reply, dated 19 November, sounds like the cry of a child:

My dear brothers ... I have received your letter on the 19th Nov., and you stated in your letter that you hired a lawyer for me and I thank you for that. But now you ask me how I happened in this trouble and I don't know absolutely nothing.

Dear brothers believe me that I don't know nothing about how I got in such trouble and how much sentence they have given me. The only thing I know is the Manager of Police told me that I was sentenced to be hanged on the 10th of March, 1916. That is all I know about this matter.

Write me often

Good-bye

Russell does not seem to have visited Gogoff – the trip would have been very expensive – but he proceeded on several fronts. He wrote to the Department of Justice suggesting that the interpreters had been inadequate for their task. Gogoff's native language was Ossetian, and Russell asserted that in fact Gogoff did not speak much Russian and that in such cases "a Russian or Jew offers himself as an interpreter claiming that while he cannot understand the Ascetanian language he can interpret for an Ascetanain who understands but does not speak the Russian or English language. In these circumstances I know from an extended experience in such matters we have a most unsatisfactory interpretation of what takes place in Court."

His second point was Gogoff's lack of counsel at the trial. "Has it not," he asked, "been a universal practice in our Canadian and all British Courts to assign counsel to prisoners charged with murder?" The fact that Gogoff kept insisting on pleading guilty was, he said, all the more reason why he should have had a lawyer to advise him. Moreover, Gogoff had not been asked if he had any witnesses or if he had any questions to ask the witnesses who testified against him. Modern readers may be surprised to learn that it was possible to convict and hang a man who did not have a lawyer to defend him, but such was the law in 1915.

The third point was Gogoff's mental state. "It is true," wrote Russell, "the learned Judge says the prisoner knew what he was doing, but is not that a question which should be answered by a Jury?" He pointed out that the witness who knew Gogoff best thought that he was insane and that other witnesses testified that his action was totally out of character. Moreover, those who testified that he was or seemed sane were not asked at the trial how well they knew him, or on what basis they came to this conclusion, while Leslie, who thought him insane, was asked those questions. Russell asked for a new trial.

The matter was dealt with in Ottawa by P.M. Coté of the Remissions Branch of the Department of Justice. Coté recommended that Gogoff be examined to determine his mental state – something that today would be done as a matter of course before the trial began – after which a recommendation for commutation could be made. Dr W.B. Clarke of Whitehorse and Dr W.G. Gabie of Skagway, neither of whom had any particular expertise in mental illness, agreed to examine the condemned man. On 3 February 1915 they reported to the minister of justice:

After conversing with him relative to himself, his early life and family history his answers were consistent and given with reasonable promptness but with reference to questions regarding his connection with the crime he would answer none ... We felt he was deliberately noncommunicative ... Our best opinion [is] that Alexander Gogoff was mentally responsible for the crime he committed and is now sane ... However we appreciate the possibility in a case of this sort that paranoia could be considered in which an individual from aberration of the mind laboring under delusions of persecution would adopt such means of revenge on the suspected persecutor. In this regard we are informed that people of his nationality adopt such measures against those whom they believe to have slandered them yet we could not reconcile the above with this case as being justifiable from a British standpoint. If what we are informed as above is true we conclude that he adopted the methods of his country in settling his grievance and so we consider him sane as he showed reason in that respect ... He appreciated the enormity of the crime as he gave himself up to the authorities and expected to be punished.

The reasoning here is interesting. Gogoff may have been deluded, but he was acting logically, in accordance with the dictates of his culture, and thus was rational. The phrase "Catch-22" begins to suggest itself here.

Russell was dismayed by the doctors' verdict and protested that Clarke was not a disinterested party. Clarke was the only doctor in Whitehorse, and he had taken Cook's dying declaration. Moreover, he had already given an opinion on Gogoff's mental condition, stating emphatically during the trial that the accused man was sane. This made no impression on the Department of Justice. Russell also collected affidavits from men who had known Gogoff both in Russia and in North America. If true, they show a man who was violent and disturbed. Alexander Gagoff, a merchant in Douglas, Alaska, and apparently no relation, recounted:

He would sit for long periods in my store brooding and dejected. On one occasion I took a walk with said Gogoff in company with one Jim Beso-loff — a countryman of mine. In a spirit of kindly feeling Besoloff slapped Gogoff on the back and told him he was a good fellow. Gogoff thereupon snatched a small board from the ground and began hitting Besoloff with it. I took the board away from Gogoff ... Some days Gogoff was very happy without any apparent reason why he should be happy and at other times without any apparent reason he would be despondent. He never seemed well balanced ... Among all the people who knew him at Douglas he was considered insane.

Alexander Aloff, another countryman of Gogoff's, testified that there was insanity in his family: Gogoff's mother, Ezdek, had "crazy spells" and had to be confined in the town hall from time to time, and Gogoff himself had "long spells of moodiness and melancholy when there was no reason for sadness, and then, without any reason that I could see," said Aloff, "he would have a happy spell and appear and act like a person who was tipsy ... His friends and relatives looked out for him and so kept him from being locked up by the authorities."

A man named Batche Basieff testified that he had worked with
Gogoff on railway construction near the Black Sea and had witnessed Gogoff's "insane spells." He would "get melancholy – soul
sick as we call it," recalled Basieff. "He was very nervous and
would jump and then he would yell and make noises and become
so that we would have to hold him. We restrained him ourselves
without any help in order to keep him out of trouble. There are no
doctors in our Caucasian villages but there are wise men who are
seers and help people by the offering of sacrifices and with cere-
monies and prayer. Some of these were consulted to help said Gogoff."

Two more men, Philip Dzaloff and Frank Zakoff, who had
known Gogoff for years, both in Russia and in North America, testified that his mother and aunt were insane, and gave accounts of
Gogoff's irrational violence. Zakoff said, "When going anywhere
with him it was dangerous to allow him to walk behind your back
– to walk after you – because he was liable to grab a stick ... and
make an assault upon you with it. He has tried to do that to me a
great many times." He also confirmed that Gogoff was prone to
spells of irrational weeping and hilarity.

At this distance it is unwise to attempt a diagnosis, but if these
men were telling the truth, Gogoff must surely have been suffering from some sort of mental disease, either a manic-depressive
condition, which is suggested by the episodes of depression and
hilarity, or perhaps a temporal lobe condition, which would explain the irrational acts of violence. Unfortunately for Gogoff,
there was no one in the Yukon who was expert in the diagnosis or
treatment of mental disease, and the government was not interested in sending an expert north to examine him. As Russell, his
lawyer, observed, most of "our leading medical men, competent
alienists" (specialists in mental illness) had "gone to the front" to
treat war casualties in France.

In the last week of February, Russell appealed to the government to take the statements of Gogoff's friends seriously.
"Surely," he telegraphed Ottawa, "this evidence [is] entitled
greater weight than medical report." He suggested that Dr
Clarke's report sounded like that of a man trying to justify his earlier diagnosis. He begged the government to postpone the execution for three months so that a proper examination by an expert
could be made.

A last flurry of excitement occurred on 7 March when Tom Gogoff, a cousin of the condemned man, arrived in Whitehorse. The police had been warned of his arrival by a telegram sent from Skagway, and it was believed that he was armed "with the intention of committing some desperate deed in order if possible to prevent the carrying out of the sentence ... as the Cossacks, fierce and independent inhabitants of the Russian steppes ... consider it an indelible disgrace for one of their number to suffer death upon the scaffold." Tom Gogoff was arrested as soon as he got off the train, and when he was found to be armed he was tried and sentenced to three months' imprisonment, with a fine of $105. At the end of the three months – there being few paroles in the Yukon in those days – he was held for an immigration hearing and then taken to Vancouver and deported to Russia.

None of the efforts made to save Gogoff had any effect on the Department of Justice, and the execution went ahead on 10 March 1915, the date set at the trial. The efforts of his lawyer had not delayed it by a day. It was reported in the press that Gogoff was a model prisoner, though apparently he lost more than twenty kilograms between his trial and execution. The sheriff reported that he had refused to talk about his crime, though he talked freely about other matters. He also "refused religious consolation," so no clergyman was present at his execution. A few days before his hanging he asked permission to go to the front, a request indicates he was still confused about what was happening to him. The Whitehorse *Weekly Star* reported the details of the execution:

With firm, unfaltering steps, marching between two stalwart members of the R.N.W.M.P. Gagoff mounted the steps of the scaffold and took his place on the trap door. Official Hangman Ellis, who came all the way from Ottawa ... adjusted the black cap. Sheriff George Brimston then asked the man who stood on the threshold of death if he had anything to say. The question was repeated in the Russian language by interpreter Zarnowsky. Gagoff answered in Russian, "No." In a clear voice Sheriff Brimston said "May God have mercy on your soul!" Immediately Hangman Ellis sprung the trap ... The drop was 7 feet, 10 inches. His neck was broken and death was instantaneous. Dr. Clarke kept his hand on the pulse, which ceased to beat in 14 minutes. The body was then cut down and placed in a box ... In addition to those whose duty required their presence, the execution was witnessed by only a half dozen spectators. The temperature was 36 below zero.

Why was Gogoff executed? There are several reasons, and they illustrate the temper of the times both in the Yukon and in Canada as a whole. First, he had killed four men rather than one, which made his crime more heinous in the minds of the public and the government; the fact that he was tried for only one murder made no difference. Second, he had not been acting in self-defence, and his act was unprovoked – or, if provoked, the provocation had been at some time in the past. Third, he had no public support. Even Labelle, who of all the killers described in this book was probably the most contemptible, was able to muster petitions from respectable citizens asking for clemency; but Gogoff had only a few relatives and friends, all foreigners, to testify that he was insane.

Fourth, he was a foreigner, a "Cossack," prey to dark, unfathomable, and in essence, non-British impulses of revenge and violence. This period saw the height of immigration to Canada; it was the era of the "men in sheep-skin coats," in Clifford Sifton's memorable phrase – people from Central and Eastern Europe who came to settle the prairies. Although they were welcomed as settlers, they caused a backlash among the Anglo-Canadian population. By remarkable coincidence, about ten days before Gogoff's fate was debated by the federal cabinet – and it can be assumed that it was a short debate – the federal minister of justice, Charles Doherty, spoke in the House of Commons on a private member's bill to abolish capital punishment. Doherty opposed the bill, stating that the murder rate in Canada was due to the rise in "foreign" immigration. Of the seventy-nine murders that had occurred between 1900 and 1914, he claimed that thirty-eight had been committed by newly arrived foreigners. "We are getting flooded," he said, "with a population who are accustomed to think that you can kill your neighbour but that your life is so sacred that the state will never touch you."[5]

In this lottery of death, Gogoff held a losing ticket. As a man, a foreigner, and a person without money, he was more likely to be hanged than those who did not have those disadvantages.[6] Finally, Yukoners wanted him hanged, and they expected him to be

hanged. The comment from the newspaper about the lack of vigilantism makes it clear that the death of Gogoff and people like
him was necessary to maintain public order. Not to hang him
would have caused a tremendous outcry in the territory. There
was no reason, therefore, why he should be spared.

Alexander Gogoff was not missed, and no one in the Yukon
mourned his passing. His execution was, in fact, a testament to the
fact that the police and judiciary in the territory kept the region
safe for the residents. But Gogoff would not have been missed
even if had he left the Yukon without murdering anyone. He was
one of the Yukon's transient "floaters," his sense of isolation exacerbated by his ethnicity and language. He bonded with no one in
the North and left no legacy of friends or contacts. In this, he sym-
bolized several key aspects of the social history of the Yukon, including the inability or unwillingness of the region's residents to
absorb the "foreigners" working in their midst – and also the continuing importance of migrant workers in the operation of the regional economy. That Gogoff was a murderer provides us with
insight into a social and cultural group that is little known and often ignored – the floating population of young males who ani-
mated the regional economy – and it tells a tale of loneliness,
isolation, minimal financial accomplishment, and discrimination.
There is nothing pretty in the Gogoff story, for it reveals aspects of
Yukon life that, in the broad light of day, do not reflect well on the
regional order.

CHAPTER SIX

"To Make These Tribes Understand": The Trial of Alikomiak and Tatamigana

Imprisonment or banishment would not be adequate,
but what about flogging?

William D. Reeve, Anglican bishop of Toronto,
suggesting appropriate punishment
for Alikomiak and Tatamigana

This chapter deals with a case of national significance, one whose importance went far beyond the boundaries of the Northwest Territories, where the killings took place, or the Yukon, where the trials were held. The trials of Alikomiak and Tatamigana were an important milestone in the extension of Canadian sovereignty over the Arctic and marked a turning point in relations between the Inuit and the Canadian authorities.

The difference between the cases of the Nantuck brothers, of Paddy Duncan (described in chapter 7), and of Alikomiak and Tatamigana shows the futility of viewing the North as monolithic. As these cases make clear, there are many "norths," each with a different social history. The reason the Alikomiak case has been included in this book, besides the fact that it is interesting in a dramatic way, is that it makes a number of useful points. For one thing, it shows that the legal and criminal history of the NWT was very different from that of the Yukon. The indigenous population of the NWT was considerably larger than the Yukon's at the beginning of the twentieth century, though no one knew how big it was, since there were many Inuit who had never been contacted by the authorities, let alone counted. On the other hand, the non-Native population was much smaller than that of the Yukon: only a few hundred fur traders, missionaries, prospectors, and, after 1903, a handful of Mounted Policemen. The most spectacular cases in the NWT involved indigenous people rather than non-Natives, and they were dealt with in a manner different from that of the Nantuck case in the Yukon.

Another point concerns the attitude towards indigenous people in the North. The Canadian authorities (in the persons of the Mounted Police, who were the first contact between the Government of Canada and the Dene and Inuit) viewed the two peoples differently. Pejorative comments in the records of the Mounted Police show that they held the Dene in low regard – as dirty, lazy, people who hung around the police and Hudson's Bay Company posts looking for handouts. A police officer comparing the Dene of the Mackenzie Delta with the Inuit, commented: "The Indians here, they are too lazy to hunt or trap and live all the year on fish ... Any money or debt they can procure goes on their backs, and then their stomach is thought of. Different with the Esquimaux; one need only go 100 miles down the Mackenzie River, and he will find the men either out trapping, or fishing through the ice ... They are not improvident like the Indians. They very seldom take debt, [but if they do] ... the first thing they do is to come in with the furs to pay what they owe."[1]

The authorities liked the Inuit, and as the cases discussed in this chapter will show, were inclined to give them the benefit of the doubt or be lenient with them in criminal matters. This was not the case with Native people in the Yukon, as was obvious from the Nantuck executions. Of course, the authorities knew, or thought they knew, what "Indians" were like, having dealt with them for generations in southern Canada. But the Inuit were new to them, and the first impressions of these people were favourable. The gold rush had created a political and judicial climate in the Yukon that was different from that of the NWT. When the Nantucks shot a white man, the road to the gallows was short; when Inuit murdered whites, they were given a second and then third chance to change their customs.

Although the authorities, especially the Mounted Police, liked the Inuit better than the Dene, it would be hard to argue that the Inuit were intrinsically the more likable. There are basically two reasons for the difference in attitude towards them. First, the Inuit culture was more like European culture than Dene culture was. The police were accustomed to having First Nations people hanging round their posts asking for handouts (and they had a predictable idea of why they did this). The Inuit, on the other hand, did not often beg, and if they borrowed something they usually paid it back. They seemed to have in their culture some northern version of the Protestant work ethic, a fact that inclined the authorities to view them with favour.

The second element is a difference in the intensity of contact between Europeans and Dene, and Europeans and Inuit. When newcomers came to the land of the Dene (with the exception of the very earliest explorers such as Samuel Hearne and Alexander Mackenzie), they came to stay. They came to set up fur trade posts, to bring Christianity to the First Nations, and to look for gold or other valuables. Thus, from about 1800 they were in a close commercial and religious relationship with the Dene. The intensity was even greater in the Yukon, which in the mid-nineteenth century had a population of perhaps 7,000 First Nations[2] and only a handful of Hudson's Bay Company traders. Then, suddenly, around 1890, about a thousand outsiders arrived, and then between 1897 and 1899 nearly forty thousand more poured in. There were bound to be pressures and conflicts.

The intensity was much less when newcomers contacted Inuit, both on the north slope of the Yukon territory and along the Arctic coast of the NWT. Explorers came and went, and a few would-be exploiters such as Martin Frobisher clashed with the Inuit, but until the end of the nineteenth century there was very little sustained contact between them and outsiders. Consequently, the authorities came to the wrong conclusion – that Inuit were better than Dene – and when sustained contact did occur, it was discovered that these people also had a darker side.

In July 1923 two Inuit men, Alikomiak and Tatamigana, were tried for murder on Herschel Island, a small island in the Beaufort Sea, just off the north coast of the Yukon Territory. Uninhabited, it is now the Yukon's first territorial park, but at the beginning of the century it had a lively existence as the centre of the whaling industry in the Western Arctic. It had the best natural harbour for hundreds of kilometres along the Arctic coast, and because of the distance from their home port in San Francisco and other West Coast cities, the ships came for voyages of two or three years, wintering at Herschel Island. At the height of the industry, around 1895, there were about a dozen ships and more than 150 crew, as well as a number of Inuit and a missionary and his family resident on the island in winter.

After repeated appeals to the federal government from William C. Bompas, Anglican bishop of the Yukon, who complained that the Inuit were being debauched by liquor and sexually exploited by the whalers, a two-man detachment, consisting of Sergeant Francis J. Fitzgerald and a constable of the North-West Mounted Police, was established on the island in the summer of 1903. Fitzgerald, a veteran of Yukon service, spent the rest of his career at Herschel Island and became famous when in the winter of 1910–11, as leader of the "lost patrol," he and his three companions lost their way and starved to death in an attempt to set a speed record on the Fort McPherson – Dawson patrol.

The whaling industry was on its last legs in 1910, and by 1914 no more ships came north to hunt the bowhead whale. But the Mounted Police detachment on Herschel Island was kept open, since its original purpose had not really been to watch over whalers or protect Inuit. The post was there to show the flag – to proclaim the sovereignty of the Canadian government over the Western Arctic. Because significant areas of the Arctic had been explored by non-Canadians, particularly Scandinavians, Canadian sovereignty had to be based on occupation and administration rather than on claims arising from discovery.

For the same reason, other detachments were established in the Central and Eastern Arctic after the First World War, extending the nominal authority of Ottawa over regions as remote as Bache Peninsula in east-central Ellesmere Island, which at 79°N was the most northerly police post in history and also the most northerly post office in the world at that time. Although mail delivery was only once a year and although there were only two police and an Inuit family as residents, the existence of the place was an important demonstration of sovereignty.

A crucial demonstration of sovereignty in the Canadian North was enforcing criminal law on the indigenous people. In the Arctic, the federal government and the police were at first inclined to take a lenient view of Inuit who broke the law. The official view was, sensibly, that it was unreasonable to expect the Inuit to obey the law before they had been told what it was. Nevertheless, it was Ottawa's wish that its sovereignty be emphasized in the Arctic through enforcement of the law, and it was the Mounties' duty to see that this was done. Enforcement was not an easy task, for the distances were huge and the land only recently explored by Europeans. As late as 1914, members of the Canadian Arctic Expedition had met groups of Inuit in the Central Arctic who had never (or only very recently) met a non-Inuit. A third difficulty was the unusually high rate of violence and murder among the Inuit of the Central Arctic. As Sidney Harring points out, the contact period, roughly 1910–20, saw six Europeans and about forty Inuit murdered among the Copper Inuit, and all this violence took place in a community of seven hundred people.[3]

Although the official attitude at first was to deal leniently with these people, attitudes hardened when the violence continued. Three cases show this change. In June 1912 two explorers, H.V. Radford, an American with northern experience, and George Street, a young man from Ottawa, were killed by Inuit at the southern end of Bathurst Inlet, apparently because Radford, who was notoriously bad tempered, had threatened and struck an Inuk who was acting as their guide. The police sent out an expedition to investigate, but it ran into difficulties, and not until the winter of 1917–18, when the crime was nearly six years old, did they obtain solid information about the event. The government accepted the fact that the Inuit, in killing these men, were simply following their own law and tradition, and the expedition to find the men responsible was more an expedition of exploration than one of punishment. It seems never to have contacted the actual killers, but it did reach their families and explained to them the error of their ways and warned them that Canadian law was now to be obeyed.

Late in 1913 two Oblate priests, Fathers Rouvière and Le Roux, were killed in similar circumstances near Bloody Falls on the Coppermine River (the site was named not for this murder but for an incident a hundred and forty years earlier, when Samuel Hearne's aboriginal guides killed a band of Inuit there). Le Roux had threatened one of the Inuit guides, and both priests were killed by Sinnisiak and Uluksuk. In this case the police located the killers fairly quickly. News of the murder became known in 1914, a patrol was sent out in 1915, the killers were contacted and arrested in 1916, and they were brought south for trial in 1917. To the astonishment and chagrin of the Mounted Police and the Oblate order, there was public feeling that these priests had disturbed the primitive inno-cence of Inuit and had got what they deserved. When Sinnisiak and Uluksuk were tried in Edmonton in the summer of 1917 for the murder of Father Rouvière, they were acquitted. Only when they were subsequently tried in Calgary for the murder of Father Le Roux was a conviction obtained.

Sinnisiak and Uluksuk were convicted of murder, but in keep-ing with the government's policy of educating the Inuit to obey the law, they received a light punishment. They were sentenced to life imprisonment at the police detachment at Fort Resolution, NWT, where they were not confined and were kept busy in doing odd jobs around the post. When the Tree River detachment was established in 1919, they were employed as dog-team drivers. Af-ter two years they were released and permitted to return to their band, by which time they had acquired a certain arrogance and enough surplus goods from the police to make them rich men in their communities The impression left with the Inuit may well have been that crime was taken lightly by the government or even rewarded.

In 1920 there was yet another incident in which a European was killed by Inuit. This was the Robert Janes case (which has been brilliantly analysed in a recent book),[4] in which a trader was killed by Inuit near Cape Crauford in northern Baffin Island in March 1920, again because he had behaved aggressively. Janes was a Newfoundlander who had a good deal of northern experience, having been second officer on the Canadian government vessel *Arctic*'s voyage to the north in 1910. He had tried prospecting and exploring in the Eastern Arctic during the First World War, and had set himself up in 1916 as a trader on the northern end of Baffin Island. His personality was such as to invite disaster in that re-gion. He was so unpleasant to his assistant, Thomas Holden, that the man fled from him and died trying to reach home.

Janes lived with an Inuit woman, Kalluk, and was intensely jeal-ous of any Inuit who paid her attention, threatening to shoot one of them. On one occasion he was seen beating her because she wanted to go to a dance. "When warned that his threats and aggressive manner might alienate the Inuit, Janes declared that 'he would shoot any native if he misbehaved,' appearing to take pride in the fact that they feared him."[5] Such stupidity beggars belief, for Janes must have heard of the murder of the explorers and the priests. The best explanation for his behaviour is that his arrogance, abusiveness, and violence were so profound as to amount to mental illness. Eventually he went too far with the local Inuit, and very reluctantly and full of fear, they shot him. The authorities were informed, and the police came to the region to investigate. Three Inuit were tried and one was imprisoned for the killing.

Three separate cases of this kind would understandably incline the government to increasing severity. When the fourth murder occurred, therefore, the authorities were no longer in a forgiving mood, especially as one of the victims was a Mounted Policeman. The detachment set up at Tree River in 1919 had been placed there to demonstrate Canadian sovereignty and enforce the law in the Coppermine – Coronation Gulf region. The post showed the clear desire to "prevent murders of whites and to stabilize commercial and government activity in the Arctic,"[6] which was what sovereignty was chiefly concerned with. The Tree River post was manned by two members of the RCMP: Constable D.H. Woolams and Corporal W.A. Doak, who was in command. There were three other white men there, employees of the Hudson's Bay Company's post at Tree River.

In December 1921 Doak, accompanied by Inuit employees of the police, went on patrol to Kent Peninsula to investigate a number of killings of Inuit by other Inuit. After a short investigation – the community was, as always in such cases, completely cooperative and forthcoming with information – he arrested Alikomiak, a young man of sixteen to nineteen years of age, and Tatamigana, whose age is not known. He returned to Tree River with the two men and with Ikalukpiak, a man he arrested at Grace Bay on the return trip for an unrelated killing. Doak and Woolams did not confine the three men (which would not have been easy, since the detachment did not possess a lock-up), but put them to work and gave them complete personal freedom. It never occurred to the two Mounties that the Inuit might turn on them. The police by this time had developed a contradictory view of the Inuit: they were

Alikomiak, photographed under arrest at Fort
Good Hope in the summer of 1922 (NA, PA-102577)

primitive and violent, fond of infanticide and other forms of killing, but once brought under the control of the government, they
were believed to be docile.

On the night of 1 April 1922, while Woolams was off on patrol,
Alikomiak shot the sleeping Doak in the upper leg and sat for
some time watching him die of blood loss. Early the next morning
he shot Otto Binder, the Hudson's Bay Company trader, who had

come to call on the policeman. When Woolams returned from patrol he seized the unresisting Alikomiak and tied him up. In the summer Alikomiak and Tatamigana, along with some other Inuit, were taken to Herschel Island for trial.

The motive for Doak's murder was an echo of the earlier fate of the two explorers and the two priests. Binder was killed to keep him from exacting revenge for Doak, though it was later claimed that a quarrel over a woman was a contributing factor. Alikomiak's statement, made on 17 April 1923 , a year after the incident, through an Inuit translator working for the police, has the ring of truth; Sinnisiak and Uluksuk had said much the same thing several years earlier:

I was scared of Doak as he sometimes gave me little hard jobs. One time we went to haul meat and Doak made me run beside the sled with him. I rode on the sled at times and so did he. It was deep snow and I could not keep up. Doak spoke to me but I could not understand him and do not know whether he was angry with me. I was afraid he might use the dog whip on me though he never threatened or hit me with it. Doak gave me boots and lots of things to fix and I did not like it [this was women's work]. One time he gave me seal skin long boots to fix the bottoms and I had done one when he told me that I had not done it right and for me not to fix the other boot. I was mad and did not feel good inside. The next day I think I like to kill that man. The morning after I worked on the boots I went to [the] Police store house and got Agnavik's rifle ... [Doak] was still asleep ... I shot him in the left buttock as I did not want to kill him right away as I wanted him to get mad. I wanted to wound him as there was [a] revolver beside his bed and I did not care if he shot me as I did not want to go west to Herschel Isl ... I did not want to go to a strange country ... I was afraid Binder would see Doak and want to kill me ... I shot to kill him.[7]

If this account is true, and there is no reason to suppose it is not, Doak showed very poor judgment in his treatment of Alikomiak, and it is difficult to know why he expressed impatience with the man or gave him women's work to do. After all, the earlier murder cases were well known to all members of the force, and one would have thought that they would have been particularly careful to avoid the mistakes of Radford and Street and the two Oblate

Corporal W.A. Doak on patrol in 1921 (NA, RCMP papers, access
1996–400, neg. 880)

fathers. Admittedly, Alikomiak seems to have been especially sensitive to what he considered abuse – Doak never struck or even
shouted at him. This, at least, was the official version of events. A
somewhat different story was given by the ethnographer Knud
Rasmussen, who discussed the case a few years later with some
Inuit from the region: "Corporal Doak is described by all as a de-
cent man; but he was in the habit [of] playing on the feelings of
the accused Alekámiaq by assuming a brutal and terrifying manner, despite the fact that they could not speak to one another. According to what the other Eskimos told me, Alekámiaq by and by
got the idea that Doak was going to kill him, so he decided to fore-
stall him."[8]

In July 1923 Alikomiak was tried at Herschel Island on a number of charges, as was Tatamigana.[9] There were four trials involving the two men, and they were brief by modern standards, for all
were completed in a period of four days, including one day
wasted on a mistrial. Tatamigana was tried for killing a man
named Hanak and wounding another man. They were tried separately for the murder of another Inuk named Pugnana, and Alikomiak was tried for the murder of Doak and Binder.

Sidney Harring, in his study of the case, remarks that these trials were "designed to legitimate some official policy, but were actually pre-decided."[10] In this instance, the official policy was at

least as old as the Mounted Police themselves. The North-West Mounted Police had been established by the government of John A. Macdonald in 1873 in response to an atrocity that occurred in what is now southwest Saskatchewan, where a group of drunken wolf hunters from Montana had murdered more than twenty Assimiboine. What alarmed Ottawa was not so much the fate of the Native people but the notice the incident gave to the world of the government's powerlessness either to prevent such murders or to punish those who committed them. The NWMP was founded to show the flag, to demonstrate Canada's sovereignty over the newly acquired prairies. The force has been described as a semi-military organization, but it is more accurately described as being semi-political. On the prairies the NWMP enforced Macdonald's "national policy" – they made sure that settlement was peaceful and orderly, that the Native people moved to their reserves in a timely fashion, and that the Canadian Pacific Railway was not delayed by workers' strikes or Native protests.

In the Yukon during the gold rush, the police made sure that British-style authority prevailed over American-style popular democracy. Later, between 1903 and 1925, the flag was unfurled in the Arctic. It was not until the First World War that police duties were extended to such matters as national security – investigating putative German spies and the like. When Doak and Binder were killed, the police were the main – indeed, the only – representatives of Canada in the Arctic, and an attack on them was an attack on Canadian sovereignty in the region. It was for these reasons that the trial of Alikomiak and Tatamigana took on some of the characteristics of a show trial.

Thus, the trials that took place at Herschel Island in July 1923 were carefully planned, both for their political impact and for logistical reasons. The island was chosen because it was easily accessible and was the only community along the Arctic coast which had buildings of any considerable size – they were left over from the whaling days. Judge Lucien Dubuc of Edmonton, who was also a stipendiary magistrate of the NWT, was sent north as judge. A student of the territorial judiciary later described Dubuc as "a compassionate individual who was suited to the task of introducing the Inuit of the Mackenzie delta to only the broad principles of the 'white man's justice.' There is no evidence, however, that [he]

Judge Lucien Dubuc, who presided over the
Alikomiak trial (NA, PA-019353)

delved extensively into Inuit customs or their mode of living.
Rather he introduced the formal trappings of the white man's justice leaving it to later Magistrates ... to try to apply, with sensitivity, the substance of the white man's law to the Inuit."[11]

Dubuc was accompanied by T.L. Cory, solicitor for the North-
west Territories Office of the Department of the Interior, who was
appointed counsel for the accused, and I.B. Howatt, acting for the

crown. The jury was selected from white residents of the communities along the Mackenzie River, who travelled with the court party. Preparations were made for the likelihood of a conviction. The travel season in that region was short, and it was realized that if the verdict was guilty it would be impossible to hang anyone for a year – until travel made it possible for the hangman to come to Herschel Island in the summer of 1924. To avoid such delay, which would have weakened the whole point of the proceedings, the hangman, Special Constable Gill, accompanied the party, and because of the shortage of suitable timber on Herschel Island, a portable gallows was taken along as well.

Private correspondence from government officials and others before the trial began indicate that example and deterrence were the main goals. Cortland Starnes, assistant commissioner of the RCMP, commented that the previous policy of leniency towards Inuit who killed outsiders had not worked, and there was a danger that these people would conclude "that crime is a thing to be rewarded by the White man." He recommended that steps be taken to "impress upon the Eskimo that such disregard for human life will not be tolerated and those found guilty of committing murder will be adequately punished."[12]

Perhaps the most remarkable comment made before the trial came from T.L. Cory, the lawyer appointed to defend the accused. His employer, the Department of the Interior, was the arm of government most concerned with the establishment of peace, order, and good government in northern Canada. Moreover W.W. Cory, the deputy minister of the interior, was his father. Presumably T.L. Cory was appointed for the defence partly because he drew a government salary and would not have to be paid extra for the task – Ottawa was very conscious of such costs in those days. Doubtless the trip to such an exotic locale appealed to him. But one would not have to be a conspiracy theorist to suppose that the main reason he was appointed was that he was not expected to overexert his talents on behalf of the accused or make emotional post-trial statements in the press.

In September 1922, before his appointment as defence counsel, Cory had written a memorandum to his immediate superior, O.S. Finnie, director of the NWT branch of the Department of the Interior, echoing Starnes's opinion that harsh public measures were required:

The numerous murders committed by Eskimos in the last year or so, clearly indicate that kindness and clemency have not had the desired effect upon the native population and I am strongly of the opinion that a court ought to be sent into the N.W.T. in 1923 to try those accused of murder. The cases should be tried midst the accused's local surroundings where the Native will feel the influence of the law, and those found guilty should receive the utmost penalty ... As kindness has failed in the past I strongly recommend that the law should take its course and those Eskimos found guilty of murder should be hanged in a place where the natives will see and recognize the outcome of taking another's life.[13]

A few months later he was appointed to defend these same men.

Of the transcripts of trials that took place at Herschel Island in the summer of 1923, only the three capital cases have been found in the records: *R v Alikomiak* for the murder of Pugnana; *R v Tatamigana* for the murder of Pugnana; and *R v Alikomiak* for the murder of Otto Binder and Corporal Doak. The first two were short, almost perfunctory affairs. The facts were not in question, since the Inuit involved had made full confessions to the police soon after their arrest. Tatamigana was called as a witness to testify against Alikomiak, and vice versa. The proceedings were conducted in English, with the police translator interpreting for the benefit of the accused, and the result was never in doubt. The transcripts are brief: only fifteen and nineteen double-spaced legal-sized pages, respectively, including charge, evidence, summation, and verdict. Both trials took place on the same day, 17 July, and each must have taken no more than a couple of hours. In one, the jury deliberated for nineteen minutes, and in the other they took eight minutes to arrive at a verdict of guilty. No witnesses were called for the defence in either case, and the judge delivered a summation (which must have taken only a few minutes) to the effect that the facts were clear enough but that he did not wish to influence the verdict.

The third murder trial, which took place the next day, was a different matter. Its transcript was longer, fifty-one pages, since Alikomiak was on trial for two killings. As well, the judge addressed the jury at much greater length. As with the first two trials, the accused had made a full confession, no witnesses were called for the defence, and Cory's cross-examination was confined to minor points of fact. In his summation, he apparently made an impassioned plea for the accused on the grounds of his ignorance of the law, but this was not recorded in the transcript, which says only "Mr. Cory replied on behalf of the Defence."

Cory's defence has been harshly criticized by one student of the case, who characterizes it as "neither incisive nor crisp … aimless. Seemingly seduced by tangential issues, he examined on matters wholly irrelevant to the central issues of the case. To blatant hearsay he made no objection."[14] It seems possible that if Cory had pursued a number of technical and jurisdictional matters, the verdict might have been different. Judge Dubuc admitted as much, commenting later: "In the hands of a less scrupulous lawyer there would probably have been an acquittal … and this expensive expedition would have ended in a gigantic fiasco and miscarriage of justice."[15] However, Cory, who was not in any case a criminal lawyer, knew his role, and no embarrassing acquittal occurred.

Judge Dubuc's address to the jury was fully recorded and is highly interesting as evidence of the official attitude towards the case and towards the Inuit. It is clear from the record that there was no thought at all of incorporating Inuit ideas of justice into the trial or of tempering the judicial process to northern conditions – as later judges, notably J.H. Sissons and W.G. Morrow, began to do following the Second World War.[16] Dubuc began with a nod towards British justice, "which has been the envy of all other Nations, and which has conquered the admiration and respect of all the individuals and even the nations which have sought its protection." He then complimented the jury:

Gentlemen of the North, you who live on the edge of civilization, as it were, in that "No-man's land" between the civilized and uncivilized portion of our great country, who endure all the hardships incident to this rugged country of ice and snow, with its every day privations; blazing the trail that the path may be clear and easier for those to follow. You have been selected … to listen and to weigh the evidence presented to you because you have a personal knowledge of the ways and customs of these nomads and unruled Eskimo who travel these shores … You will notice that the panel chosen to help at these trials is composed of Traders, Trappers, Prospectors, Captain of Ships and moreover, some of them are married to Natives, so that it represents every phase of northern life, and thoroughly represents the sentiment of the North; that is why I expect from you a true verdict in true conformity with the evidence, having at the same time regard also to a justice which will be understood by these Eskimo.[17]

He then got to the real point of his speech:

I am further satisfied that you shall not fail to bring a correct verdict because you have not forgotten I am sure those undying principles of British fair play which go with British justice, for although you may feel that you should have some consideration for the simple mentality of these primitive people, yet you also feel that you owe a duty to your country, who extends to them its generous protection in every way.

One of the victims, Otto Binder, was a northern man like yourselves, a member of the oldest trading company in the North, a Company who has been the pioneer of civilization in Western and Northern Canada, and whose kindness and benevolency to the natives in the past, and even now through its self sacrificing Agents at different posts, is, in many cases, not sufficiently appreciated.

The other victim, Corporal Doak, was an Officer of the Royal Canadian Mounted Police in the north, one of those lonely and fearless sentinels for Law and Order, posted somewhere on some barren and desolate point in the Polar Sea. A man whose duty was to prevent if possible, and if not, to detect and help in punishment of crime. This adds interest to this case and to the charge against the accused because we are all concerned in the protection of those silent men who traverse and patrol these lands of ice and snow, and who are always on guard for us; we are interested in the safeguarding of those whose duty it is to protect us. Corporal Doak [who was] one of the ablest and kindest members of that distinguished Force ... was brutally murdered, defenceless in his sleep, in one of the most cold-blooded manners known in the annals of the Force, a victim of his kindness to the accused. While he had the accused in his custody he was protecting him at the same time from his own people, who wanted retribution for an alleged previous murder.

The blood of Corporal Doak does not cry out for vengeance, and it is possible, when he turned on his death bed to look in the eye of the aggressor, that his last thought, in that moment's awakening before his eternal sleep, may have been one of Christian forgiveness; let us hope so. But at this trial the personality of the individual must be laid aside. It is your duty as Jurymen who have taken the oath as such to decide according to the evidence, and make these tribes understand that the stern but at the same time just hand of British justice extends also to these northern shores. We want it plainly understood in the minds of these people that one of our most important laws is for the protection of human life which flows from the Divine command "Thou shalt not kill."

It is all very well to plead for mercy and play on your sympathy for these uncultured tribes, but murder amongst all people ... has always been a crime of the most hateful and punishable character. When such eloquent and sentimental appeals are made to you, do not forget the innocent victims Otto Binder and Corporal Doak, beloved by all those who have known them, who have been cowardly murdered. Remember that after all it is hands drenched with the blood of his own tribe and of his two white benefactors which are lifted to you to plead for mercy. Remember that this is not a court of mercy but is a Court of Justice, and mercy should be given only by a Higher Tribunal after proper representation is made to it, I mean the Governor General as representing the King.

I will now leave this view of the case which is painful to us all, but I could not let it pass in silence after the eloquent, emotional, and so sentimental appeal of the Counsel for the Defence on behalf of the accused. I am myself a man of the West, I have travelled long enough among the frontiersmen and pioneers of the North to know that under their rugged and stern appearance, there beats a heart as tender as it is human, a heart that warms up quickly to all human sufferings and weaknesses. I know how a sympathy and forgiveness that knows no bounds flows generously from those who themselves have endured so much of life's hardships and privations. I have learnt to appreciate how far a northern man will go to help a neighbour who is in trouble, but today, Gentlemen, the country is making an appeal to your honour as good Canadians to do your duty fearlessly, and you should not therefore let yourself be unduly swayed by sentiment of pity and mercy alone.

I speak now with a knowledge of what I say and for a special purpose, because it has come to my ears that some members of the Jury had already expressed before the trial ideas of mercy and acquittal unmindful no doubt of the consequences. Our Government has not undertaken this expensive Judicial Expedition to have exhibited here a mockery and travesty of Justice before these primitive people. You have a duty to perform as Jurymen, a duty to your Country and to our Laws, and a duty to yourselves. We are leaving this Island very shortly after these Trials and the result of your verdict shall fall on you who are to remain here, and it is you who shall have to bear the consequences.

A student of the case commented about this remarkably histrionic and one-sided speech, that it was "graphic, admittedly; stirring, undoubtedly; in the nature of an unbiased and unemotional jury address, assuredly not!"[18] Today it would surely lead to a successful appeal for a new trial. Dubuc went on to explain the law in the case. He praised the counsel for the crown and the counsel for the defence, and one again exhorted the jury men to do their duty. The jury retired, deliberated for eighteen minutes, and returned a verdict of guilty.

Although Judge Dubuc expected to leave the next day, he was delayed several weeks awaiting the steamer that would take him back up the Mackenzie River. On 11 August, the day before his departure, he sentenced both men to be hanged on 7 December. Back in Edmonton he wrote, on 22 September 1923, a report on the trials to the secretary of state in Ottawa, in which he recommended strongly that no clemency be shown to either of the convicted men, while at the same time suggesting alternatives to traditional punishment:

Imprisonment in the North for the Eskimo is nearly impossible and is not taken seriously by them ... For the Eskimo, every day of his life is a fight and struggle for food and existence under the most rigorous climatic conditions; so that, being fed and housed with the Police ... is not only a reward, but an honour ... Close confinement in our Penitentiaries outside would mean to them sure death within a very short time.

It is my opinion that the Criminal Code be amended if possible, empowering the Judge to sentence a criminal Eskimo to imprisonment on bread and water and inflict the lash; that this form of punishment be continued in effect for a few years until these people are more civilized. To be whipped is to be treated like a dog and is to them the greatest humiliation; such a sentence would be real punishment and one they could understand. If this cannot be done, and long terms of useless [jail] have to continue to be administered, power should be given the Judge to see to it that the family of the men sentenced does not suffer (for they are nomads, have no chiefs, and do not live in groups) and to leave their families unprovided for is to sentence them to perish ...

With my experience and the study of the character of the Eskimo, and having in view the protection of the white men visiting the North country ... and lastly the brutal and cowardly murder of Otto Binder and Corporal Doak, I feel it my duty, although very painful to me, to recommend most respectfully, but most earnestly, that the Law follow its course.[19]

No one at the time remarked on the significance of the fact that it was only Alikomiak who was condemned for killing whites; Tatamigana was sentenced for killing one of his own people. This might have been taken as an example of even-handedness on the part of the government and is perhaps the reason, though the records are silent on the point, why Tatamigana – who had not even fired the shot that killed Pugnana, though he had plotted it with Alikomiak – was also sentenced to hang. Perhaps the government wanted to make an example of him to demonstrate that the law would protect the Inuit in the same fashion as whites.

The cases of Alikomiak and Tatamigana attracted a great deal of attention in the newspapers and amongst the public. The government received petitions and letters recommending clemency, both from members of the general public and from people with northern experience. The typical argument rested on the idea that the Inuit were primitive, childlike, and ignorant of the law. An undated letter from E. Maitland of Plummer, Ontario, expressed the idea eloquently: "Although a woman, I am not one who favours the abolition of the death penalty ... but it seems not unreasonable to sympathize with the ignorant, primitive people, standing confused and bewildered in one of our law courts, and so simple-minded and remote from the subtleties of 'civilized' law proceedings that they told a straight-forward tale, which practically convicted themselves."[20]

Wilfred Grenfell, the medical missionary, commented publicly on the case, stating: "To hang an Eskimo for murder is the same of hanging a little child ... The Eskimos are an extraordinarily intelligent people ... but they are totally ignorant of law and the consequences of its violation. Ethically, the Eskimo is just like a child of seven years. You would not hang a child of seven years, would you?"[21] One wonders how much he had learned about Inuit culture during his thirty years of service on the Labrador coast.

Some northerners also commented on the case, notably James R. Lucas, Anglican bishop of Mackenzie River, within whose diocese the murders had occurred and who had witnessed the trials, and Isaac O. Stringer, bishop of the Yukon. Both made the argument that the condemned men should not be executed for breaking laws that they knew nothing about and should instead suffer life imprisonment. But the government had heard these arguments in previous cases and was not prepared to yield to them again. Lucas had another point to make. In a letter of 17 September 1922 to Raoul Dandurand, acting minister of justice, he wrote: "It will not enhance the reputation of the White man among them, if they think that it was fear of meeting a similar fate that led them to take their countrymen away where it would be safe to kill them ... The execution of these two men will jeopardize the lives of White men who may be living amongst the tribes of Eskimos whence these murderers came." William D. Reeve, bishop of Toronto, suggested corporal punishment as an alternative to death: "Imprisonment or banishment would not be adequate, but what about flogging? I am inclined to think that the application of the lash would have a greater moral and deterrent effect than anything else."[22]

It was suggested in the press and elsewhere that Alikomiak was only sixteen years old, but the police secured a statement from a trader who had known him for six years and swore that he was at least an adolescent when he first met him. It was also suggested that Otto Binder had started the sequence of events by stealing the wife of a local Inuk, a rumour that sparked a petition from members of the Hamilton, Ontario, branch of the Council of Women, who sympathized with men who had "followed their own natural light in regard to right, in avenging this transgression against home and wifehood." This accusation was denied by the police, who presented statements from witnesses to disprove it. Even if true, it would have had little bearing on the murder of Doak.

Although the bishops and a number of others protested the sentences, the newspapers generally supported them, and, not surprisingly, the government refused to commute them. Accordingly, an RCMP patrol was sent from the northern Yukon to Herschel Island in the late fall of 1923 with the news that there was to be no mercy, and the two men went stoically to the gallows on 1 February 1924. Knud Rasmussen described their last hours:

One evening late in winter, while following their customary occupation of making salmon nets, they were informed that they were to be hanged next morning at three o'clock. Young Alekámiaq received the news with a smile. The other man, who was somewhat older, felt as if he was choking and asked for a glass of water; having taken a drink he too was ready to meet his fate. Just before they were to be executed they gave the wife of the police sergeant some small souvenirs carved in walrus ivory, as a sign that they bore no malice towards the police. They ascended the scaffold with great calmness and met death without fear.[23]

What conclusions can be drawn from this episode? The most important and most obvious, as has been noted by other commentators,[24] is that these were clearly show trials, carefully staged for public effect. Everything about them, from the location to the sentencing, was designed to send a message that Canada's sovereignty over the region was to be enforced. The question arises, however: For whom was the show put on and to whom was the message directed? The immediate answer would seem to be the Inuit. But for a number of reasons, this seems not to be the whole truth. It is just as likely that the government's purpose was to demonstrate to the Canadian public as a whole, as well as to the world, that the old laissez-faire attitude towards the Arctic had ended and that a new activist era had begun.

It is significant that the trials of Alikomiak and Tatamigana took place at a time when the government was busily involved in establishing police posts in a number of remote spots in the Arctic for the purpose of demonstrating sovereignty, the basis for which under international law was more than a little questionable. In some places, such as the Bache Peninsula on Ellesmere Island, there were no inhabitants at all, so the demonstrations of sovereignty were confined to operating a *pro forma* post office. But in the Western Arctic, the Alikomiak case provided the opportunity for an actual criminal trial – one of the best demonstrations of sovereignty possible.

The assertion that these trials were show trials for southerners as much as for the Inuit is reinforced by the sentences themselves. Many people, both at the time and since, have commented that it was wrong to hang men when they were ignorant of Canadian law; this was the main point made by those who signed petitions asking for clemency – the convicted men were "simple," "primitive," "ignorant of the law," and so forth. But, after all, the punishment among the Inuit for killing was the same as it was in the Canadian criminal code. Inuit who killed their own people could expect to be killed in return, and murder and retribution were extremely common among the Copper Inuit of that era. Rasmussen described a "small snow-hut camp of fifteen families ... [containing] not a single grown man who had not been involved in a killing in some way or other."[25] It was the proceedings, not the sentence, that were alien to the Inuit.

In this regard, it is surely significant that several observers who knew the Inuit well had suggested that corporal punishment would be a more appropriate punishment than hanging. Judge Dubuc and three bishops of the Anglican church, one of whom was present at the trial, recommended other punishments – life imprisonment, bread and water, flogging – that would have seemed more terrible to the Inuit than hanging. Although Dubuc was admittedly no expert, at least two of these men knew the North very well at first hand – better, apparently, than the government did. At first glance their advice seems merciful. But as these men themselves said, such punishment, from the Inuit point of view, would be a far more severe penalty than hanging.

Execution was the usual Inuit way of punishing murder, while corporal punishment was not only unusual but as all three murder cases had demonstrated, it was something the Inuit feared and resented. Being taken from their country to an unknown place and never returned was even worse. Indeed, one reason Alikomiak gave for shooting Doak was that he did not want to be taken to Herschel Island for trial. The bishops and the judge were thus not squeamish liberals balking at a couple of salutary executions. On the contrary, they were suggesting culturally devastating punishments, which might well have had the deterrent effect the government claimed it wanted.

Why, then, did the government not accept the advice of the judge and the bishops and modify the punishment to something far more humiliating and perhaps more effective than hanging? Part of the reason must be that the trials were for southern consumption, and in the south a flogging followed by imprisonment at hard labour would have seemed insufficiently harsh. The federal government had been sensitive ever since the Alaska boundary dispute of 1903 to the charge of being weak in upholding Canada's authority in the North. By hanging Alikomiak and Tatamigana, it not only showed Canadians that it would brook no further violence from Inuit, but it demonstrated to foreigners that the government intended to be a strong force in the region.

This case may also be seen as a precursor to the current practice of imposing culturally relevant sentences in some criminal cases involving First Nations people and the use of sentencing circles in such cases. In 1923 well-informed northerners suggested that hanging was the wrong penalty to impose on Alikomiak and Tatamigana – not because it was cruel but because, given the cultural context of the Inuit, it was not harsh enough or was inappropriate. Although this suggestion was not adopted, the fact that it was made at all is of considerable significance.

CHAPTER SEVEN

"A Drunken Impulse":
The Paddy Duncan Case

He has not the intelligence of the white man and lacks the
same power of control while under the influence of liquor.

> The Department of Indian Affairs, commenting
> on Paddy Duncan's request for parole, 1946

The Paddy Duncan case[1] of 1936 is the last chronological case
dealt with in this book, and it is in some ways the most interesting.
The interest lies not in the details of the crime or its detection but
in the light it sheds on the social history of the Yukon and, in particular, the territorial patterns of race and racial relations. The
Duncan case was one of Native-Native violence, which was not
very common in the Yukon before 1950 but became far too common after that time. Not coincidentally, it is the only one covered
here in detail in which the killer was not hanged. It is also the only
one dealt with in this book, other than the Katy Joe case, in which
both killer and victim had been born in the North. In the other
cases, the role of bureaucracy was to make a recommendation on
clemency, but Paddy Duncan was the subject of bureaucratic attention throughout the length of his imprisonment. The role of the
press was different too, in that the newspapers treated Duncan as
the subject of good human interest stories rather than as a public
scourge to be purged from society. This was partly because the papers that covered his case were in southern British Columbia,
where he was imprisoned, rather than in the Yukon, where he had
committed his crime, so there was no hostile feeling about him
among the papers' readers. There was also the fact that the killing
of a Native person by another Native created much less alarm

among the general public than an interracial murder would have done.

We know more about Paddy Duncan than about most men convicted of murder in the Yukon. This is largely because he was not hanged but was sent to a penitentiary, from which he was eventually paroled, a process that generated much paperwork over the years. Because the penitentiary was in British Columbia and because he was an elderly prisoner with an indigenous background and was something of a "character," the Vancouver newspapers made him a minor celebrity, and in due course he had his fifteen minutes of fame. And since he was a Native person, the federal Department of Indian Affairs also took an interest in his fate. Unlike Elfors or Gogoff, who seemed to appear from nowhere, commit the crime, and then fade from memory, Paddy Duncan had his roots in the North and was a member of a group of people about whom a great deal is known.

By 1936 the Yukon had shrunk to a shadow of its former glory. Already by 1921 its population had declined to just over 4,000, of whom about 2,500 were non-Native, and it did not rise significantly until the 1940s. Despite the fact that Canada was in the midst of the Great Depression, the Yukon was not particularly poor. The price of gold had risen, and the territory's mining industry – its only source of wealth other than government and transportation – was fairly prosperous. But everything was on a very small scale. It did not take many men to operate the huge dredges that scoured the old creeks where thousands had once dug and sluiced by hand. A few other mines continued to operate, notably the lead-zinc operations in the Mayo-Elsa region. There were also train crews and steamboat crews (in summer) manning the transportation network; the Mounted Police were still there, though in greatly reduced numbers; and there was a vestigial civil service and a small tourist industry based on big game hunting. That was about it for non-Native activity.

The Native people, who had been there long before any fur trader or prospector came to the Yukon, were still there, and some took advantage of the new economy in ways that did not affect the seasonal pattern of their lives. For instance, they could cut cord wood for the Yukon River steamboats at times that did not interfere with their hunting, and many did this for cash to supplement their trapping income. Some Native people fell afoul of alcohol and gravitated to the Yukon's little towns, where they cadged food, reinforcing white people's racist stereotypes about them. But in most cases, the events of the forty years since the discovery of gold in the region had not changed the lives of the Native people in any fundamental way. Most continued to follow a seasonal hunting and gathering life, taking from the newcomers what they needed. The only really dramatic effect on them was that of disease. The newcomers had brought new illnesses, a process which began before the gold rush; as a result, an indigenous population which has been estimated at 7,000 in the mid-nineteenth century had been reduced to 1,500 a hundred years later.

Yukon First Nations therefore maintained a social distance from the newcomers. Consequently, there was very little conflict between the races. The Nantuck case was a dramatic exception. The contrast to the Australian Outback and the American West, where there was far more violence between indigenous people and whites, was notable and shows how tiny and limited the European presence in the Yukon was during this period, how peaceable and retiring the First Nations were in the Northwest, and how the territory was big enough for the races to keep their distance. It also shows how effectively the Mounted Police kept order. The police did this, in large measure, by keeping non-Natives (especially those trying to sell liquor) away from the First Nations and by maintaining their role as "protectors" of the indigenous people.

It was only after the Second World War, with the rapid dislocation of aboriginal life under the assault of the social welfare state and the legalization of the aboriginal use of alcohol, that the First Nations of the Yukon began to crowd the territorial jails – far out of proportion to their numbers. Before 1950, fewer Native people had found themselves in court, and generally it was for different offences. The sad modern litany of social pathology – spouse and child abuse, suicide, and other contemporary problems associated with alcohol – is a modern rather than historical problem in the Yukon. Before 1945 the police were somewhat (though, as this case shows, never completely) successful in keeping alcohol out of Native hands. Over the years, they prosecuted dozens of Native people, mostly men, for possession of liquor or public drunkenness, and they prosecuted a large number of whites for supplying the li-

The Dalton Range, photographed from the Dalton Trail in 1898. A view of the country from which Paddy Duncan came (NA, PA-40001)

quor. A few Native people appeared in court charged with other minor offences, such as assault, petty theft, and violation of hunting regulations, but major crimes were uncommon.

In the Yukon in the late 1930s, the small non-Native society was concentrated in the narrow confines of the Yukon River valley, from Carcross in the south to Dawson City in the north, with an offshoot up the Stewart River valley to the Mayo-Elsa-Keno mining region. Outside this corridor, the rest of the Yukon, a region of more than 483,450 square kilometres, remained the preserve of the First Nations where, unless they committed a really serious breach of Canadian law, they were left to their own devices. This meant, among other things, that their own social traditions, including enforcement of behaviour through group consensus and insistence on apology and restitution by offenders, remained in place as a mechanism of self-government.

Paddy Duncan lived in Champagne, a collection of log houses west of Whitehorse, on a pack trail that led to Burwash in the west part of the territory. Another trail ran through it, a route that went from salt water at Haines, Alaska, past the spectacular and mountainous Kluane country, and north to Selkirk and eventually Dawson. This was Dalton's Trail, founded by Jack Dalton during the gold rush as an alternate to the Chilkoot Pass route. The Natives of Champagne (a community supposedly founded by Dalton in

Members of the Champagne band setting their weirs across the stream to catch salmon near the village of Klukshu in 1949 (NA, PA-172812)

1902) lived by hunting and trapping, participating in the small gold and silver "rushes" in the area, and occasionally guiding a rich sportsman on a trophy hunt in the St Elias Mountains.

Although mostly undisturbed by the twentieth century, the people of Champagne were not unaffected by it. By the mid-1930s, they could drive to Whitehorse, for the trail was usable by cars in summer. They dressed in manufactured rather than "traditional" clothing, relied heavily on technology – rifles, canoes, gasoline motors – for hunting, and increasingly ate processed food. But they still followed the ancient seasonal rhythms, fishing for salmon, hunting moose and other game, and trapping fur-bearing animals, all according to the proper season.

Champagne, together with the nearby settlement of Klukshu, had a total population of only sixty-four, according to the Department of Indian Affairs figures for 1944. The region was occupied by the southern Tutchone, but it had traditionally been contested by the richer and more powerful Tlingit of the Alaska panhandle. The Tlingit had historically used their control of the mountain passes, which joined the coast to the interior, to dominate the southwestern Yukon. Before the gold rush, they had dictated trading conditions to the Tutchone, using a combination of diplomacy and violence to control communications with the interior.

Before the arrival of European outsiders in the mid-nineteenth century, these people had governed themselves according to their own customs. When quarrels between individuals resulted in violence, the usual response was to separate them, but when murder occurred, a stronger response was called for. The ethnographer Catherine McClellan described the policy of the southern Tutchone: "In case of what was construed as murder ... it was felt essential that both sides negotiate formally in order to see that the loss of life was fairly compensated for. Apparently either the death of a social equivalent of the victim or else a payment in good equal to his worth would be satisfactory compensation."[2]

Paddy Duncan was a member of this society. He was born in 1877 near Dalton Post, a trading establishment on the Canadian-American border. The highway between Haines, Alaska, and Haines Junction, Yukon, runs by the site of the post, but when Duncan was born the boundary had not been surveyed or even firmly established, so no one knew or cared which country he was born in. Much of his early life was spent at Klukwan, near Haines. According to the Mounted Police, he was a "Coast Indian," his father coming from the American side of the border, his mother from the Canadian, a common pattern that was often related to trade and political relations between tribal groups.

In his early twenties, he and others of his people were able to profit from the Yukon gold rush when several hundred stampeders tried to reach the goldfields by way of Dalton's Trail and hired Duncan and others as guides and packers. Fifty years later, Stan Cameron, a prospector from British Columbia, recalled Dalton's work: "On July 8, 1897, eight of us set out from Victoria with 54 head of cattle and 15 horses. At Haynes Mission in Alaska, we hired Paddy Duncan as guide. He took us 100 miles to Dalton Post – and you couldn't wish for a finer guide or a livelier companion. We all thought the world of him."[3]

After the gold rush, Duncan had a number of different jobs. He worked as a miner and hunter on both sides of the international boundary and actually assisted in marking it when the boundary commission visited the region in the years before the First World War. He acted as a guide for the Mounted Police for a number of years and participated in several small gold rushes in the Kluane region, continuing into the 1930s to work a property he had claimed.

In the fall of 1936 Paddy Duncan was about sixty years old. The records state that he was 5ft 6in tall and weighed 155lb. The fact that none of the other murder files carry such statistics shows partly that attitudes had changed by the 1930s, and partly the fact that Duncan had been sent to prison, where such matters were important. He was slightly stooped and walked stiffly. His most notable physical characteristic was his ears, which were pierced according to the custom of his people. He could not read or write, which was understandable, since he must have had little contact with English speakers until he was past his teens. His spoken English was reasonably good, and he could sign his name, though not easily. Like most of the Yukon's Native people who belonged to a church, he was Anglican. Little is known about his family, except that by that time he was a widower and had two daughters living in Alaska.

Although he did not live permanently in Champagne (he moved freely throughout the southern Yukon), he visited the small community regularly to trade and socialize. It was for one or both of these reasons that he went there in September 1936, bringing a boat from the village of Dezadeash for Joe King, with whom he stayed for a while. Towards the end of October he moved in with Joe Kane, to whom he was distantly related by marriage. He borrowed a 30-30 Winchester rifle from Kane and went hunting for a few days. When he returned, on 29 October, he put the rifle at the head of his bed, helped prepare supper, and sat down to eat and smoke. Sometime during the evening the Kanes (Joe, his wife Lily, and their two sons, the curiously named Harton and Parton, who lived nearby) brought out some liquor – illicit, of course, since all liquor was forbidden to Native people at the time – and what the police later described as "an all night carousal on home brewed intoxicants" got underway.

This kind of affair, what the press used to refer to as a "drinking party," was in part the result of the official policy towards indigenous people and alcohol. Since it was illegal for anyone to sell or give liquor to Native people, and illegal for them to possess or drink it, it was difficult for Natives to develop the habit of moderate drinking as a social pleasure. When they managed to get liquor from whites, it was from bootleggers or from men who wanted to sleep with their women. Or they might make home brew, a beverage not meant to be sipped and appreciated. None of this was conducive to the responsible use of alcohol, and the society that forbade them its use "for their own good" was quick to point to bouts of spectacular drunkenness as evidence that they were not sufficiently responsible to be permitted legal access to it.

In the early evening of 29 October, Joe Kane left the house, then returned with a small pot of beer, and Duncan and the Kanes settled in for a night of drinking and talking. As Duncan later described the evening, "We sat down and talk fun all the way through. We talk fun – laughing – joshing each other. After while all gone that pot. We drink it up. I am pretty well loaded up – maybe all of us – maybe – I don't know." Harton and Parton Kane left to buy some home brew beer from Reginald Lowe, a clerk at the Taylor and Drury Company's general store. They bought two quarts, and later another two gallons (about nine litres), for which they paid $3.50. Eventually everyone fell asleep, Harton Kane returning to the nearby cabin he shared with his wife Grace. No one later recalled any quarrelling or fighting.

But early the next morning, something went wrong. Lily Kane got up and started a fire. Paddy Duncan awoke and asked for a glass of water while Lily, looking out of the window, saw that Harton and Grace were walking towards Parton's house. Lily went out to join them. The three Kane houses were close to each other, and it took only a moment for the family group to get to Parton's cabin. Just as Grace reached the door, she heard a shot. Turning, she saw her husband Harton fall to the ground, and Paddy Duncan standing behind him, a rifle in his hands. She pulled her husband, who was bleeding badly, into the house, while Lily leapt at Duncan, pulling the rifle from his hands and shouting, "You hurt my son. Let go." Dragging Duncan across to her own cabin, she called to her husband, "Paddy Duncan shot my boy. You hold him. Don't let go of him." Thinking that Duncan might try a second shot, she hid the rifle in a cache behind the house, while Duncan struggled with Joe Kane, shouting that he wanted to "see the boy he had shot."

Grace and Parton then ran to the RCMP detachment where, smelling strongly of home brew, they awakened Constable D.A. Dunlop with the news of the shooting. Dunlop ran to the cabin and found Harton lying on the floor wrapped in an eiderdown sleeping bag. Writhing in pain, a bloody froth on his lips, he muttered to the constable, "Paddy Duncan, he shoot me." Meanwhile, the rest of the family milled about, speaking wildly in Tutchone, too distraught to give Dunlop a coherent account in English. The police officer gave Harton a quick examination and discovered that he had indeed been shot in the back and that the bullet had exited through his stomach. He bundled Harton into his car and prepared to leave for Whitehorse.

Before leaving, however, he took steps to set the legal machinery in motion. He found Paddy Duncan in Joe Kane's cabin and arrested him. Duncan was still showing the effects of his binge but was able to walk without assistance and was "clear and collected" in his speech. He surrendered without a struggle, telling Dunlop, "He after me, I get him." A short search turned up the rifle in the meat cache behind one of the cabins. Duncan was placed in the detachment's cell and put under the supervision of Lowe (the trader who had sold the group the home brew), assisted by John Carroll, another local resident.

About an hour after the shooting, Dunlop left for Whitehorse with Harton, a trip that would have been impossible a few weeks later except by sleigh, since the road was not kept open in winter. The trip, which must have been a torment for the wounded man, took more than eight hours, from 8:00 AM until 4:30 PM. Why a journey of less than a hundred kilometres took so long is not clear – it was a rough wagon road, and Dunlop would have to have driven very slowly. The initial delay is explained by the fact that Dunlop must have felt that taking Duncan into custody was more important than getting the victim to a doctor. At the Whitehorse hospital, a doctor examined Harton and declared there was nothing that could be done for him. He died seven hours later, at 11:15 PM.

Duncan was charged with murder, and the Whitehorse RCMP telegraphed Ottawa asking that the government hire a lawyer to defend him. The Department of Justice agreed to pay for his defence, estimated to cost about $500, and Willard Phelps, a Whitehorse lawyer, was hired to prepare for the trial. If it is true that "justice delayed is justice denied," then Paddy Duncan could have had no complaints about the speed with which his case was handled. In the late 1930s, criminal cases of this type were still pushed ahead with great speed. His trial began on 2 December 1936, less than five weeks after the shooting. And like the earlier murder cases dealt with in this book, it was astonishingly brief by modern standards. It began in the morning, and statements, evidence, cross-examination, summation, deliberation, verdict, and sentencing were all completed in time to permit judge, counsel, and jury (still in that year made up of only six men) to be home for their evening meal.

C.E. McLeod appeared for the crown, and Judge Charles Macaulay presided. The trial began with Constable Dunlop describing the crime scene and Duncan's arrest. Then the Kane family testified, with George Chambers, a local trader who knew the Kanes, acting as interpreter for the older family members. Reginald Lowe testified about selling home brew to the Kanes; by doing so he incriminated himself, and he was later convicted under the Indian Act and given six months, the maximum sentence for selling liquor to Native people. The only witness whose testimony was not already known was George Joe, another local resident, who spoke to the question of motive. Paddy Duncan, he said, had talked to him that September about buying a new rifle, not for "moose or caribou, but for his life or another's, one of the Kane boys." The prosecution ended its case with testimony from E.E. Hildebrand, a Whitehorse doctor, who described the victim's final hours and the cause of his death.

There was only one witness for the defence, Duncan himself. He stated that he could remember nothing about the events surrounding Harton Kane's death, and he denied that he had threatened the lives of the Kane brothers. During cross-examination, McLeod suggested that Duncan seemed to remember some events clearly – he claimed to have removed the shells from the rifle the previous night – but was blank on other aspects of the killing. McLeod repeatedly pressed Duncan to tell what he actually knew, but Duncan said he needed an interpreter: "I do not understand much English. If I tell you anything you understand what I tell with good interpreter here. What he tell me I understand. Without it can't do nothing." But an interpreter was not provided, nor did the defence counsel ask for one (an omission which today would likely lead to a new trial on appeal), and Duncan continued his testimony in English. After a few more questions, the evidence was complete.

Judge Macaulay's summation made it clear that he believed that Paddy Duncan had committed the murder. "In regard to the shooting," he said, "I think there can be no question in anybody's mind but that Harton Kane's death was caused by a bullet fired from a rifle in the hands of Paddy Duncan." He "deplored that a white man should have supplied the liquor to these Indians," but said that although "this was what led up to the tragedy," he could not ask the jury to consider a verdict of manslaughter: "Drunkenness does not reduce a charge of murder to manslaughter if there are not other circumstances that would justify it."

The jury left the courtroom at 4:30 PM and returned forty minutes later with the verdict: guilty as charged, but with a strong recommendation for mercy. Judge Macaulay then gave the sentence the law required: Paddy Duncan was to be "kept in confinement until the 23rd day of March 1937, when he would be hanged by the neck until he is dead." But Macaulay, strongly seconded by the crown prosecutor, added a recommendation for mercy.

In view of the evidence, the verdict was a foregone conclusion, and despite the absence of a credible motive there was really nothing to be said in Duncan's defence. There was no allegation of self-defence or anything that might have excused the deed. The court officials expressed sympathy for Duncan, but it was tinged with the racial assumptions of the era. Writing to Ottawa about the case, Macaulay commented: "These Indians in this district have not the intelligence of white men, and when they consume liquor they seem to lose their sense entirely." McLeod also blamed the affair on the Indians' weakness for liquor:

There is little doubt in my mind that the shooting would not have taken place had not the accused, as well as others of the Indians involved, been in at least a semi-intoxicated condition that morning as a result of drinking home brew which had been sold to them by a white man. Morally I feel that the man who sold the beer shares in large measure responsibility for the murder ... I was unable to prove anything like an adequate reason or motive for the shooting. I believe it to have been done upon drunken impulse, and that in the case of an Indian the ends of justice would be served by a punishment less severe than death.

The RCMP now moved Duncan to the territorial capital, Dawson City, where he was lodged in the police guardroom to await execution or the commutation of his sentence. There seems to have been no thought of an appeal. Duncan was never in much danger of execution, for a recommendation for mercy from judge and jury were virtually a guarantee of commutation, especially in a case involving intraracial killing among Native people. Local support for mercy was strong, and even the jurors sent a telegram to the federal cabinet urging commutation: "Not one of us believe that murder was premeditated but under the judge's charge felt we were obliged to bring in the verdict of murder and believing that our very strong recommendation for mercy part of our verdict would save from the scaffold otherwise our verdict would have been manslaughter."

Many local residents, familiar with Duncan's character and the facts of the case, added their voices to the pleas. The Reverend G.A. Cross of Christ Church (Anglican) in Whitehorse collected signatures on a petition, which included the names of the jury members and many prominent citizens. As Cross observed in a scrawled note at the end of the petition, "These persons constitute a majority of the citizens of Whitehorse, being almost all the adult white people at present in the town, and including most of its leading citizens, professional men, merchants, teachers, minister, office workers, government employees, railway men, airplane pilots and also manual workers." As expected, the federal government complied with community wishes. On 1 May 1937, three weeks before the rescheduled date for his execution, Paddy Duncan learned that his sentence had been commuted to life imprisonment in the RCMP guardroom at Whitehorse, a facility hardly suited to the role.

However, Duncan did not serve his term at Whitehorse. Instead, he was sent south to the British Columbia penitentiary in New Westminster, the infamous and now demolished Okalla prison. Here he became a model prisoner, quiet, inoffensive, and peaceful. In the spring of 1941 he signed a letter (with an X) to the Indian agent for northern British Columbia, Harper Reed, asking for release from prison. The letter pointed out that his murder of Kane was the first time he had been in trouble with the law, that he had provided loyal service to the RCMP over the years (he had acted as an interpreter for them, and at trials involving First Nations people), and that his conduct in prison had been exemplary. He ended with the plea: "I am an old man, and have very few years of life left to me, and I so long to be back in my home country where I might spend the remaining few years of my life among my own people."

Reed had known Duncan before the killing and was sympathetic. He passed on the letter, noting that a "certain amount of pity is felt for him." But George Jeckell, who as controller of the Yukon was its virtual governor as well as its Indian agent, did not second the appeal. Nor was the Department of Indian Affairs sympathetic: "The Department does not consider that the public interest would be served by any further remission to this Indian." Undeterred, Duncan continued to apply for parole, and his requests were echoed by a small group of supporters. In 1942 he offered information on large mica deposits in return for freedom. The government took the offer seriously enough to send someone from the Department of Mines and Resources to interview him, but nothing came of it. Meanwhile, the prison officials noted that he was getting frail and that "His sudden death would not be surprising."

Duncan made yet another attempt in 1944, but it also failed. The prison report noted, "This prisoner is well behaved & his industry very good ... Age 76 years. Appears too early [for release]." The following year the report noted that Duncan was "suffering from chronic myocarditis & now unable to work. Maintains innocence of the crime – Seems to be getting pretty feeble. Specifically recommended by Warden – will go back to Yukon when released. Says health with be better there – 73 years old."

Although the authorities could never seem to remember his age – in fact, he was sixty-seven in 1944 – it was clear that their determination to keep him locked up was beginning to weaken. In 1945, nine years after the murder, the annual report on him noted: "Apparently he was intoxicated at the time of the offence as he still maintains that he did not shoot the victim and he can't remember anything regarding the argument which was supposed to have taken place. Very feeble might be a good risk now."

He survived prison by keeping a low profile, playing solitaire, checkers, and horseshoes, and looking at the pictures in magazines that he was unable to read. The prison chaplain helped him with his letters, which became more frequent as the tenth anniversary of his incarceration approached. In one letter he spoke of his longing for the wilderness of his home: "I couldn't see anything but cement walls and sky. At noon I would look at the moon and wonder what she was seeing in the Yukon bush on the other side of the big wall." He appealed for release on account of age: "I am asking for a parole because I am now an old man. I am 78 years of age [he was actually 69 when this was written] and should like to be able to spend the rest of my days with my children and grand-children. I have money to take care of myself and my children will give me a place to stay if I prefer. I have been in the Penitentiary for over nine and one half years and it is my hope that you will recommend my release."

As the months went by, the prison, Indian Affairs, and Department of Justice bureaucracies pondered his case from time to time, seeing it as a classic example of the evil impact of alcohol on "Indians". An internal report prepared in 1946 said of Duncan that "he has not the intelligence of the white man and lacks the same power of control while under the influence of liquor." That home brew played a major role in the murder of Harton Kane obviously played in Paddy Duncan's favour, but not enough to secure his release after only ten years in prison.

In 1947 Duncan came in contact with Andrew Paull, president of the North American Indian Brotherhood and one of the leading aboriginal activists in British Columbia. Paull was taken with the case – an aging man protesting his innocence, who longed only to return to the North before he died. Noting that the Roman Catholic bishop of the Yukon supported Duncan's continued request for freedom, Paull reiterated the point that the prisoner was unusually well behaved and trustworthy in the penitentiary and was hardly a threat to Canadian society. Moreover, wrote Paull, playing a familiar tune to the paternalistic government, "Most Indians in the north do not read, and if he was sent back he could tell them orally what he had seen and how the white men punish bad Indians. If he died his people would not learn of this, so let him out to tell them what British Justice is."

Paull tried a different and contradictory argument in his correspondence with W.P. Gallagher, director of the Remissions Branch of the federal Department of Justice. Paddy Duncan, Paull argued, "is innocent of the crime for which he was sentenced to life imprisonment." According to Paull, who admitted he knew little about the case, "Native Indians in northern B.C. and the Yukon practice witch craft, and will take revenge on the friends of some one that has harmed them, which is sometimes imaginary. Paddy Duncan is of the opinion that the friends of the boy who died were mad at some of his relatives and took revenge on him." Paull went on to observe, correctly, that Duncan had lived a trouble-free life before the murder. At one point Duncan had apparently been told that he would have to serve ten years before a request for remission would be heard. In the spring of 1947, the ten-year period was up, and Paddy Duncan desperately wanted to go home.

Paull's intervention and continued pressure added urgency to a case that otherwise would likely have been given less attention. While Gallagher of the Remissions Branch was quick to point out that there was "no indication that he was innocent of the offence," he commenced a full review of the sentence. But as events moved towards a parole, a difficulty was discovered that had nothing to do with Canadian law. Investigations in the Yukon revealed that there were objections in Duncan's community to his early release. The RCMP reported: "The Indians and half-breeds do not think Duncan should return to Champagne, Y.T., where three of the brothers of the murdered man are living. There is a certain spirit of revenge still apparent." R.J. Meek, Indian agent in the region, recommended that if Duncan was released, he should be sent not to Champagne but to Dalton Post or, better still, across the border to live with his brother in Haines. The Department of Indian Affairs, noting the possibility of violent revenge, felt that it was better that Duncan should not return home.

Time was running out for Duncan, who now was over seventy and in uncertain health. Once more Andrew Paull came to his defence. He and his family visited Duncan in Okalla in May 1948 and once again heard his pleas for release, which were made more urgent by Duncan's discovery that one of his daughters had died while he was in jail. Paull could not resist the case, writing again to the Department of Justice asking for mercy for the prisoner. He was, he stated, "willing to take him and be responsible for him and keep him in my house until he is dead and after he is dead, I will buy a coffin and bury him." But the bureaucracy did not trust Paull (who had recently lost his position as president of the North American Indian Brotherhood), commenting that he "is not to be relied upon to carry out his undertakings, although, of course, he might do so in the present case." Others wondered why Paull would accept such a potentially onerous obligation. One observed that he might " have some private arrangement for compensation from Duncan or his friends."

Finally, on 3 July 1948, approximately six weeks after Paull's latest offer and more than eleven years after Paddy Duncan had been sentenced to life in prison, he was granted a "ticket of leave," as parole was then officially called. Duncan's freedom came with stringent conditions: that he live under the supervision of Andrew Paull, that he refrain from the use of alcohol and, most significantly, that he not return to the Yukon Territory. Duncan could not go home so was not as free as he wished, but he was now ready to move outside the walls of the penitentiary. He also had some $600 available to him – not a princely sum, but enough to see him through the first months of freedom.

On 8 July, as Duncan prepared to leave the prison, he was met by W.S. Arneil, Indian commissioner for British Columbia. Arneil was impressed with Duncan who, he said, "creates a most favourable impression and is most appreciative of his parole being granted. He is known as an exemplary prisoner." But Duncan was not happy about being relocated to North Vancouver. "The old man," Arneil wrote, "is simply burning his heart out to return to the Yukon." He apparently hoped that, once outside the prison, he would be permitted to continue on to the Yukon. Arneil opted to defer Duncan's departure – the ticket of leave was good for thirty days – until a means of dealing with his "return to the Yukon obsession" had been managed and proper arrangements made.

At this point the newspapers took up the story. Andrew Paull, adept at using the press for his own publicity, had arranged to have some journalists on hand for Duncan's release. It was a good human-interest yarn: aged Indian longs for return to northern woods; killer grown old in jail turns to the ways of peace, and so forth. According to the *Daily Province*, Duncan reacted violently to the news that he was to live in Vancouver. "No, no no," he screamed, "I go home. I go home or I stay." And he refused to leave the prison. The paper ran a story written by Clyde Gilmour, then a young reporter and not yet the country's reigning expert on recorded classical music. His story[4] emphasized the unusual fact that Paddy Duncan was refusing to leave prison, preferring continued incarceration to freedom in North Vancouver. His spokesmen, Paull, was described as "founder and honorary President of the North American Indian Brotherhood, doughty Squamish tribesman and courtroom warrior who has fought for his people all over Canada."

Gilmour described the situation in the overwrought terms common to that era: "There were tears in Paddy's faded eyes when he walked into the office, but he blinked them back with fierce determination." Apparently, Duncan talked of his remaining daughter, now a grandmother, and his brother: "'I want to see them again,' the Indian said today, while sitting meekly in the warden's office. I want to see home. Don't want to stay down here. They treat me good here, but I want to go home:" Duncan was "wearing a prison-made grey, single-breasted suit, black ankle boots, blue shirt and grey tie. He laid his brown fedora hat on his lap and peered incuriously through steel-rimmed glasses." Paull, speaking for the distraught Duncan, commented: "Paddy would just as soon spend the rest of his life here in prison than stay anywhere except his old haunts in the Yukon. And I can't say I blame him."

Duncan's dogged determination to go home played well in the newspapers. How often had a prisoner serving life imprisonment turned down an opportunity to leave permanently? Duncan put aside his grey worsted "freedom suit," specially purchased for the occasion, and again put on his prison denims. He just wanted to go home.

The *Daily Province* stayed with the human-interest story – much to the chagrin of the Department of Indian Affairs. To the bureaucrats, the problem lay with Andrew Paull who, one said, "has some connection with this paper and, I understand, is on their payroll." The follow-up story, published on 10 July 1948, was decidedly less inflammatory but still tried a few tugs on the heartstrings.

Other newspapers told the story differently. The *Victoria Times* satirized Duncan's decision to remain behind bars: "Many a man or woman, weary of the unceasing struggle against the world, with the rising cost of living, the effort to make ends meet, and the continual competition for survival, will be moved to admire the aged Indian's decision. Three meals a day, a bed, a roof overhead, medical care and freedom from income taxes – these surely are attractions adequate to outweigh certain small disadvantages."

The difficulty for the authorities lay in their belief that if Duncan were to return to the Yukon, he might be the victim of a revenge attack, which was undesirable for several reasons (of which his personal safety was not the most important). After further hesitation, the Department of Indian Affairs agreed to a revision of the terms of his parole, provided that he did not become a charge on the department's welfare rolls, but it stipulated that its final decision would be contingent on discovering whether the old animosities still flourished. The fear of revenge lingered, although several officials, including Arneil, expressed the hope that it might "be found possible to permit this old man to return to his friends and relatives in the Yukon."

The government did not relent, and eventually Duncan changed his mind. On 22 July 1948 the Vancouver *Daily Province* reported: "There is an 80 year-old [*sic*] Indian heart that beats a little faster in Vancouver today. Paddy Duncan walked through the cold steel gates of the B.C. Penitentiary Wednesday afternoon. His faded old eyes danced and his hickory-lined face wrinkled into a happy smile." Duncan went to Andrew Paull's house, carrying with him $150 in cash, having left four $100 Dominion Government war bonds and another $75 with the Indian Affairs Branch for safekeeping. He was free, but his cherished dream of returning to the Yukon remained on hold. Paull, however, continued his efforts. Only five days after Duncan left jail, Paull was writing to the director of the Indian Affairs Branch, pointing out that Duncan now wished to return to his home in Alaska – not to the Yukon. He also collected evidence to the effect that the family of Harton Kane, specifically Jimmie Kane, bore no lasting grudge and did not intend to exact revenge.

Free but not yet satisfied, Paddy Duncan continued to press the authorities for permission to return home. The news coverage of his delayed departure from prison had turned him into a minor celebrity, ensuring that his case received prompt attention. Duncan did not settle easily into Paull's home, and pined for the chance to head north. His nerves frayed by his impatience and his sorrow, he contacted his sister and received word that he was welcome to return to her family's care. Meanwhile, Paull kept up the pressure at the national level. During a May visit to Ottawa, he sought – but did not receive – an audience with the federal solicitor general so that he could make the case for Duncan's quick return to the Yukon.

R.J. Meek, Indian agent for the Yukon, was pressured to survey the scene again and determine if it was safe to permit Duncan to return. Meek delegated the task to Constable R.H. Martin of the Haines Junction detachment of the RCMP. It took Martin a few weeks and two trips along the Haines road to Klukshu to locate Chief Johnny Fraser and members of the Kane family. When he asked Fraser and two of the victim's brothers, Parton and Bobby Kane, how they would react to Duncan's return, they walked a distance away and talked together. Then they came back to Martin and "stated that if Duncan would follow the old Indian custom and upon his return to the Yukon sponsor a big party and invite all the local members of the Wolf and Crow tribes that this would express his desire to return to them as a good friend and they felt that if this was done by Duncan he would be welcome among them, however, failing this they thought it would appear that Duncan did not want to make friends and as a result there would be bad feelings between the local Indians and Duncan."

As a result of these investigations, Meek reported to Ottawa that Chief John Fraser of the Champagne band believed "that 'Indian law' had been satisfied and that the likelihood of revenge by the brothers of the murdered man is now very improbable." Meek failed to track down Duncan's brother, who supposedly was at Haines, but learned the sad news that Paddy's remaining daughter had passed away in late August 1948. Meek ended his report with the words that Paddy Duncan had waited years to hear: "It is my personal opinion that it is now safe to allow Paddy Duncan to return to his former home in the Yukon." Separately, Meek reported: "The conditions under which Duncan could be received into the Band appears to be traditional with the Indians of this area."

Duncan's saga continued its bureaucratic path. T.R.L. MacInnes, secretary to the Indian Affairs branch, had been on the verge of recommending that the conditions on Duncan's ticket of leave be lifted, but Martin's report raised new apprehensions. MacInnes recoiled at the "requirement" of a big party. "It would be difficult, if not impossible, to keep liquor out of such a party," he protested, "and it is quite likely that it might end up in a further row and possible violence. Furthermore it would probably result in the old man wasting what little money he might have available for his needs." Duncan, he ruled, should remain with Paull.

B.C. Indian Commissioner Arneil thought the opposite. Claiming familiarity with the tribal custom of holding "a celebration at various points to renew completely the friendship of the Wolf and Crow Tribes," he stated that the friendship was in "no way strained either by the Duncan-Kane case or any other recent event." Arneil argued that the Kane family (Crow) and Duncan's relatives (Wolf) saw the need for a reaffirmation of friendship, that the prospect of difficulties arising was remote, and that Duncan's family would cover the costs. All that the Crow people wanted was to have Paddy Duncan "state that he has returned to his people and the district friendly towards everyone." There was mounting evidence that he would be welcomed back into the North, added Arneil. This evidence included communications from the Kane family, support from the Alaska Native Brotherhood, and further reports from Duncan's family.

Further investigation by Meek supported Arneil's case. He travelled to the Klukwan settlement near Haines, Alaska, in the company of Dr Douglas Leechman, an anthropologist with the National Museum of Canada. They ascertained that Duncan would be welcomed back at one of the "totem houses" – Frog House, Killer Whale House, Raven House, etc. – and that "by some law of totemism, Paddy Duncan would entertain his Band or tribe." Meek downplayed the "party" appellation for the gathering, pointing out that guests brought their own food and that "while drinking might take place, it is by no means inevitable." Meek and Constable Martin agreed that the likelihood of difficulties was small.

The interminable debate inside the government over the case began to extract a toll on Duncan and his friends. He had recovered from a serious skin disease, which had required hospitalization, and had returned to Paull's home. This now caused difficulties. By late October, Paull was compelled to write to Ottawa requesting an immediate decision. "My wife," he wrote, "is getting tired of him cooking etc. – and I fear she may have a serious breakdown. While I am willing to help Paddy Duncan and other Indians, my wife comes first in my duties." With Agent Meek's report now in hand, T.R.L. MacInnes finally, on 28 October 1948, recommended that the restrictions on Paddy Duncan's return be lifted. When so informing the director of Remissions Branch, Department of Justice, he could not resist a small jibe at Paull: "One reason why it might be better to do so is because Andrew Paull apparently now wants to get rid of responsibility for taking care of Duncan, something I apprehended and suggested in earlier correspondence."

Another month passed before the wheels of justice concluded their spinning. On 20 December Duncan's ticket of leave was amended, permitting him to return to the Yukon Territory. On 30 December he boarded a Canadian Pacific steamship bound for Skagway. Paddy Duncan was going home. But he was not completely in the clear, for he had to abide by the other conditions on his ticket of leave, most noticeably the rule against drinking, and he was obliged to report to the territorial Indian agent on a regular basis.

Duncan arrived in Whitehorse on 3 January 1949, reported to Indian Agent Meek and, the next day, checked in with the Whitehorse RCMP division. Duncan's original plan – to return to Dalton Post to live – had had to be abandoned, just like the settlement itself, which was a ghost town. Finally back in the Yukon, Duncan now expressed a desire to return to Juneau, Alaska, where he wished to live with his brother, Peter Duncan. Preliminary investigations with U.S. Immigration had already been undertaken, but Duncan also needed Canadian approval to leave the country. Having finally been granted an amendment to his ticket of leave so that he could return to the Yukon, Duncan now wanted it cancelled altogether, conditional upon his being accepted into Alaska!

The exasperation of officials in Ottawa was palpable, even in their normally drab internal correspondence. M.F. Gallagher, director of the Remissions Branch, asking for comments on the appeal by the Indian Affairs Branch, testily noted, "It is hoped that this further request is not due, to a great extent, to restlessness on the part of this Indian and it would be a precursor to numerous additional appeals by him." MacInnes commented: "it was a good way to get rid of him but then I mentioned that we could not just simply shoo our Indians over to the United States when we desire to dispense with them on this side." Officials informed Duncan that, should he be granted permission to move to Alaska, he could not expect further support, including medical assistance, from the Canadian government.

Duncan was nothing if not determined. His nephew David Hotch informed him that he was welcome in Haines, even offering to send money to cover the costs of the trip. Meek remained sympathetically disposed towards the appeal and recommended that Duncan be permitted to relocate, especially "as all Duncan's relatives and tribal connections are in the Haines area." And so, in mid-April 1949, the Canadian government once again amended Paddy Duncan's ticket of leave, this time permitting him to take up residence in Alaska, "so long as his presence in Alaska is not found objectionable to the United States authorities."

Finally, Paddy Duncan could go home. He went to Haines in the spring of 1949, moving in with his family. Elderly and in failing health, he travelled little in the area. There is no record of his returning to the Yukon, although the summer road between Haines and Haines Junction on the Alaska Highway would have made passage fairly easy. As well, there is no record of his holding the often-discussed celebration marking his return to the North, though he may have done so. From the Canadian government's perspective, the case was now resolved. Duncan's last years would be passed in Alaska, among his own people and without financial draw on Canadian resources. This was as both Duncan and the Canadian government wished.

The memory of Paddy Duncan's killing of Harton Kane has survived, especially among Harton's relatives. Even now, almost seventy years later, it is easy to detect strong feeling in their discussions of the events of October 1936, both because of Duncan's failure to make proper restitution and formally apologize, and because the Canadian judicial system placed its entire emphasis on punishing Duncan and did nothing to help the family cope with its loss.

Paddy Duncan's case does not have a prominent place in the folk memory of the Yukon Territory. Few non-Natives have heard of the events at Champagne in 1936, and only a handful of First Nations people are familiar with the murder, the prison sentence, and the subsequent discussions about Duncan's return. The nature of the crime itself – a drinking party that turned to murder – was neither dramatic nor particularly unusual, and was hardly the stuff of legend. Duncan's real motive for shooting Harton Kane in the back remains unknown, though there are stories of personal rivalry between the two men.

Yet the story is significant, particularly for what it reveals about the absorption of Yukon First Nations into the criminal justice system. Until recently, the Duncan-Kane affair was one of the last examples of aboriginal law being taken into account in the handling of criminal matters in the Yukon. Only in the 1990s were aboriginal customs, such as the sentencing circle, once more tentatively introduced into the system. Although Duncan's arrest and trial were conducted completely according to the formal criminal justice system, nevertheless the authorities felt in 1948 that a party held to heal the differences caused by the event would be appropriate – a fact that shows they were willing to adopt at least some of the concepts of aboriginal justice in bringing closure to the case.

In the Canadian North, although aboriginal law had been supplanted as an effective instrument of social control by the arrival of the Mounted Police and the Canadian judicial system, as Paddy Duncan's efforts to return to the Yukon reveal, the territory's First Nations still expected that indigenous customs and considerations would be observed before such a serious matter could be considered to be entirely closed. Under these terms, Paddy Duncan's killing of Harton Kane remains, at least in part, a dispute that has not been fully culturally resolved.

CHAPTER EIGHT

A Miscellany of Murder

It is quite probable that when the facts of the present affair have
been brought to light it will be found that some petty jealousy
or equally trivial cause led to the killing.

The *Klondike Nugget* on the Slorah case

There were many reasons for murder in the Yukon, and the previous chapters have illustrated the more important ones. So far, however, sexual crimes of passion have not figured in this account. This is mostly because there were not many of them, which, given the overwhelmingly male nature of the population in the gold rush days, should not come as a surprise. There were not very many women in the Yukon Territory in the early period, a fact that caused women to be valued, though at the same time there was considerable competition for their favours. For the same reason, it was a profitable place for prostitutes, and Dawson City saw liaisons which – though of course they existed in communities everywhere – seemed particularly common in the North. Robert Service's poem "The Shooting of Dan McGrew" is a sanitized version of one of them.

The real cases involving what the Victorians called the "demimonde" were anything but glamorous, generally involving alcohol, betrayal, and violence, and the victims were nearly always women. Often the cases also had very strong overtones of social and economic class. An example from the gold rush period involved Pearl Mitchell from Boston, who in 1899 came to Dawson City as a member of Frank Simons's "Sapho" dance company. In Skagway she met James Slorah, a Canadian-born resident of Seattle, a widower supporting three children. The couple lived in Dawson City for a while, then moved with the dance company to Nome, where the gold rush was in full swing. There they may have married (the papers were inclined to be arch about their marital status), and eventually they returned to the Yukon, where both got work at the Orpheum – James behind the bar and Pearl on the stage.

One day in October 1900 their relationship erupted into fatal violence. Pearl, according to the *Klondike Nugget*, "seemed happy enough – happy as such women ever are, which is but a thin covering of assumed gayety for the thing beneath the surface." At work, Slorah appeared to be well, though later he seemed "haggard and out of sorts."[1] That morning, Pearl was visiting her friend Susie Vernon when Slorah arrived and ordered her to return to the room they shared at the Orpheum. Pearl did so, but then came back to Vernon's room, saying that she did not need any more sleep. Slorah followed her, and the two quarrelled. Then, without warning, he pulled out a handgun and shot her twice in the head. Vernon fled the room, screaming for help, and as she did so she heard another shot from the room.

Someone called the police, and when Constable Borrow arrived shortly thereafter he found Pearl on the bed, bleeding heavily; within thirty minutes she was dead. Slorah lay on the same bed, half-conscious from a self-inflicted gunshot wound. Regaining consciousness, he mumbled that the dead woman was his wife.

The episode was fodder for Dawson City gossips, and the *Klondike Nugget* wrote about it in terms which suggested that the murderer and his victim were virtually members of another species. "Among the class to which both Slorah and the woman belong," sniffed the paper, "very slight causes often lead to murder or suicide, and it is quite probable that when the facts of the present affair have been brought to light it will be found that some petty jealousy or equally trivial cause led to the killing."[2]

The tone here is interesting, clearly suggesting that while important people kill for serious reasons, the lower classes, the vulgar and degraded, to which both Slorah and "the woman" belonged, kill for nothing much at all. What else could be expected from such people? The casual contempt expressed by the newspaper gives the lie to the assertion, often made by writers about the Yukon, that there were no class differences in the North

– that it was one big egalitarian community, that people were judged on character, not class, and so forth.

A police inquest called to investigate the affair quickly reached the conclusion that Pearl Mitchell had been shot by her lover, and Slorah was held in jail on a charge of murder. Susie Vernon, the chief witness, was a longtime acquaintance of the victim. The two had known each other on the western dance circuit and had travelled together from Butte and Helena, Montana, to Spokane and Seattle before heading north to the Klondike. Deemed a flight risk, she was ordered to post a $500 bond, and since she could not, she too was held in jail.

The trial took place in mid-November, a month after the crime, as was the usual pattern in the Yukon. As with all these trials, there was a great deal of public interest: "The trial is attracting much attention and the courtroom was packed almost to suffocation during the entire day. People in the back end of the room standing upon benches in order to see the testifying witnesses and counsel, and others crowding the doorways and occupying generally every inch of standing room outside the railing."[3] By the time the trial began, Slorah had recovered from his head wound, which must have been superficial, and not only protested his innocence but had an implausible version of events, which was different from that of the police and witnesses. He claimed that Pearl Mitchell was a violent woman, given to "cranky spells," and that she had often struck him – with hair brushes, beer bottles, or "anything within reach." He claimed that on the day of her death she had hit him and then come at him with a gun. They had wrestled over it, and it had gone off as they fought for it. He claimed that during the fight he was hit again on the head: "After this, I don't know if I was struck again or not. I think I heard a pistol shot, but everything turned black to me, and it seemed that I had fallen down stairs and someone had lifted me up. That's all I remember until I came to."[4]

Susie Vernon told a different story, though inconsistencies in her testimony weakened its effect. She portrayed Slorah as a violent man and heavy drinker, and told stories of fights between the couple in which both were the aggressor. On one occasion, she said, Pearl had hit Slorah over the head with a water pitcher. She said that she had thrown a blanket over her head during the fatal quarrel and had not seen the shooting.

The trial was enlivened by some nastiness between F.C. Wade, the crown prosecutor, and a lawyer named Bleecker, who conducted the defence. In a summation that lasted for more than two hours, Bleecker assailed Wade, claiming that he had "made the trial a struggle for professional pre-eminence rather than with any thought of doing justice to the prisoner." Wade's summation, which was almost as long, ridiculed the defence's attempt to resuscitate the character of the accused, characterizing Slorah as a "box rustler" (what we would call a "hustler" in taverns), "the lowest type of humanity who ever came before an intelligent jury charged with a crime."

The jury was out for twenty-five minutes, then returned with a guilty verdict, which Slorah received calmly, saying simply, "I have nothing to say, except that I did not commit this crime." His lawyer stated that he would appeal on the grounds that the jury had been influenced by statements made outside the courtroom, and also that the indictment was incorrect, since the accused should have been charged with the murder of his wife, Pearl Slorah, not of Pearl Mitchell. This sort of tactic was never successful in northern trials, and the judge, Calixte Dugas, brushed it aside, sentencing Slorah to be hanged on 1 March 1901. There was, the *Nugget* reported, "a death like stillness in the room for a moment, during which all eyes were turned upon the condemned man, but he gave no sign whatever – not so much as changing color, or by the movement of an eyelash, and when he left the room he did so with a firm step and an erect head."[5]

Slorah had friends in town, and they circulated a list asking for contributions to finance an appeal. The *Nugget* was cynical and dismissive of the process:

The time [for appeal], however, seems to rest largely with the attorney, whose only incentive to undertake cases, in view of the fact that that is the source of his livelihood, is one of monetary consideration. For this reason, the "proper time" is when the friends of the condemned man come forward with the money, and although March seems some distance away yet, it must be remembered that a great deal is necessary to be done, and that soon, if an appeal is to be taken.[6]

By the end of December enough money had been raised to allow Bleeker to launch an appeal, the cornerstone of which was the claim that crown witnesses had socialized and even shared drinks with members of the jury, thus tainting the trial.

Although the appeal did not result in a new trial, Slorah was not hanged. Late in January 1901 James Pope, undersecretary of state, telegraphed William Ogilvie, commissioner of the Yukon, to tell him that the death sentence had been commuted to life imprisonment. The *Nugget*, changing its tune considerably, commented: "The commutation of the sentence was generally received by all classes with satisfaction as there has prevailed a general feeling since the trial that guilty or not guilty the evidence was not conclusive enough and not of the right character to warrant his execution, and there has been at all times a feeling that there is evidence in the case which has never come out."[7]

The paper continued to follow the case, and after the commutation, a reporter visited Slorah in his cell and described him in a passage of purple prose: "His eyes were filled with tears and his voice, always low, sank until it was almost inaudible and trembled as he talked, although he bore up quite bravely, and strove to subdue his feelings, which, guilty or innocent, were quite natural to one in his position."[8] Saved from the gallows, he nevertheless faced life, or at least many decades, in the British Columbian penitentiary.

No one seems to have spoken up for Pearl Mitchell, and of course there was no women's support group in the territory to demand a harsh sentence for her killer. Had she been a middle-class victim of a rape-murder, there would have been a huge public outcry and a demand for justice and vengeance, but since she was a victim of domestic violence and a member of the demimonde, no one seems to have been very troubled by her death. Those who crowded the courtroom did so not out of sympathy for her but to see the show of the trial. As the newspaper suggested, her fate was common enough among "that class of people" to which she and her killer belonged.

Even more socially outrageous lives were highlighted in a murder-suicide that had fascinated Dawson City in the early months of 1899. David Evans, a young man from Wales, had arrived in the Klondike in the summer of 1897, had acquired some valuable property, and was living off his investments. Late in 1898 he took up with Libby White, a married dance hall girl, who had come north alone from Colorado. Their relationship was stormy. The press later reported, with some delicacy, that "the woman's promiscuous tendencies occasioned several quarrels during the two months they [had] been together." In the early hours of 3 February 1899, Libby White "made a proposition to Evans to which he strenuously objected." He "refused to sink to the level of promiscuous cohabitation which the woman desired." In the ensuing quarrel, which "fermented his jealous rage beyond the point of endurance," he struggled with her, shot her in the back of the head, and then turned the gun on himself. Since "the woman" was clearly a deviate by the standards of the day, public sympathy lay with Evans.

Later that year a similar incident took place in the same room. Maud Roselle, an actress, was described in the press as "about 25 years of age, of a happy disposition, exceptionally bright," with "a quick, keen sense of humor that made her a favorite on the stage." Her lover, Harry Davis from Emporia, Kansas, was around thirty and a man about town. Early on the morning of 12 August 1899, after a long evening in which the pair drank separately but heavily, Maud entered the hotel room in which the earlier shooting had taken place and found Harry waiting for her. She told him that she was going to break off with him. He pleaded with her, to no avail. So he pulled out a gun and shot her and then himself. The incident played only briefly in the papers – no one was surprised when people of that sort did such things.

More conventional murders continued to occur, fuelled by the greed and turmoil of the gold rush. Charles Hubbard's shooting of Tom McNamee in May 1900 is a good example. McNamee had been in the North for several years. His brother James was one of the richest men in the Klondike: having come north from Juneau in the early stages of the rush, he had been lucky enough to get a claim on Eldorado Creek. Tom had funded his brother, and when he learned of his good fortune he came north too, expecting a 50 per cent share of the riches. The brothers quarrelled, and Tom launched a lawsuit, hoping to get about $125,000. Since he had little money, he turned to others for financing. One of his backers was Charles Hubbard, who had known the brothers in Juneau and apparently put up $5,000 for legal expenses.

Before the case had gone very far, James paid Tom $20,000, and Tom dropped the case. The local newspaper speculated that he settled for such a small sum because the Yukon judicial system looked to be incapable of dealing with a complex civil case of this kind.[9] But rather than using the money to pay his lawyers and the debt he owed Hubbard, Tom McNamee skipped town, heading down the Yukon River towards Alaska.

Hubbard was furious; he had funded McNamee for nearly two years, draining his own resources in the process. As soon as he could, he left Dawson City with a travelling companion named Bryson. They stopped at each settlement along the river and learned that McNamee was at Fort Yukon. When they arrived there, Hubbard immediately confronted McNamee to hand it over demanding his money. McNamee refused to hand it over and challenged Hubbard to shoot him. Whether he meant it or not, it was the wrong thing to say, for Hubbard immediately fired at him. The shot missed, and McNamee fled to a nearby cabin. Hubbard ran after him, pulled open the door, and shot him dead. Then he walked to a nearby saloon, put the gun on the counter and said, "Here, take this. I have no further use for it. I have got my man."[10]

Fort Yukon is in Alaska, but there were no legal officials anywhere near the place, so the case was initially handled by a citizens' committee in the manner of the miners' meetings that had dealt with crimes in the Yukon before the arrival of the Mounted Police. Hubbard told the committee: "It is a sad story, and I am sorry now I shot him, but he owed me $5,000 for which I held his note, and I couldn't help it."[11] The committee seemed sympathetic, but he was taken to Rampart House, near the international border, and then to Circle, Alaska, where he was tried in August 1900. The Dawson paper was sympathetic to him:

It is authoritatively stated by those who are in a position to know that his plea will be justifiable homicide, and in this the jury is expected to coincide ... It seems one of the most aggravated cases imaginable ... When Hubbard reached Circle it is said of him that he was penniless and that his very clothing was in rags. He had no shoes, and the old moccasins he wore hardly sufficed to cover his feet. Under these conditions it is not to be much wondered at that he shot the man who, though having plenty of money, merely insulted him when asked to pay what had been loaned him as an act of friendship.[12]

As well as being a personal tragedy, this case illustrates the inter-connectedness of the Northwest, something that has already figured in some of the cross-border incidents discussed in this book. Here, three men started out from the Alaska panhandle and crossed the international border into Canada. One was lucky enough to be in Juneau when the first word of the great 1896 gold discovery reached the outside world and, staked by his brother, he rushed north to find wealth. Later, the brother and a third man followed him to claim a share of the riches. When trouble ensued, Tom McNamee fled back to a different part of Alaska, but he found the border was no protection from the vengeance of his former friend.

The border did have meaning, however, because in Alaska, Hubbard was treated gently, at least initially, by an ad hoc citizens' committee. Had he been tried in Dawson City, he would either have been hanged or given life imprisonment, despite the justice of his complaint. By crossing the border into a more libertarian country that had a strong community focus to its justice system, Hubbard had made a good choice. The region, though a single social environment, was cleanly split into two entirely different government and legal systems.

One of the better-known Yukon murder cases is the O'Brien case. Its fame rests on its brutality and on the fact that a book has been written about it.[13] It was unique in the history of killings in the Yukon in that it is the only instance in the territory's history of classic "bushwhacking," in which men lay in wait in ambush to kill strangers for the purpose of robbing them. The Mounted Police officer who wrote a general synopsis of the case[14] called it "one of the most hideous and unprecedented cold-blooded murder cases ever perpetrated in the confines of our Dominion borders," one that (naturally) exemplified "the highest traditions of the N.W.M.P. in solving a crime by persistency, determination, thoroughness, and justice."

George O'Brien was a bad character, an Australian, according to the police, who had lived in Birmingham, England, where he had served most of a seven year sentence (1888–94) in Dartmoor prison for shooting with intent to do bodily harm. Released, he turned up in the Yukon in 1898 and was imprisoned for theft, serving a year in the Mounted Police barracks jail (where everyone did hard labour on the woodpile). Released in December of that year, he was told to get out of the country. Instead, he formed a partnership with Thomas Graves, about whom little is known, and on Christmas Day 1899 the pair lay in wait on the trail near Minto. After some time, three men came along the trail: Ole Olsen (a lineman with the government telegraph line at Five Fingers), Fred H. Clayson (an American merchant from Skagway, who had come to the Yukon to buy gold), and Lynn Relfe (an American, aged about twenty-five, from Tacoma, who was working as a bartender in the Monte Carlo saloon in Dawson City).

Forensic evidence gathered by the police told what happened next. O'Brien had a pair of binoculars, and when he saw the three men approaching he and Graves hid beside the trail about thirty metres apart. When Olsen, Clayson, and Relfe were between them, they jumped out, rifles cocked, and ordered their victims to take a side trail that led to the river. When one of them, probably Clayson, made a break for it, O'Brien and Graves shot all three, dragged them to the river, cut a hole through the ice, and stuffed them in, after rifling the bodies for a few articles of little value. The bodies were not found until May. But unluckily for the killers, Olsen had arranged to have Christmas dinner with his friend Corporal P. Ryan of the Hootchikoo Detachment, and when he failed to show up, a search was launched, the murder site discovered, and a chain of evidence established.

Suspicion immediately fell on O'Brien, who had been seen loitering around the area. A man with the colourful name of Kid West was brought from the Washington State penitentiary at Walla Walla, and he testified that while in jail in Dawson City the year before, O'Brien had proposed that they rob and murder men on the trail and hide their bodies in the river. O'Brien was arrested on 4 January on an unrelated charge – theft from caches, which was a serious offence in the Yukon – and was held in jail on that charge while the police worked up the case for murder. No trace was ever found of Graves, and the police came to the conclusion that O'Brien had killed him to keep him quiet.

A photograph taken in June 1901 shows a crowd of men (women would
not have participated) standing outside the old courthouse in Dawson
City during the O'Brien trial. The new courthouse, just being finished, is
in the background (NA, PA-16308)

O'Brien's trial began on 10 June 1901, and because of the tremendous amount of forensic evidence that the police had collected (there were about four hundred exhibits) it lasted until
22 June. O'Brien was convicted and was sentenced to hang on
23 August. An appeal launched on his behalf by Charles Bethune,
an Ottawa lawyer (acting for Bleecker and Dejournel of Dawson
City, the lawyers for the defence), was quickly dismissed. The review process in Ottawa seems to have been unusually quick, for
among the men mentioned in this book, he was the only one
hanged on the date set by the trial judge for his execution. Mr Justice Dugas, in forwarding his report to the Department of Justice
in Ottawa, observed: "A great anxiety has existed throughout the
whole territory about this case, the result of which is a great satisfaction to the whole public: the murder having been one of the
most atrocious known in the history of crimes."

As was noted earlier in this book, there were killings in the
Yukon that resulted in convictions for manslaughter rather than
murder. Because the files on these cases were not preserved, it is

A different view of the same event shows men peering through the
windows as the trial progresses (NA, PA-16269)

difficult to tell how many killers were convicted of manslaughter
or were acquitted altogether. However, the records of at least one
case – the Sarga case – have been preserved because, in that instance, there was a question of extradition from the United States
that involved diplomatic exchanges at the highest level, even
though the killing was quite ordinary in motive.

John Sarga was born in Greece (the records do not say when) and
left that country in 1896, arriving in Dawson City a year or so later –
too late to stake a valuable claim. Instead, he took out a "lay." The
lay system was reputedly invented by "Big Alex" McDonald, the
Nova Scotian-born mining entrepreneur who made a fortune by
staking and buying up claims and then letting other men work
them for a share of the profits. It was, in short, the Yukon version of
the southern U.S. agricultural pattern of sharecropping.

In the spring of 1899 Sarga was working "a lay upon a bench
claim ... known as Bench on Right Limit of Bonanza off of creek
claim number six below discovery, in the second tier."[15] He had
been working on this lay for about two months when Louis Ballos,
also a Greek, approached him and asked if he could buy in on the
lay. Ballos agreed to pay Sarga $100 from the profits of the lay for
becoming a partner in it. But after two months of work, when Sarga
asked for the money, Ballos refused to pay on the grounds that the

lay was not as rich as he had expected. There was a quarrel, and the
two men agreed to go to Dawson City and let some members of the
Greek community there settle the dispute. Early on the morning of
25 June, while Sarga was washing his face outside a Dawson City
cabin, he was approached by Ballos, as he later described:

He was very angry because I told our countrymen about the hundred
dollars. He said "What do you make so much fuss for? Do you think now
that I will pay you?" He … rushed at me and struck me several times in
the face, blacking my eyes and causing my nose to bleed a great deal …
Our countrymen came out of the cabin and I left the dispute to them to
settle, but they were friends of Ballos and came from his county in
Greece, so they only laughed at me and would do nothing. Then Ballos
and I made up, and decided to work together. I told Ballos that we would
let the Hundred Dollars drop, that I did not want the money.[16]

A week later, on 2 July, the two men were camping near the mouth
of Bonanza Creek, and in the evening, after they had eaten, Ballos
took up the matter of the dispute, still resentful that Sarga had
told the other Greeks about it. According to Sarga,

I said "Let it go, you know you are wrong in that matter." Ballos at the
time had a revolver in his scabbard strapped to him. He always carried a
revolver. Ballos then swore at me … we quarreled, and Ballos made a
move to pull his revolver. I picked up a stick that was in the wood pile
near the fire, and struck Ballos on the left side of the head just above the
ear. He did not fall, but wavered and seemed dizzy. He kept on pulling
his gun and got it out of the scabbard, when I sprang forward and
grabbed his hands, and tried to take the revolver from him. He was a
much stronger man than I so I caught hold of his hand with my teeth and
bit a piece out. He turned loose the revolver and I got it and jumped back.
He started toward me and I was afraid he would get back the revolver, so
I emptied the revolver into his body, shooting him six times … I scraped
up the sand with my hands and covered the body.[17]

What Sarga did not say in this statement was that after shooting
Ballos he beat him severely with a stick, put him under a pile of
brush, and set fire to it, presumably to conceal his identity. When
the body was eventually discovered, it took the police some time

to establish which partner it was. Sarga said that at first he thought of going straight to the police but instead decided to go to Nome, where gold had just been discovered. The day after the killing he left Dawson on the steamer *Rideout*, and within a few days he was mining the beach at Nome.

Ballos's remains were not discovered until early September, and the Mounted Police soon learned that Sarga was in Nome. They sent information to the American authorities, who arrested Sarga, took his statement, then sent him under guard to Puget Sound (it was late October by this time, and too late to send him back up the Yukon River). The Puget Sound police then handed him over to the Canadian police in Victoria.

It was at this point that the international complications arose. The Mounted Police wanted to bring Sarga back to Dawson City for trial, but in the winter of 1899–1900 the Alaska boundary dispute was entering a delicate phase. It had always been difficult to send uniformed Canadian officials over the neck of Alaskan territory that lay between tidewater at Skagway and the international boundary at the Chilkoot and White Passes, but the Mounties still needed to go there from time to time. Although Soapy Smith, Skagway's ruling gangster, had been shot to death in the summer of 1898, there were still plenty of bad characters in the town. Because of a certain amount of tension when police officers crossed this piece of land, the policy was to send them in plain clothes rather than in uniform. It was for this reason that the Yukon Field Force – the two-hundred-strong contingent of the Canadian army that had come to the Yukon in the summer of 1898 to help police the territory – had avoided crossing Alaska by taking the old telegraph trail north from the Stikine River to the southern Yukon.[18]

In view of this delicate situation, the Canadian authorities decided to ask the U.S. government for permission to have Sarga escorted north through Skagway in charge of a uniformed police officer. Why the authorities did not simply send him via the passenger steamers that went up the Yukon River is not known. Although that route also went through Alaska, there were no communities of gangsters along the way. Perhaps it was the cost; the police were always cost-conscious, and tickets along this route at the height of the rush could cost a thousand dollars. But there were, as the police noted, "a number of men at Skagway who never lose an opportunity or spare an effort to make trouble between Canadian and United States officials."[19]

During the winter of 1899–1900 there occurred a four-cornered correspondence between the offices of Joseph Pope, Canadian undersecretary of state, Lord Minto, the governor general, Lord Pauncefote, Britain's foreign secretary, and John Hay, the U.S. secretary of state. The seemingly absurd path of communication resulted from the fact that Canada at that time did not have a Department of External (now Foreign) affairs. All diplomatic relations of the British Empire were conducted by the Foreign Office, and formal communications between Ottawa and London went from the Canadian government through the governor general's office to the Foreign Office in London – an arrangement that continued until after the end of the First World War. The case actually resulted in a significant exchange of diplomatic information. The police, through these channels, requested that the Americans grant formal permission for an officer of the NWMP to conduct a prisoner through Skagway to the Yukon. In November 1899 Secretary of State Hay informed Lord Pauncefote that this could not be done:

It would give me great pleasure to comply with your request but I regret to say that this consent if granted ... would not afford the protection desired by the Canadian authorities. There is no Law of Congress authorizing the President or this Department to give the permission requested, and such permission even if granted, could not avail to prevent the Courts, upon the fugitive reaching American soil, from releasing him by the writ of habeas corpus. It appears from an application made by our Minister in London to Lord Salisbury in 1878 that the British Government labours under the same embarrassment.

I am informed that this subject was fully discussed by the U.S. and British Joint High Commission and a Treaty Stipulation was formulated and tentatively agreed upon to obviate this embarrassment, and it is to be hoped that a way may be found at no distance day when the relations of the two countries in this respect may be placed on a better footing.

Eventually the Canadian authorities took a chance, and a plainclothes police officer brought Sarga (who had signed a paper agreeing to go back to Dawson) across Alaskan territory.

Sarga's trial took place in November 1899 (complete with an interpreter) and it provided much titillating detail for the newspapers, especially when evidence of the murder was produced. The victim's bones were brought into court, but they had not been well prepared or preserved, and their smell was so offensive that the windows had to be opened. Sarga pleaded not guilty by reason of self-defence, but his attempt to destroy the body and his flight to Alaska told against him, as did the fact that he had emptied the revolver into Ballos. He was found guilty of manslaughter and sentenced to seven years in prison.

The press, as always, reported the outcome of the trial in tones of deepest satisfaction, pointing out that justice had once more been done in the Yukon: "To those who have followed the case in detail the sentence of seven years will appeal as being wise, just, and consistent ... And now Sarga has lost, or is losing his identity as an individual and becomes known, not as John Sarga or 'Little Joe,' but simply by the number which will be assigned to him with his convict's garb, and when next he comes through the prison door it will be in a suit of half yellow and half black, and his occupation will be a laborer doing government work without compensation or liberty."[20]

Another case involving "foreigners," this time Italian immigrants, took place in 1914, but its outcome was very different from that of Sarga and Ballos.[21] On 11 June of that year the body of a man was found floating in the Yukon River near Whitehorse, the head so badly battered that it was some time before the victim was identified as Dominic Melis, aged forty-five, an Italian immigrant who had worked at the Pueblo mine. The killer, as the police discovered after a thorough investigation, was the dead man's partner, Romolo Cesari,[22] and the crime had taken place the previous February. The two men had worked as labourers in the mine and lived together in a cabin that was part of a rooming house in Whitehorse. Cesari, it was later judged, was mentally unstable, and the partners had begun to quarrel in the winter of 1913–14, particularly over the invention of a machine to be used in mining (the police called it a "perpetual motion machine"). Cesari feared that Melis would steal the machine and cheat him out of the money he expected to make from it. Very unwisely, he made

Romolo Cesari, photographed while in confinement
at the police station in Whitehorse early in 1915
(GA, NA-1663–23)

statements to a third man in which he threatened to kill Melis and
discussed ways in which he might do so.

Exactly when the murder took place was never ascertained, for
Cesari maintained his innocence to the last, but the police investi-
gation made it fairly clear what had happened. Some time in early
February, Cesari had attacked Melis with a heavy blunt instrument,

perhaps the back of an axe, breaking his skull in several places, as well as his jaw and nine ribs. He then trussed Melis to several poles cut from trees (the police later matched the poles to the stumps), dragged him to the river, and shoved him under the ice at a place where the ice would not melt until well into the spring. A burial in some distant spot would have been better from the point of view of concealing the body, but the permafrost must have made it impractical or too difficult. The problem with putting victims' corpses in the river was, of course, that they were usually discovered. It was later determined that the body had probably been released by the ice only about two weeks before it was discovered, which accounted for its good state of preservation. Cesari eventually went north to Dawson City, where he was arrested.

The case against Romolo Cesari was entirely circumstantial, and the police had to do a considerable amount of work to make it credible. Cesari's statements to the third man were damning, but the police went to the trouble of obtaining the records of supplies purchased at the local store before and after Melis's death, and these showed a change in the two men's relationship:

At the store of P. Martins it was noticed there by the clerk Mr. McPhee, and Mr. Martin that they were living in the same cabin, and that they were starting to buy their provisions, each one for himself, that it was Cesari, that came and ordered that a lot of groceries that had been charged up to Melis, by himself (Cesari) be changed to his name. The slips still show the alteration. Evidence was given, showing the conflicting stories told by the accused as to where Melis had gone to ... Then there is the hurried arrangements to go away to Dawson. The leaving of the sack at Martins store, with his own articles mingled with that of the deceased. The sack is marked "Cesari," and he leaves no word that it [is] to be called for by Melis, this is not consistent with the work of a man that expects his partner to return in a few days.[23]

Because the evidence was all circumstantial, the trial took longer than usual – six days – for the case had to be made from a great many details. Fifty witnesses were called, all but one for the prosecution. As happened sometimes with these cases, the press sought to find interest, and even entertainment, for its readers in the colourful details that came out at the trial. It happened that Cesari had a glass eye, and this gave the newspaper reporter who took notes of the proceedings an opportunity for some dramatic writing. When the bag stored at Martin's shop was emptied in court, the reporter noted

The change which came over Caesari [*sic*] when the articles above mentioned were produced was apparent to everyone in court. Previous to that time he had worn a semi-amused smile during all the proceedings, but when the goods identified as having belonged to Melis were emptied on the table, his face turned an ashen color and both his eyes became glassy. (One of them is of glass and they looked alike.) He soon recovered, however, and assumed the careless, buoyant air that was so noticeable when the hearing first opened.[24]

The one defence witness, Mike Sinnett, tried to throw the blame on persons unknown, but he "told his story in such a way as to convince the court and Jury that he was lying, and that the story was one that had been brought on by a large imagination, and also a lot of whiskey drinking."[25] Cesari testified in his own defence, but not effectively. Mr Justice Macaulay, in his charge to the jury, instructed them on the matter of reasonable doubt: "They were to remember that the element of doubt necessarily entered into all human transactions and that if every doubt were entertained and they were to rely on matters of absolute certainty, no murderer would ever be convicted on circumstantial evidence."[26] The jury deliberated for an hour and forty minutes, then returned a verdict of guilty, after which the death sentence was passed, the date being set for 5 February.

Cesari was not hanged, however, for on 1 February 1915 a telegram arrived from Ottawa commuting his sentence to life imprisonment. As the Whitehorse paper put it in a headline, "Hanging Is Off: Hemp Stretching Billed for Tomorrow Will Never Take Place."[27] Cesari had spent part of the time after his trial in raving and shouting abuse at the police, and had written a series of increasingly incoherent letters in Italian to his parents, who still lived near Rome. He had also written to other relatives, to the Italian consul, the governor general, and the "President." These were his own efforts. His lawyer, presumably acting *pro bono*, does not seem to have taken part in any proceedings after the verdict.

In these letters, which are so incoherent that at one point it was noted that "a portion of this letter could not be translated, the interpreters stating that there was no sense to it," he begged for

Constable William Leslie Pritchett on duty in the Whitehorse jail, conducting a death watch over Romolo Cesari before his reprieve, early 1915 (GA, NA-1663-24)

mercy, protested his innocence, suggested there was a conspiracy against him because of his nationality, and offered to trade the secrets of his mining machine for a pardon. The Yukon authorities had come to believe he was insane, an opinion confirmed by Dr W.B.Clarke. But the commutation of his sentence did not entail his removal to a mental institution. The order simply stated that he was to serve the rest of his life in the jail in Whitehorse, though presumably he would soon have been moved to British Columbia.

However, he served little of his sentence. Ten days after the hanging was to have taken place, Cesari tried to escape. He waited until evening, when his two police guards removed the shackles binding his legs in order to put him to bed. As one constable knelt in front of him to remove the leg irons, Cesari pushed him aside, threw a table at the other police man, and bolted for the guard-room door, running towards the bush. The policemen ran after him, fired two warning shots and then, as Cesari continued towards the forest, shot him twice, once in the hip and once in the small of the back. Cesari fell, was taken to hospital, and died the next day. At the inquest, held a day or two later, the police testified that they had read Cesari Rule 16 of the prison regulations: "Every

Constable Craig of the Royal North-West Mounted Police posing in front
of the cells in the police guardroom at Whitehorse, early 1915
(GA, NA-1663–21)

convict who attempts to escape either from the prison or when
working outside, is liable to be shot." They also testified that they
considered him dangerous, not because he was too insane to know
what he was doing but because he was delusional, and they said
they had shot him because once in the bush, it would have been
difficult to recapture him. This satisfied the authorities, and Cesari
was buried at government expense, and forgotten.

The theme of insanity runs through many of the Yukon murder
cases. As already noted, Yukoners could not work up much rage
over murders of women of "questionable" character, and the
same was true of killings by mentally ill people. In a land where,
according to popular belief, winter and the lust for gold produced
cabin fever and other forms of madness, examples of mental illness elicited a fairly calm public reaction.

An early example of a case involving insanity dates from
May 1899 and was characterized by the *Klondike Nugget* as "the
most heinous murder which has yet occurred to stain the record of

the Yukon Territory."[28] This sounds alarming, but the paper tended to describe most murders this way at first – the proof of public reaction lies in whether the papers kept up the tone of suppressed hysteria. One reason for the tone was that the victim worked for the newspaper. James Prater, the murdered man, was a 32-year-old pressman from Seattle who shared a cabin with three other men, including Arthur Goddard, with whom he had travelled north in 1898. One morning the other two roommates, Hill and Anderson, left Prater and Goddard alone in the cabin. When Hill returned around 10:30, he was met by Goddard at the door, naked, telling him that Prater's neck had been cut. Hill called the police, who arrived to find Prater dying, his throat cut open and the side of his skull crushed.

Goddard readily admitted that he had attacked Prater with a hatchet but did not say why. The police searched the cabin and found a straight razor covered with blood. When they showed it to Goddard he simply said, "I was his partner and he was a traitor to me." This made little sense: Goddard was unemployed, living off his victim's charity, and the police quickly decided that he was insane.

Goddard was charged with murder, and his lawyer indicated that a plea of not guilty by reason of insanity would be entered. Goddard had a family back in the United States and was well connected, his father being a prominent businessman from Wisconsin. Apparently, Goddard had had an accident as a child, hitting his head on a tree, and this had required the insertion of a steel plate – a serious and rare operation in the nineteenth century. The newspaper reported: "Those who know him best say that ever since his misfortune befell him Goddard has periodically been mentally unsound … Indeed, it is safe to assume that he will never be tried for his crime, for if he is not dead before the day of the trial arrives, he will likely have his sanity ordered into by Judge Dugas, which will legally establish his insanity." As if to prove this, Goddard's mental health deteriorated; he sat silent and brooding for hours, then exploded into ranting and violence. On several occasions the police had to subdue him physically. When his father arrived from the south, Goddard did not recognize him. The father commented to the press, "I know of no civilized government on the globe where a crazy man is hanged for murder."

The Yukon was one place on the globe where this did happen, or perhaps it would be fairer to say that Canadian justice had a very restricted definition of what constituted legal insanity. But in this case, unlike the later Gogoff case, the murderer was considered insane even by the strictest definition. The trial was a formality. Several doctors testified to Goddard's condition, and the prosecutor acknowledged it. Without leaving the courtroom, the jury declared him mentally unfit to stand trial, and he was sent to an asylum. There were several differences between this case and that of Gogoff. Goddard was an American, and Gogoff was a foreigner from a land that most had never heard of. Goddard came from a good family; Gogoff's family were peasants and his mother was reputedly as crazy as he was. Gogoff's crime was premeditated, which suggested that he knew what he was doing, while Goddard's was inexplicable.

At least one murder case involved a nationality that was even more foreign to Canadians than Gogoff's. For many years, the Chinese and Japanese were subject to severe discrimination, both legal and social, which was in some ways even worse than that directed at First Nations. During the First World War, few people in Dawson outside the small community of Japanese-born residents knew or cared much about Rokuichi Yoshioka and his wife Hisha. The two lived on a small farm outside town, where they raised foxes, apparently with the intention of taking the skins back to Japan. Hisha worked part time in town, in the office of Dr LaChapelle and also for Shuzaburo Kawakami, a local merchant, but the couple was perennially in financial difficulty. Yoshioka's credit had run out, and he was planning to return to Japan with some skins for sale.

Late in June 1917 Yoshioka told an acquaintance, Frank Ishimoto, that his wife was missing, and Ishimoto and three other men went to look for her. Yoshioka was acting oddly, sending the four men off to search but showing little concern himself. While the men were searching, Constable H.W. Stallworthy[29] of the RNWMP encountered Yoshioka standing on a Dawson street weeping and asked what was wrong. "My wife, somebody kill her, I think she is dead,"[30] replied Yoshioka. Stallworthy accompanied the distraught man on the ferry across the Yukon river to West Dawson to his ranch, where he found Hisha "lying on her back with her legs wide apart with her dress turned up thus exposing her person." The constable believed that the woman had been "outraged" and noted that she had been stabbed in the chest. An autopsy revealed that she had also been shot in the back and was pregnant.

Yoshioka blamed the attack on Percy James, a First Nations man who worked for him, and accused him also of stealing a dog team, some money, and some other things from his house. James was from the Peel River region. He had moved to Dawson City looking for work and like many others of his people had found an employer who was willing to hire a Native short-term. Yoshioka's flimsy story soon fell apart. A search of the surrounding area turned up the body of Percy James, three dead dogs, and a rifle in a pit about three hundred metres from the cabin. James had also been shot in the back. Two of the dogs had been shot, and the third clubbed to death. Yoshioka was charged with murder.

The trial took place on 6 August 1917. Although there was no direct proof, there was plenty of circumstantial evidence. Yoshioka's neighbours testified that he was unhappy with his wife and had stated that she was sick and "he wished the damn bitch was dead." He had also unwisely stated that he stood to gain $5,000 from an insurance policy on Hisha, and in fact he did have a $2,000 policy on her life. Others stated that they believed he had been beating her.

The defence simply stated the accused's version of the events, which was highly fanciful, or at least not supported by any evidence. He claimed that two Japanese pimps named Izumi and Manibi, on whom he had earlier informed to the authorities, were in the Dawson region and had killed his wife in revenge. If not them, then it must have been a local farm foreman "who was always trying to have connections with his wife." His lawyer, Austin Fraser, suggested that the marriage had been happy, and he too put forward implausible explanations for the event.

In rebuttal, crown prosecutor J.P. Smith waxed sarcastic and made much of the one piece of concrete evidence – James's bootlaces, which had ended up in possession of the accused, taken off the dead man's boots. Smith ended by rather generously reminding the jury that although the case was strong, "if there was any doubt in any one link in the chain of evidence ... it should be given to the accused as he was a stranger in a strange land." The jury took just over two hours to reach a verdict of guilty.

Since Yoshioka was not insane by the standards of the day, there was little chance of commutation. The usual review of the case in Ottawa took place on 19 November, and Yoshioka was hanged on the twenty-third. He offered no last-minute confession or statement, disappointing those who hoped for moral lessons from the hanging. The police officer in charge of the execution noted that he "showed a most callous disposition throughout the whole period of his incarceration, and met his sentence unmoved."

The Yoshioka case documented a social world that was only loosely connected to mainstream Yukon society. The killer and his victim had contacts with the small, self-contained Japanese community but apparently not with the larger population. The trial involved two groups of "outsiders" – the Japanese Canadian and the First Nations community – so did not strike at the core of gold-mining society. The case was sad, but murder among people on the margins, even when brutal, attracted no lingering attention.

Murder cases in the Yukon, as elsewhere, revolved around a number of simple human weaknesses: greed, anger, lust, drunkenness – four of the seven deadly sins if drunkenness can be substituted for the traditional gluttony. The other three – pride, envy, and sloth – do not seem to have motivated people to kill. There was a fifth reason for murder, insanity, a weakness of a kind different from the others. When First Nations people in the Yukon killed one another, white society always assumed that the real culprit was alcohol, taken in such quantities that any further motive was unclear. Paddy Duncan was heavily drunk when he committed his crime, so drunk that neither he nor the witnesses could give any reason for it, though he talked vaguely about a grievance. This was convenient for the authorities, since alcohol, though it did not excuse killing, provided a rationale for it and thus did away with the need for further investigation: Indians got blind drunk, and someone was killed. Why? Because they drank too much. Case closed. When the Katy Joe murder took place, some observers assumed that it was just another case of this kind. But it was not.

Katy Joe was born Katy Jack about 1885 (the records are vague about the exact year of her birth, just as she was). She was born near Dalton Post on the Yukon-Alaska boundary, a region that was very isolated then but is now easily accessible by way of the Haines Highway. This road runs from tidewater at Haines, Alaska, 250 kilometres through spectacularly beautiful country to join the Alaska Highway at Haines Junction. This was the region where Paddy Duncan had been born eight years earlier. Katy's father, John Jack, moved his family in 1903 from Dalton Post to the nearby community of Champagne and lived there until his death from influenza in 1919. In the year of the family's move, Katy, at the age of eighteen, married Hutchi Joe.

Her entire life was marked by tragedy. Although as a girl she was what the police later called "a normal Indian,"[31] her brother Charlie Jack, nicknamed Sloppy, a year older than she, was "an imbecile from birth." The police reported that her father had suffered from syphilis, which may have damaged his children, though four others seem to have been unaffected by it. Katy Joe had six children. The first was born dead, the next two lived, but the fourth died soon after birth, by which time Katy Joe was "in a precarious condition": "The side of her face, and neck, also her tongue were swollen badly and apparently her memory was affected, as on getting better she inquired for the baby, remembering that the child was born but remembering nothing further; since that time she has had two more children but has never been really well and has had spells of sickness in the head when she apparently knows or remembers nothing, though she has never previously known to be violent or show any symptoms of wishing to injure anyone."[32]

Early in the morning of 18 October 1922, in the small Native community of Hutshi, Katy Joe fired four shots from a rifle through the window of a cabin where Hutshi Jim, his wife Kitty, and their child were sleeping. Kitty Jim was killed almost instantly, while her husband, shot in the thigh, reached through the broken window and wrestled the rifle out of Katy's hands. Their neighbours, Field Johnson and Dixon John and their wives, roused by the shots, ran from their cabins and held Katy Joe until her husband arrived and led her away. The police were called and took her to Whitehorse.

Katy Joe was held in prison in Whitehorse, where on 10 November she tried to kill herself. She pried a long splinter from the wall or floor of her cell, put it in her ear, and hit herself on the head with the slop pail that was kept in the cell for her use. The police doctor was called, examined her, and reported that no damage had been done except that her ear had bled. The inspector ordered that a closer watch be kept on Katy Joe and that the slop pail be removed. During the months of her imprisonment she was visited more than thirty times by the doctor. He and the police matron reported that she said almost nothing (she spoke virtually no English), though she would follow instructions, and stood motionless for hours in her cell.

The coroner's jury had already dealt with the facts of Kitty Jim's death on 4 November 1922. One of the jurors[33] was the druggist, McPherson,[34] who appears in this book three times: once in the Gogoff case, once in the Cesari case, and finally in this case. Presumably this was more than a matter of chance, for the authorities would have found it useful to have at hand a middle-class businessman who was able to leave his pharmacy for a day or two when called for jury duty.

In June 1923, charged with murder, Katy Joe was tried before judge and jury.[35] Her lawyer, appointed by the court, was Willard Phelps, who later defended Paddy Duncan. It was a small society, for Duncan himself served as interpreter at this trial,[36] as he did at others involving First Nations people. Phelps, who was paid $150 for his work, was the leading lawyer in the community.[37] At Phelps's request, Judge Macaulay ordered the jury to consider not whether Katy Joe had killed but whether she was mentally fit to stand trial. The first witness was Katy's husband, Hutchi Joe, who, questioned by Phelps, testified that she had had spells of illness even before he had married her eighteen years earlier. Soon after their marriage she had a more serious attack:

Next was in town of Hutchi. I am married not very long. In the first place get sick. We had the flu that time. I am sick too. My wife sick. My wife went out and I don't know where go. Tell my brother Jim and her brother Hutchi Charley and lot of men ... we go look for her down on the flat at Hutchi. That three years ago. We find her way down around the lake, about half mile from village. She was running around, and we take her back home ... She was just trembling all over. I talk to her but she not answer me back ... We have to watch her for about a week after that ... That was the worst time I see her.

Further testimony revealed a dismal tale of death, disease, and misery in the family:

Q When that baby [the oldest] die how was your wife?

A She just about like dead that time – heart drop. Baby was sick the same way first, and I brought my wife in town at time and baby too.

Q When you say sick what you mean by that?

A She get on bed and stand up and don't know what she is doing.

Q How long that last?

A A long time – about 20 days I guess.

Q How many times you see your wife that way since?

A 2 times.

Q Any [*sic*] see any of her relatives that way?

A The three children [her siblings?] same way. Children not talk to me. They all dead. One died here.

Q You knew the father and mother of your wife.

A Yes.

Q How are they?

A The father an mother both get sick the same way. One brother [Charley Jack] sick the same way too …

Q Where is he?

A Dead now, die this spring. He sick same way my wife. Same sickness she had all in family …

Q Did the doctor ever see her?

A Yes, doctor [Paré, the police doctor] see her at the time she sick and I brought her in town …

Q How many times you see her in Whitehorse [after her arrest]?

A 4 or 5 times. I try to talk to her and she would not talk. 3 or 4 times I went to barracks but I could never speak to her.

Hutchi Jim testified along the same lines, and Emma Reddick, who had been taking care of Katy in prison, testified that she was like a "simple child."

Dr Duncan McKenzie, who had examined Katy Joe three times in the police barracks, testified that she was mentally incompetent to stand trial. His authority was *Clouston's Clinical Lectures on Mental Diseases*. Sir Thomas Smith Clouston was indeed an expert. His book had gone through six editions, though the last was published nearly two decades earlier, in 1904, perhaps not coincidentally the same year that McKenzie had graduated from the University of Toronto medical school. He brought his copy into court and read from page 305 on the subject of "mental stupor":

A morbid condition in which there is mental and nervous lethargy – in which impressions on the senses produce little or no outward appearance. In which the faculty of attention is or seems paralysed. In which there is no sign of originating mental power. In which the higher reflex functions of the brain are paralysed. The voluntary motions are almost suspended, but the patient usually retains the power of standing, walking, masticating, and swallowing. Symptoms. A typical case of this condition: stands or sits for hours in the same attitude. When spoken to takes no notice. Shows no active desires, passions or affections. Does not speak nor move nor show interest in anything. Expression of the face is vacuous.

Another physician, Dr Norman E. Culbertson, who was in charge of police patients at Whitehorse, confirmed the diagnosis.

The judge then charged the jury to determine Katy Joe's fitness to stand trial, remarking, "Your duties will be very light … I think it would be insulting your intelligence for me to attempt to deal with the evidence any further." The jury retired and brought in a verdict "that this woman is not fit to assist in her trial on account of insanity." The judge then directed that the indictment for murder be withdrawn and that Katy Joe be confined to the police barracks to await the pleasure of the gold commissioner.[38] Judging from the briefness of the transcript, the trial, which began at 10 AM, was probably over before lunchtime. In July, Katy Joe was taken to the British Columbia mental hospital at New Westminster, for there was no facility in the Yukon that could accommodate people in her condition.

In the final chapter of Katy Joe's life something happened that had not occurred before: someone in white society who was not an official actually took an interest in her welfare. This was Harry Eskrigge, a veteran Yukon prospector, who had participated in the great gold rush. Why he interested himself in Katy Joe's case is not known, but since he spent winters "outside," as many miners did, he had the time do so. In December 1925 he wrote to his friend Percy Reid, the Yukon's gold commissioner, about her condition:

In the fall of 1922 the Indians had a big drunk at Hoochi village and Big Kitty was charged with murder ... She was taken out to the Insane Hospital at New Westminister July 1923, and during all this time has not had one visitor. Today I called to see her, and was quite shocked at her condition. When the matron brought her in my presence the woman fell down. Her lower limbs seem to be going back on her and her sad eyes still haunt me. She doesn't know much English and kept telling me I want to go home to Champagne ... She is sane enough, it was the Boose [sic] that caused the affair.

Eskrigge suggested that she be returned home, and he cited as precedent the two Inuit who had been sent north after their trial in Alberta for killing the two Roman Catholic priests. Three days later he visited her again and spoke to the doctor, and again he reported that she was not insane.

This request touched off correspondence between Gold Commissioner Reid, George Black, MP for the Yukon, John Hawksley, superintendent of Indian Affairs at Dawson City, and officials in the Department of Indian Affairs and the Department of Justice in Ottawa. Although Eskrigge's idea was well meant, there was an insuperable problem, which the Department of Justice pointed out: If Katy Joe was no longer insane, she could not simply be sent home; she would have to return to Whitehorse to be tried on the original charge of murder. She might be declared not guilty by reason of insanity, but that of course would lead to other difficulties, perhaps another period of incarceration in a mental hospital. It was what a later generation was to call a Catch-22 situation, and it did not look as though Katy Joe would ever see home again. In March 1926, Eskrigge had Harry "Shorty" Chambers, postmaster and trader at Champagne, talk to members of Katy Joe's community, and they agreed to contribute money if she was released and said they would have her looked after, perhaps in a cabin in Whitehorse, where some women of her nation lived.

During the winter of 1925–26 the bureaucratic correspondence ebbed and flowed, but eventually Katy Joe solved the problem herself by dying, in May 1926, of what causes the file did not record. Percy Reid wrote Eskrigge to give him the news, commenting: "After all the trouble you took, it has now come to naught, but I suppose the poor old girl [she was forty-one] is better off than she would be anywhere in this world, consequently we should envy her rather than express pity."

A number of lessons can be learned from the Katy Joe case. The first is the remarkable tendency of white observers to assume that the killing was fuelled by alcohol. Eskrigge, who was sympathetic, spoke of a "big drunk," and Superintendant Hawskley's initial report of 21 November 1922 referred to the rumour that the shooting was "principally attributed to intoxicants." When medical evidence was brought forward that Katy Joe had bought medicine for her condition from a trader, one of the questions was whether the medicine contained alcohol, which it did not. In fact, alcohol played no part at all in the affair, as Hawksley reported in January 1926: "Regarding the statement that the murder was done during a fit of intoxication. I was present at the preliminary trial in the Police Court also at the Territorial Court trial, the evidence given by the witnesses called shows that it was not a case of intoxication. No trace of intoxicants was found by the police who made the arrest." This must be true, for if alcohol had been a factor, as it was in the Duncan case, evidence would have been brought out to that effect; it was always the first thing the authorities thought of when a crime involving Native people occurred.

The second lesson is the fact that Katy Joe lived her short and sad life totally ignored by the authorities until she committed the crime that led to her incarceration, a crime arising from mental disease exacerbated by neglect, with the motive totally unknown. In the Gogoff case, the killer had a deranged grievance against the victims, and Paddy Duncan may have borne a grudge. But no one ever knew what motivated Katy Joe. Whatever her mental condition was, and the doctor's diagnosis of "mental stupor" seemed reasonable at the time (though it might just as well have been venereal disease), she had lived her entire life in a state of mental disability, and no one who came in contact with her – physicians, police, Indian agents, merchants, perhaps clergymen – had taken official notice of it or done anything about it. Unless Native people committed crimes against white people, they lived their own lives in the Yukon in those days, left to their own devices, to sink or swim. Any wardship on the part of the state was more theoretical than real.

One final case deserves attention, not because it sheds much light on Yukon society but because it is probably the best known murder case connected with the Yukon. This is the case of Albert Johnson, the "Mad Trapper of Rat River," which began in December 1931 in the Mackenzie Delta region and after a running gun battle, in which one of his pursuers was killed, ended two months later in the northern Yukon. The case still arouses interest, and Dick North's account of it is still in print after thirty years.[39] The case has everything going for it: an irresistible title, a chase through an arctic winter using dog teams and airplanes, the famous photograph of Johnson's corpse with a snarl frozen on his face, the wounded Mountie rushed to hospital by dogsled, and finally a "mystery," so beloved of the media – the trapper's identity was never proved to everyone's satisfaction.

The case is used as an Internet Web resource for university and high school students.[40] Rudy Wiebe wrote a novel about it,[41] and Hollywood has filmed the story.[42] One can even buy a painting of the Mad Trapper.[43] There is a large sign by his grave in Aklavik, and another along the Dempster Highway. There is a Mad Trapper Pub in Inuvik (and another in Golden, British Columbia, perhaps a different mad trapper), and a Mad Trapper Bowling Alley in Whitehorse. It is the only Yukon murder case that has its own display in the Yukon Archives in Whitehorse. None of this is true of any of the other Yukon killers, which proves, presumably, that it takes more than a homicidal personality to guarantee immortal fame – the killer also needs a catchy nickname. But the Albert Johnson case will not be dealt with here, for it is already well documented, and it tells us little about Yukon society in the 1930s, though it is an interesting example of the introduction of technology and the airplane to northern police work.

Conclusion

This book deals with notable murders – crimes that attracted a great deal of attention locally and sometimes nationally. It is the high-profile cases, the Nantucks, Fournier and Labelle, and the others, that permit an examination of issues and tensions within northern society. But the point needs to be made that these cases do not illustrate the typical way in which people in the Yukon were killed by others. One of the most common causes in the early twentieth century was not robbery, a lovers' quarrel, or madness – it was death by shooting in a hunting accident. In at least eight instances in the period under discussion (and probably in several more, since the records are unreliable), a Yukoner mistook another person, usually a family member or a friend, for an animal, most often a moose. Here was a uniquely northern cause of death: a man, anxious to add five hundred kilograms of free meat to his winter's cache, shot incautiously at a partly obscured target and killed a human by mistake.

No charges – not of murder or even of carelessness – were laid in these cases. Neither the police nor society considered the shooters to be murderers. They lacked what the lawyers call *mens rea*, criminal intent, and their feeling of guilt was considered sufficient punishment. Near Carcross in 1912, Sheridan Johnson died in such an accident. In 1939 Johnny Jackson of the Teslin area mistook his brother for a moose and shot him to death, as did Dawson John when he killed his friend Joe Jacky in 1918 along the M'Clintock River. Charles Petit killed his trapping partner Alex Swanson in similar circumstances in 1916.

There were also a good number of deaths arising from quarrels between friends and family members, most of which did not result in murder charges or convictions. In May 1899 two brewery workers, William Bennet and Arthur Braemer, got into a fight, and Bennet hit Braemer over the head with a blunt object, killing him. He was found not guilty by reason of self-defence. In 1900 C. Hill and John Blair got into a fist fight over a dog. Hill shot Blair, turned himself in, and was acquitted on grounds of self-defence. In July 1912 Eugene Vaglion, aged forty-five, shot his brother John as well as John's wife and two daughters, aged nine and seventeen. They had been quarrelling for some time. The unusually atrocious nature of this deed would probably have led either to execution or to incarceration for mental illness, but Vaglion turned the gun on himself and died.

Alcohol, as the Paddy Duncan case shows, often played a role in Yukon violence. In 1926 Jackie Macintosh and Pelly Jim were drinking in a cabin near Whitehorse when a fight broke out and Macintosh stabbed Jim in the neck, killing him. Macintosh fled the scene, heading into the bush, a reaction that caused a brief but intense spasm of fear among the non-aboriginal residents of the southern Yukon. The concept of the "renegade Indian," out of control and dangerous, was part of the folklore of the Yukon, despite the fact that except for the Nantuck case, indigenous violence against newcomers was virtually unknown. The fact that the Mounted Police were chasing Macintosh added to the general apprehension. However, there was no basis for the panic. There was never any evidence that Macintosh planned more violence against anyone, and within three days the police had him in custody. He was found guilty of manslaughter and sent to the New Westminster penitentiary to serve a three year sentence.

Given the value of the gold involved in the great rush, it is perhaps surprising that there were so few murders for money. The O'Brien and Fournier-Labelle cases have already been mentioned as exceptions, and some reasons for the low murder rate were suggested: the geography that made it hard for anyone to escape, the strong police presence, and so forth. There were quite a number of shootings, some of which resulted in conviction and execution. An argument between D.J. McFee and John Sipkus, his employer, over a small amount of money resulted in the police being brought in. McFee was furious when the police arrived to question him. He stalked and shot Sipkus, then turned the gun on himself, dying in hospital a short time later.

Similarly, Herbert Davenport, the American captain of a scow operating on the Yukon River in the summer of 1900, was the victim of a fit of rage. Alexander King, an American passenger, became angry when Davenport was unable to avoid running aground on the many sandbars that dotted the Yukon River. Furious at the delays, King pulled out his gun and shot Davenport. Contrite about his actions, King turned himself in to Dawson police headquarters the next day. He was quickly brought before Judge Craig and charged with murder. The jury found him guilty, and he was hanged on 2 October 1900.

Lovers' squabbles and, in particular, male jealousy relating to women, figured prominently in the annals of Yukon murders. Sexual tensions were high during the Klondike gold rush, and the women, particularly the prostitutes and dance hall girls, sometimes became the focus of violence. As we have seen, David Evans, furious at what he saw as the promiscuous behaviour of his lover, shot her in the head and then shot himself; and Harry Davis, when his partner threatened to leave him, shot her and then killed himself. The Slorah case also has already been mentioned. Then there was W.F. Smith who, angry with his wife and C.M. Kelly for reasons unknown, shot them both at the Black Hills Roadhouse on the Whitehorse-Dawson trail in January 1913. Like Evans, Davis, and many others, Smith then killed himself.

Insanity or mental instability – often described in the popular literature of the Yukon as "cabin fever," but not demonstrably more severe there than in southern settings – contributed to a significant number of deaths, as the Gogoff and Goddard cases show. Ethnicity, as the Gogoff case also demonstrates, proved to be an important factor in the pattern of Yukon murders. But for the most part, First Nations people killed fellow aboriginals, and newcomers killed fellow newcomers, though there were a few exceptions – most notably, the high-profile Nantuck case. Only one of the murders (the Yoshioka case) involved a non-Native killing a Native person, but this was a sign more of social distance than of a predilection towards racial equality.

Overwhelmingly, murders occurred within ethnic groups and, more often than not, among friends, family, and acquaintances. The Sarga case is an example of this. Similarly, a violent fight between Scurvy Shorty and George Joe of Carmacks resulted in Joe's death and Shorty's arrest for murder (though he was found not guilty of manslaughter). Although the Yukon was a culturally complex social environment, with many different ethnic groups and nationalities represented, nearly all violent deaths involved intragroup conflict. There is no compelling evidence that any of the murders examined here originated in racial or ethnic struggles.

What is important in this survey of violent death and murder in the Yukon is not only what is evident but what is missing. As we have seen, women were particularly vulnerable to acts of jealousy or rage by their lovers. Murder-suicide was surprisingly common, but it received little newspaper coverage and attracted minimal police attention; the death at his own hand of the murderer eliminated the need for an investigation, trial, and punishment. In most cases, to the degree than this can be ascertained, the event that triggered the deed was small and relatively inconsequential – except to the murderer and victim, of course. Petty squabbles, immediate disputes, and affairs of the heart accounted for most of the Yukon murders. It is also important to note that there were no vigilante deaths, very few acts of robbery or theft, and, as already noted, no racially motivated murders. Dan McGrew notwithstanding, there were no gunfights in Western fashion, no shootouts in the goldfields, and no pitched battles between rival companies, gangs, or ethnic groups. The police were involved in only a small number of the deaths, including Albert Johnson's and that of James Croteau, who was killed in 1939 by the RCMP officers who were attempting to apprehend him.

Canadians like to attribute the seeming tranquility of the region to the presence of the North-West Mounted Police and the quality of Canadian justice. The first factor is true, not only because of the quality of the police presence but because of the sheer size of the force, especially during the height of the gold rush. But the argument based on quality relies too much on the mythology about the American frontier and the presence of the occasional desperado, such as Skagway's villain, Soapy Smith. Although no systematic study has yet been undertaken of murder and violence in Alaska, evidence gathered from Canadian newspapers reveals much the same pattern on the American side of the border. There were several dramatic exceptions, such as the 1899 murder of Bert Horton and his wife near Haines Mission on the Lynn Canal. This murder, which the police attributed to theft and the newspapers to "native bloodthirstiness," had a "Canadian-style" outcome. Far from the stereotype of American frontier vigilantism, the result was that twelve Native people were arrested, six of whom were released and the other six found guilty. The apparent ringleader, named Hanson, was sentenced to be hanged (later commuted); the others received penalties of between twenty and twenty-two and a half years in jail.

There were other Alaskan cases that attracted considerable attention, more for their uniqueness than their representativeness. In 1912, for example, a Japanese foreman named Itow killed a Caucasian worker at Juneau, driving a sword through his body because Itow had learned that the man planned to quit his job. Then there was the Prohibition officer, Seneff, who shot and killed John Bernard in September 1923. Bernard had started to walk away from the Sullivan Roadhouse near Healy, and his unwanted departure caused Seneff to shoot him. It was not treated as a murder. In 1911 Joe Campbell murdered two men, Gus and John Nelson, along the Yukon River. They were probably shot when Campbell was robbing them. He was captured and sentenced to life imprisonment, but he escaped from jail in 1917. In 1905 two Seattle businessmen, Robert Ball and William Deppe, quarrelled over the presidency of the Great American Marble Company. At the end of the debate, Deppe lay dead. In 1930 an Austrian called Black Matt Berkowitch, angry that Phil Dohme had testified against him in court, shot Dohme dead near Ketchikan and then killed himself.

In 1925, an Eskimo prisoner, Mike Eqwana, attacked and killed the prison guard F.K. Fleckenstein and fled from his cell. In 1900, showing that the vigilante tradition was alive and well in Alaska, Martin Servert was grabbed by a crowd shortly after he had killed Steve Fredigno in Lituya Bay. They hanged him immediately, dispensing a little frontier justice in the process. There were also a few supposedly "classic" northern murders, such as the killing of Frank Musgrove and a man named McCarty during a dispute over a mining claim at Cold Foot on the Koyukuk in 1904.

Except for this handful of dramatic cases, the violent deaths in Alaska arose mostly from the standard, mundane frustrations and angers of everyday life. U.S. Army Private Hollander killed an aboriginal man, Paul Kadasham, in a fight over a Native girl. Willie Horton, in 1940, got in a fight with Willie Mills over a woman, shot Mills, and then attempted to kill himself. George Hardy, in a 1930 American reprise of an all too familiar scenario, shot his wife in a domestic dispute and then turned the gun on himself. In 1924 Paul Fromming shot and killed his neighbours, John and Alex Vanaja, and then turned himself in to Anchorage authorities. In 1899, Mailo Cegara argued with Joseph Riley over firewood that Cegara had cut. Cegara showed his displeasure by shooting Riley in the back three times. Jack Friehage murdered his common-law Native wife, Emily Big Joe, beating her to death with a carpenter's clamp when she refused to join him in drinking; he paid for his crime with a twenty-year prison sentence. A dispute over a dog led Bert Taylor to kill A. Chisel at Skagway in 1927. In 1900 Dan Carolin killed Joseph Muldowney of Rampart after Muldowney had assaulted Carolin's "squaw wife"; he later received a presidential pardon and was released from his life sentence.

Affairs of the heart – or of lust – claimed a number of victims, including Ted Fogleman, killed by Voleny Stevens, who was said "to be with" Fogleman's wife. Similarly, Ernie Bryson of Haines was angry that his wife was spending too much time with a neighbour, R.H. Ferry, and in 1922 he shot Ferry and then turned himself over to the authorities. In a scene reminiscent of several Yukon murders, an aboriginal man, Charlie Axson, who was mentally "unbalanced," killed Richard Cavanaugh, another Native, when Cavanaugh walked past Axson's Petersburg home. Axson attempted suicide immediately afterwards. The death of Sam Heninger at the hands of Richard Albert, which occurred after a drinking party near Yakutat in 1933, was likewise an occurrence familiar across the North.

Without a systematic analysis of Alaskan murders – the ones recounted here were identified from newspaper stories in the Yukon press – it is improper to generalize too confidently about the different conditions in the Canadian and American Northwest; but the available evidence suggests that the standard image of Canadian peace and order compared with American violence and disorder needs to be redrawn. People killed for much the same reasons on both sides of the border and at roughly the same rate according to the population. There were robberies on both sides, though there were a few more deaths related to struggles with police on the Alaskan side and several more multiple murders. Most of the murders in both territories had the same causes: they were acts of passion or insanity, alcohol-related conflicts, or petty disputes that unexpectedly erupted into violence. Patterns of ethnic violence were also much the same: most Native murders and violent deaths involved other Natives, but in both countries there was a small number of incidents of Aboriginal people killing whites. The one significant difference (and it is hard to know from the small sample how much importance to attached to the data) is that three American murder cases involved Caucasian people killing Native people; there were no such murders in the Yukon before 1940.

Murders, even banal ones, take us deeper inside regional societies than we could otherwise get. The reaction to high-profile cases illustrates the most fundamental insecurities within the local population. And in the Northwest, it is clear that people feared for the security of their land and worried about the difficulty of controlling thieves in the vast open spaces; they recognized their vulnerability to local people who "went bush," faced with long, dark winters and crowded quarters, and they watched with trepidation for an eruption of violence along the aboriginal and non-aboriginal divide. From these cases, a more nuanced portrait emerges of northern life than is readily available in the standard accounts and records. The Yukon Territory and Alaska hosted tense societies, made more so by cramped quarters, economic uncertainties, large gender imbalances, and the vagaries of Aboriginal-newcomer relations. Drink figured prominently and often violently, as did volcanic eruptions of jealousy over the real or perceived loss of a woman's affections.

At root, of course, many of the elements of the violent disputes mirrored those in all societies: men asserting control over women, struggles of passion and lust, violence unleashed by drinking, and battles with friends and colleagues over money. What stood out about the Yukon and, it appears, Alaska was the relatively small number of murders during this period before the Second World War, the surprisingly small amount of interethnic violence (supporting the argument that Native and non-Native people spent comparatively little time in each other's company and watched one another warily), and an overwhelming sense of vulnerability to violent offenders, which ensured that the police, or other residents, acted quickly.

Reviewing the history of murder in the Yukon during this period, one is struck by the banality of violent death. The vast majority of the cases emerged from very simple domestic situations. There was a handful of robberies and a small number of people who, mentally unbalanced, destroyed the lives of family members and friends. But from Edward Henderson, who killed his travelling companion in a rage over endless teasing about his bladder infection, to Paddy Duncan, who murdered a close friend in an alcohol-induced outburst, most of the murders were far from the stuff of Perry Mason, Agatha Christie, or *Law and Order*. The Mounted Police nearly always got their man, or woman, for the simple reason that the perpetrator was immediately known and often at hand.

Only in a small number of highly publicized cases did the police have to track down the offenders and return them, shackled and bound, for trial. The continent-wide fascination with the Royal North-West Mounted Police search for Albert Johnson in 1932 – a case which started with Johnson's murder of a policeman in the Northwest Territories and ended with the mysterious murderer dead on a frozen river in the northern Yukon – illustrates the inherent interest in acts of gratuitous violence and flight. The public's reaction to those cases – Nantuck, Labelle and Fournier, Albert Johnson, George O'Brien, Alexander Gogoff – reveals the deep societal horror at unprovoked attack and the demand for swift and sure retribution. All societies live in fear of premeditated and random acts of violence, and they insist that their governments protect them from potential offenders and deal swiftly with those who cross the line.

In the Yukon before 1940, society's demands were met promptly and efficiently. Police and the courts worked quickly to bring offenders to justice and to exact punishment. Juries, judges, and the national government often showed restraint in exacting retribution. Although the rationale was usually rooted in the racial stereotyping and ideology of the age, the courts forgave First Nations offenders for some of their actions, clearly expecting less moral behaviour from aboriginal people. And since Native people lacked effective medical attention, the authorities played more loosely with those claiming insanity as a defence. An aboriginal offender such as Katy Joe was excused her crimes in part and was sent to an asylum for what was called treatment, though it was really life imprisonment. A more aggressive offender, such as Gogoff, whose sanity was likewise in dispute, benefited from no such mercy.

Murders reveal the tragedy of everyday life. They bring into sharp relief the jealousies embedded in personal relationships – and the much greater likelihood that women will pay the price for a lover's rage. They document the disruptive and pervasive impact of drunkenness, a trigger for many violent actions throughout the Yukon's history. Yet within a general pattern of homicide, the murders in the Yukon varied little from those in other North American societies. However, some of them spoke to the northern experience.

Violence on the gold rush trail was sparked by frustration and the heat of the passionate stampede to Dawson City. The hard-drinking frontier society created more than its share of alcohol-related deaths, and a few of the murders (although this is difficult to know in the absence of forensic psychologists) appear to have been rooted in the loneliness, isolation, and darkness of the sub-arctic winter. On a handful of occasions (the Nantuck trial, for instance, and Jackie Macintosh's short-lived flight from justice), a deeply embedded racial fear of aboriginal violence emerged, only to be largely subsumed by social isolation and separate economic worlds. There is evidence, too, in the cases involving Eastern European and Japanese offenders, of the racial and ethnic barriers within Yukon society, and of the cultural divides that separated a small and seemingly homogenous region. Battles over business affairs, from mining claims to commercial transactions, highlighted the financial imperatives of gold rush and post-Klondike northern life. The smell of gold, we have long known, fuels great emotions, and it is hardly surprising, given the magnitude of the Klondike gold rush, that robbery, gold, and the pursuit of opportunity would be factors. More broadly, the male-dominated mining society reared its head in a pattern of jealous rage influenced by the small number of women in the region.

The crowds that gathered at public executions in the Yukon, the frenzied reportage of murder trials, and the sharp demands to the police and government that offenders be arrested and punished forthwith illustrate the complex juxtaposition of terror and fascination that surrounds murder. People wanted to know why murders occurred, and they sought assurances that they were safe. Canadians, in particular, worried about the advance of the stereotypic American Wild West and sought assurance that their frontier would be different. Trials and hangings revealed the blood lust, itself a mix of vengeance and morbid fascination, that lurked just below the surface of northern society. Executions and long-term imprisonment, especially when the prisons were many hundreds of kilometres away, satisfied the demand for retribution. Vigilantism was unheard of in the Yukon (and very rare in Alaska too). The police did their job, both by preventing acts of violence and, just as reassuringly, by moving quickly to arrest and bring to trial those accused of murder.

Patterns of murder changed dramatically after the Second World War. The incidence of violent death during the construction of the Alaska Highway and the northern defence projects in the 1940s had been surprisingly small, given the scale and speed of the American "invasion" of the Canadian Northwest. After 1950, the onset of the mining boom and a period of accelerated government investment in the Yukon Territory led to a greatly increased territorial population, from 8,800 in 1950 to 21,000 in 1975. Changing conditions within First Nations communities brought massive social unrest. The collapse of the fur trade, an intrusive welfare and residential school system, and economic and social marginalization in a fast-growing and wealthier Yukon society resulted in a surge of violent acts within the aboriginal population. Importantly, however, the pattern extant since the gold rush of minimal violent confrontations between First Nations and other Yukoners continued; aboriginal people in the Yukon, as elsewhere, took out their anger and frustrations on themselves and within their communities. The surge in population meant that there were more murders, a handful of them pieces of high drama, but not enough to make the Yukon an anomaly within Canada in terms of the incidence of violent acts. Drunkenness (and, increasingly, drug use) remained a critical feature in northern life and continued to play a crucial role in the pattern of violence in the territory. Women continued to suffer disproportionately at the hands of men, maintaining a pattern with a long and troubled history.

Murders offend, disturb, and fascinate. Often banal, typically unexpected, always shocking, they highlight the vulnerability of human existence, the evil that hides within all societies, and the finality of individual brutality. The history of murder in the Yukon illustrates the degree to which the territory shared the tensions and violent capabilities of all human populations, but it also shows that the Yukon produced its own frustrations and societal fault lines, which pushed individuals over the edge. Each case a tragedy, the effects of the act of murder reached far outside the territory, drawing in family members and friends of both the victims and the perpetrators, while demanding a response from the police and government and sparking an immediate public response, testing the resolve of the regional society, and making and remaking stereotypes and assumptions about the North.

Understanding murder, murderers, and the community's reaction to acts of violent death brings us closer to the essence of human relationships and societal structures. By observing the line between survival and death, struggle and fatality, order and chaos, punishment and revenge, love and hatred, soundness and insanity, and self-control and frenzy, we begin to see the veins of anger, pain, composure, ethnic tension, mental instability, greed, and self-interest that lurk within all peoples and all societies. In the process – in identifying the various forms of behaviour, worries, and approaches that the Yukon shared with other regions, as well as those that were specific to time and place – we begin to explore, at a different, more intense level, the social fabric of a subarctic society that was enduring enormous change and tension.

Studying Violent Death: An Analysis of Historical Scholarship on Murder

While bookstore shelves sag under the weight of books on "true crime" and murder mysteries, professional historians are much less likely to venture into the unusual, violent, and often confusing world of murder. Popular historians have written graphic accounts of infamous murders by the hundred, but scholars, with some notable exceptions, have avoided writing about these occurrences. Such neglect is perhaps due to the view that murders are isolated incidents that have no meaning deeper than the anecdotal; or perhaps it is professional squeamishness, a reluctance to join the ranks of what some academics consider to be hacks. It is not that these events passed unnoticed in their time, for almost all murders generate a considerable amount of contemporary comment, but historians have generally considered them to be ephemeral events of limited lasting significance. Looking at the indexes of five major Canadian history textbooks aimed at university students, it is interesting to see that not one of them contains an entry on "murder." And a perusal of their contents indicates that there are very few discussions of famous murders in Canada's past, except for political killings such as the shooting of D'Arcy McGee.[1] There is certainly a huge academic literature on murder, but it comes mostly from the disciplines of sociology, psychology, and criminology rather than from history.

Although the balance between popular and historians' professional writings on murder is skewed against academic works, a
significant body of work has in fact emerged. It is important to
note that a fair portion of the scholarship is interdisciplinary.
Criminologists, psychologists, anthropologists, and others have
looked to the past for explanations about murderous behaviour.
Similarly, historians have drawn on the insights and analyses of
psychologists, sociologists, and feminist scholars in endeavouring
to understand historical phenomena. The result is a small but rich
body of Canadian and international scholarship on the history of
murder, offering methodological and conceptual models for the
historian of violent death. In this appendix, we focus on Canadian
scholarship in the main, with the purpose of placing our study of
murder in the Yukon within a national intellectual context.

As a starting point, it is useful to emphasize that the scholarly
literature on the subject of murder/homicide exists largely outside a historical context.[2] Scholars examining the intricacies and
impact of violent death generally choose to focus on contemporary events and the recent past.[3] A few, such as anthropologist Elliott Leyton,[4] whose studies of serial killers have attracted a great
deal of scholarly and public attention, reach back into earlier generations in search of patterns and meaning. *Homicide,* by Martin
Daly and Margo Wilson, weaves cross-cultural and historical examples into a complex tapestry that seeks to explain the impact of
gender, culture, economic standing, intergenerational tensions,
and other factors on the incidence of murder in various societies.
Few books do such an adroit job of combining historical and social
science inquiry in a way that challenges the assumptions of numerous areas of scholarship. On the Canadian situation, Neil
Boyd's *The Last Dance*[5] pays some attention to historical trends,
though his interest in the past is largely statistical in nature. His
work focuses generally on the emerging discipline of criminology,
and he uses history to provide a context for his analyses of contemporary circumstances. *A Criminal History of Mankind* by Colin
Wilson provides a broad cross-cultural analysis of violence, including murder, demonstrating the relevance of historical perspective to the study of this critical theme.

The view from the historical literature is not very different. The
comparatively limited amount of historical scholarship seeks,

with few exceptions, to speak to broader social, cultural, political, and economic issues. To put it simply, historians address the concerns of historians. Only a handful of them attempt to place their scholarship within the broader psychological, sociological, and criminological history. They may draw sporadically, as we have done, on insights from other disciplines, but the goal of their work is not to transform broader understandings of homicide as a societal phenomenon.[6] The gap is significant, though it is not one to which we have turned our attention in this book. The analysis of human behaviour that is possible through the consideration of historical cases has the potential to make a formidable contribution to the general understanding of why and how people murder and how societies respond to the reality of violent death. Together with other works of this sort, the historical literature provides useful insights that can speak to broader aspects of the human condition. In *Strange Things Done*, we have used the study of murder to explore generally neglected aspects of Yukon history.

Consider one of the basic challenges for the historian: finding sufficient documentation. In this context, the relative absence of detailed historical studies of murder, either as individual cases or as broader, systematic studies, is curious. The exceptions for northern Canada are the case of the Mad Trapper (which attracted writers because of the lurid details of the case and, even more, because of the apparent mystery of the killer's true identity) and the case of the two Inuit killers, Sinnisiak and Uluksuk, recorded by R.G. Moyles, which is of great cross-cultural interest.[7] The paucity of studies on the subject is odd because murders generate an unusually rich body of documentation. Police and coroners' records, court files, medical documents, newspaper accounts, along with such standard historical material as diaries and memoirs, provide diverse and useful insights into specific events. To place individual acts of violence in context, historians can draw on a vast array of qualitative and quantitative data, thereby lifting the isolated example from obscurity and using it to provide a new window on social, cultural, ethnic, and economic relations.

In Canada's case, the Capital Case files in the records of the Department of Justice[8] are a wonderful resource for historians of a certain kind of murder – those ending in a sentence of death. Similarly, American courts often provided voluminous trial, appeal,

and supporting records, thus offering the historian the raw material necessary for a successful and comprehensive reconstruction
of a particular murder. Add to these official records the public discussion of specific murders or patterns of murder, and the historian will often uncover a wealth of documentation. Newspaper
accounts, political discussions, and comments in memoirs and diaries provide an important reminder of the importance that most
social groups attached to many of the cases.

Although any historiographical typology is, by definition, con-
straining, it is possible to place most of the academic literature on the
history of murder into one of several categories. The discussion that
follows recognizes the limitations of these broad strokes but uses the
divisions to introduce readers to the diversity of this field of inquiry.

STORIES

Many of the historical accounts of murders, by professional and
popular historians alike, focus on dramatic killings. Much as the
current generation has been fascinated by the cases of O.J. Simpson,
the "Son of Sam," Hickock and Smith (the killers in Truman Capote's *In Cold Blood*), the Manson murders, and many others in the
United States, or the barbarous behaviour of Paul Bernardo and
Karla Homolka[9] and Clifford Olson[10] in Canada, people in the past
were transfixed by such classic murders as the Evelyn Dick case.[11]
There is a growing interest in the activities of serial killers, such as
Ted Bundy and John Gacey.[12] In the hands of a skilled professional,
these accounts can be both riveting and insightful, exploring the
mentality of the time and offering a compelling narrative. Typically,
however, the emphasis is on the people involved in the case, and
the intention is to tell a gripping story. The goal is simple: to explain
a well-known historical event (or resurrect from obscurity an important but forgotten case), to entertain the reader, and to get the
details as accurate as possible. These historical accounts satisfy the
reader's desire to know, and they do so in a way that enriches the
general understanding of time and place.[13]

MURDERS IN GENERAL HISTORIES

Save for major public murders, such as a political assassinations,
the history of murder rarely figures in national-survey histories.

These texts, which form the basis of undergraduate instruction and so establish the base (and often upper limit) for the students' understanding of their past, rarely give more than a passing glance at this important historical phenomenon. This is surprising, given the often intense emotions across large societies surrounding the fear of or reaction to murder. Clearly, in this instance, murders are viewed as extraordinary events, typically involving people who, by their actions, have demonstrated that they were not truly a functioning part of their host society.

PATTERNS AND SOCIAL INSIGHTS

A decades-long debate in North America about the surge (and the much less discussed subsequent decline) in the incidence of violent death sparked considerable interest in broader patterns of murder and violent behaviour generally.[14] In such studies, scholars step away from individual cases to search for patterns in the past. Their studies, like Neil Boyd's useful overview *The Last Dance*, identify and attempt to explain changes in the murder rate, the dynamics of group violence, ethnicity as a factor in murder (and in punishment for murder, a major issue for African Americans in the United States and for First Nations people in Canada), gender and the incidents of murder, and the social contexts (drunkenness, jealousy, and the like) within which the murder occurred. Such studies have attempted to correlate murders and murder rates with economic trends, social changes, class tensions,[15] patterns of immigration, and the like. These studies, if they use cases at all, focus on individual murders only to explicate broad social phenomena. Within all societies, there is a fascination with murder and, among historians, a desire to explain the prevalence (or lack thereof) within a particular culture. American scholars have long been concerned with their country's record in this regard, for the nation has experienced a comparatively high rate of violent death, among the world's highest rates of incarceration (at present, only authoritarian regimes and South Africa come close to the American level), and a compelling national interest in maintaining the death penalty. Scholars, led by Richard Brown,[16] have attempted to explain the level of violence and the high incidence of violent death within a country that, ironically, has long prided itself on a sense of community and community engagement.[17]

There are many groups in North American society – Blacks, Hispanics and Asians in the United States, women and aboriginal people across the continent, homosexuals, dissidents, and others – whose presence has been little noted in the history books. Further, the violence directed at these groups, often an endemic part of their existence, is not always well known. Historical accounts of individual murders or a set of murders provide historians with an opportunity to wrest from obscurity a critical social or cultural aspect and, through the unusually rich records often generated by a murder case, provide insights into aspects of North American life that would otherwise be difficult to identify.

In her best-selling novel *Alias Grace*, Margaret Atwood used historical records and her talents as a writer of fiction to tell the story of Grace Marks, a woman found guilty of murder in Upper Canada in the 1840s.[18] Similarly, *Walk Towards the Gallows* by Tom Mitchell and Reinhold Kramer uses the murder of the wife of a Brandon businessman by their maid, Hilda Blake, to explore social class and economic relations in late-nineteenth-century western Canada. (Blake was the only woman ever hanged in Manitoba.) This work, probably the best single work in Canadian historical writing on a murder case, provides penetrating insights into social class, attitudes towards women, assumptions about sexual mores and personal violence, and the intricacies of social life in western Canada at that time.

For a particularly interesting historiographical example of the intersection of race, murder, and the judicial system, with the added twist of providing students and others with an opportunity to assess the evidence in the murder case, see the Web site created by Ruth Sandwell and John Lutz on the death of William Robinson in British Columbia.[19] One of the more compelling illustrations of the ability of a good historian to document societal issues through the study of murder is Jill Mocho's *Murder and Justice in Frontier New Mexico, 1821–1846*; the interweaving of highly focused stories with broad social and cultural developments gives the book a sharpness and relevance that is quite rare among works on the history of murder.

Historians, particularly those interested in ethnohistory and cross-cultural relations, have increasingly used the study of murders to document the cultural meaning of and reaction to murder.

Societies are not uniform in their reaction to murder or their toler-
ance of violence in their midst. Furthermore, when murders occur
in a cross-cultural situation – either involving people from different social worlds or resulting in a member of one society being
tried by the legal system of another – they bring into stark relief
the tensions and social traumas of those complex relationships.
The earlier chapter in this book on Paddy Duncan, which seeks to
explain the aboriginal response to a murder in their midst, is a
case in point. So too is Shelagh Grant's superb study of the Janes
murder in the Northwest Territories in 1923. Her book is a richly
documented and carefully argued study that draws on both archi-
val documents and Inuit oral tradition.[20] Murder, and the documentation attached thereto, provides unusually perceptive
insights into the frontiers of ethnic relations (albeit in a situation
that, by definition, is unique).[21]

Historians of women's experiences have long argued that the
absence of detailed information and a lack of historical creativity
had assigned issues of gender to the historical profession. A series
of historians of women, including Franca Iacovetta and Karen Dubinsky, have capitalized on the usually rich documentation produced by major court cases to examine aspects of women's lives.[22]
These studies have, in particular, illuminated the historic role of
violence towards women, female agency and responsiveness in
the face of oppression, the imbalance within the court system on
matters of gender and women's rights, and male assumptions
about the role of women within families and society at large.[23]
Studies of sentencing patterns, in contrast, reveal gender discrimination in the assessment of responsibility and, in particular, in the
setting of the sentence.[24] This work has been extremely useful in
bringing women's issues to the historiographical foreground and
has proved historians with an important opportunity to probe
hitherto little known aspects of women's existence.[25]

As any aficionado of *Law and Order*, *Columbo*, or countless other
television dramas and movies can attest, perpetrators of violent
death have plenty of explanations for their actions.[26] Historians,
too, have wrestled with the claims and counterclaims about culpability and responsibility. While there are few pre-1960 examples of
the famous "Twinkie" defence (a defendant claimed that gorging
on the toxically sweet confections caused a chemical imbalance

and led him to murder), defendants and their lawyers have struggled with the question of responsibility for murder. Acts conducted while under the influence of alcohol or drugs, for example,
became the focus of a great deal of debate. So too did the suggestion that mental illness excuses an individual from full responsibility for his or her actions. The famous McNaughton rule laid
down the original parameters for insanity defences, but lawyers
have worked very hard to expand them in their clients' favour. As
historians have shown, the manner in which the courts and society at large have responded to insanity defences reveals a great
deal about changing attitudes towards mental illness.[27] Similarly,
scholars have argued that the manner in which the courts have
dealt with murders committed by abused wives – in cases raised
long before the battered wife syndrome came to be widely accepted by the courts – demonstrates a great deal about the standing of women in society at large.

RESPONDING TO MURDER

In many cases, historians are only tangentially interested in the violent incidents themselves. Instead, seeing murder as a test of society and its institutions, they focus on how the police, judiciary,
and political system coped with the murderous event, and they
examine the subsequent trial (if one occurred) and societal expectations. Canadian historians have been particularly intrigued with
the manner in which institutional responses to murders (such as
the Starchild case on the Canadian prairies[28] or the cases discussed
in this book) demonstrated the resolve, talent, and determination
of the Royal Canadian Mounted Police. In a country devoted to
the belief in the concept of the Peaceable Kingdom, and the often
self-righteously presented notion that Canada is a less violent
(and therefore better) country that the United States, such studies
have proved to be a crucial part of the nation's historiographical
armament.[29]

Conversely, in the United States, historians have taken pains to
investigate the handling of murderers, by courts and vigilantes
alike, in the American West, seeking to debunk the Hollywood-
generated image of the violent, uncontrolled, and unjust western
frontier. In both countries, the capacity of a nation to identify, ar-

rest, try, and punish violent offenders is a test of sovereignty (can a nation be sovereign if it cannot protect its citizens?) and of its institutional adaptability. Consequently, historians have long drawn on the handling of murders and murderers as a "test" of the control exercised by the nation-state over far-flung territories, states, and provinces. Studies of breaches of legal ethics or the canons of law, to turn the equation around, have been used to document the perfidy of the nation-state and its ethnic, class, and ideological interests. When people from outside the dominant ethnic group(s) are involved, these accounts often provide compelling evidence of the marginalization of subsections of the national population and the willingness the dominant groups to use their control of the instruments of authority to serve their collective interests.

The assessment of the response to murder goes beyond matters of policing and the intricacies of the judicial system; it relates, as well, to the manner in which the public at large reacts to violent death. Movies and popular fiction are filled with stories about societal reaction (and overreaction) to murder, typically highlighting vigilante action and community uproar. The media – newspapers in the nineteenth and twentieth centuries, and movies, radio, and television after the 1940s – played a critical role in determining what the community knew and what aspects of the cases drew public attention. Historical analysis of the role of the press[30] and of public responses to murder cases provide illustrations of the intensity of emotions and of the opportunities created for the manipulation of the story in the interests of race, ethnicity, politics, or community values. Angus McLaren's insightful study of attitudes to manliness in response to murder illustrates further the manner in which gender intersects with attitudes about violent death.[31] One of the most insightful studies of social response to murder, drawing on First Nations oral tradition and a sophisticated reading of the events and the aftermath of a British Columbia lynching, is Keith Carlson's essay on a gold-rush era murder in the lower Fraser River valley.[32]

The manner in which a society responds to murder and particularly the handling of murder cases by the police and judicial system reveal a great deal about the fundamental values of a population. For decades, Canadians congratulated themselves on the assumption that their frontier experience was demonstrably less violent that the American westward expansion – an idea that rested more on the prevalence of "shoot 'em up" westerns than solid historical analysis.[33] Canadian sanctimoniousness has always been in evidence on this subject, re-enforcing national mythologies about the authority and ability of the North-West Mounted Police, the inherent fairness of the Canadian legal system, and, in contrast, American lynch mobs, group violence, and kangaroo courts.[34]

On a more practical level, Canadian historians have long acknowledged that the prosecution of murder cases has been a critical element in the establishment of national sovereignty over little-populated lands.[35] As a consequence, Canadian historical scholarship has focused more on the administration of justice than on the incidents and patterns of violence and criminality.[36] Much has also been of the gentler approach (judges would say the more pragmatic) to the use of the death penalty in Canada. Again, comparing this country with the United States and finding the latter wanting in both historical and contemporary terms, scholars have been quick to emphasize the Canadian reluctance to use the death penalty, save for the most clear-cut and egregious cases, in the years before its total abolition in 1976.[37]

Studies of the differential application of legal structures on the basis of ethnicity have likewise been revealing. They have demonstrated that the Canadian system has been quite flexible in attributing responsibility and culpability to indigenous people – though for reasons more patronizing than culturally sensitive. Similar studies in the United States have argued that aboriginal defendants did not receive the same treatment as non-aboriginal offenders and that the American legal system was demonstrably unfair towards Native people.[38]

REVEALING THE UNPALATABLE

Just as murder fascinates, it also irritates and enrages family members and communities struggling with painful memories. People do not like to have old stories dredged up for public consumption. Relatives of the victims or the accused find no satisfaction in having their family's darkest moments brought forward for re-examination. The same is true of murders committed in the distant past. In the Yukon, a particularly serious example of murder among aboriginal peoples in the nineteenth century remains a matter of intense sensitivity among the communities involved. Historian Robert Weyeneth addresses this critical and delicate matter in an excellent essay on the struggles of one community with the legacy of a well-remembered but repressed episode in its past.[39] Tom Mitchell and Rienhold Kramer encountered similar familial and community resistance when they launched their investigation of the Hilda Blake case in Brandon, even though it had taken place in 1899.

Communities remember these events, and without a satisfactory resolution, the sore can fester for decades afterwards. Julie Cruikshank's excellent and sensitive discussions of the Nantuck murder case in the southern Yukon illustrates the degree to which elders remember the story – rather differently from the official account or the court record – and documents the manner in which these descriptions are preserved for subsequent generations. Her study, and that by a law student, Al Grove, are considered in our investigation of the Nantuck case. Cruikshank's work, among the most valuable in Canada on the importance of historical memory, reminds us that murder is a powerful element in the collective experience and can shape individual and group action for decades to follow.[40]

MURDER IN THE CANADIAN NORTH

A significant number of the academic works cited above relate to events that took place in the Canadian North. The police have long figured prominently in the understanding of the evolution of northern history, with works by Morris Zaslow[41] and his student, William R. Morrison,[42] establishing the foundation for subsequent work on the Mounted Police.[43] As these and other scholars have argued, a series of murders, particularly those involving the Inuit, forced the government's hand and compelled authorities in Ottawa to make a decision about the incorporation of the northern aboriginal people into the Canadian legal system. There has been very little serious historical work on murder beyond studies of the police and the assertion of official control. A few popular histories of the Mad Trapper of Rat River and the O'Brien case offer good stories but little analysis.[44] The manner in which these cases were

handled – with an understanding of the role that cultural misun-
derstandings played in the violent encounters but with a growing
determination that the Inuit and Dene understand who held authority in the region – set the framework for police-aboriginal relations in the region for decades.[45] Alaskan historians have
demonstrated a similar interest in murders in their territory,
though there has been no analysis of the role of the state, military,
of judicial authorities comparable to the Canadian studies.[46]

Murder in the American West has attracted considerable scholarly interest, with a wide variety of articles and books on aspects
of race, gender, enforcement, punishment, and justice in the history of the region. Clare McKanna Jr's *Homicide, Race and Justice in
the American West, 1880–1920* provides a useful overview. His
more detailed examination, *The Trial of "Indian Joe,"* examines a
particularly revealing example of racial discrimination in the
functioning of the western justice system. Perhaps the most important scholar involved with the study of murder in western history is John Phillip Reid. A renowned legal history scholar in the
United States, Reid has produced a series of valuable cross-border
studies of the early contact period. His investigation of cross-
cultural homicide in the fur trade documents the comparatively
effective manner in which the Hudson's Bay Company responded
to murders in British North America and the co-existence of indigenous forms of justice and vengeance long after initial contact.
Reid's Canadian counterpart, with overlapping interests in the
history of murder in the fur trade area, is legal historian Hamar
Foster. His detailed studies of the manner in which Hudson's Bay
Company officials tried to respond to murders within HBC fur-
trading territories provide excellent illustrations of the complications involved in enforcing British law in the sparsely populated
and administratively ill-served districts of British North America.
(For a further introduction to the legal history of western Canada,
see the volumes of the series *Essays in the History of Canadian Law,*
particularly volume 5, *Crime and Criminal Justice: Native Peoples
and the Criminal Law,* and volume 6, *Hard Choices and Sharp Edges:
The Legal History of British Columbia and the Yukon.*)

We have attempted in *Strange Things Done,* as Shelagh Grant did
so successfully with *Arctic Justice,* to place individual acts of violence within the mainstream of northern and Yukon history, a re-

gion where murders were far from numerous. Yet to a greater or lesser extent, each violent incident illustrated one or more important aspects of Yukon society. Historians of other areas and nations could, we would argue, make a similar effort to place murders within their general conception of the past and to capitalize on the unique insights gleaned from the pages of police reports and trial transcripts to shine the historical flashlight into the seldom seen but vital underbelly of society. Violence and murder are part of all societies, and all social groupings have developed ways of responding to such incidents. Exploring the specific cases and the general patterns provides historians with unique and potentially powerful ways of exploring social, ethnic, economic, political, and gender relations, using the violence on the fringes of society to peek under the veils of social convention and documentary limitations to learn more about the tensions that underlie any social grouping.

Notes

PREFACE

1 The Alikomiak and Tatamigana murders took place in the Northwest Territories. It was the trial and execution that took place in the Yukon.
2 Bugliosi, *Helter Skelter: The True Story of the Manson Murders*.
3 See Williams, *Invisible Darkness: The Strange Case of Paul Bernardo and Karla Homolka*, Crosbie, *Paul's Case: The Kingston Letters*, and others.
4 Milgaard, with Edwards, *A Mother's Story: The Fight to Free My Son David*.
5 There are many sources for statistics on murder, both in Canada and in other countries, for example, Schloss and Giesbrecht, *Murder in Canada: A Report on Capital and Non-Capital Murder Statistics, 1961–1970*; and Statistics Canada, *Homicide in Canada: A Statistical Synopsis* and *Canadian Crime Statistics*.
6 *Globe and Mail*, 6 September 2003.

CHAPTER ONE

1 On the history of the Yukon, see Coates and Morrison, *Land of the Midnight Sun*.
2 See Coates and Morrison, *The Sinking of the Princess Sophia*.
3 On the comparison between the U.S. and Canadian mining frontier experience, see Morrison, "Policing the Boomtown: The Mounted

Police as a Social Force on the Klondike," "Eagle over the Arctic: Americans in the Canadian North, 1867–1985," and "Imposing the British Way: The Mounted Police and the Klondike Gold Rush."

4 On the police in the Yukon, see Morrison, *Showing the Flag: The Mounted Police and Canadian Sovereignty in the North, 1894–1925.*

5 Several Web sites concerning the Bodie claim state that when it had a population of 10,000 there was a "murder a day," but this must be an exaggeration of both the population and the murder rate. See <http://www.photo.net/ca/sierra> and <http://www.virtualtourist.com/m/35563/b8012/>, both 8 October 2002.

6 The period 1897–1901 – the Nantuck, Henderson, and O'Brien cases, involving seven victims. See Morrison, "Policing the Boomtown," 87.

7 A good explanation of the Canadian jury system is Vidmar's, "The Canadian Criminal Jury."

8 Strange, "The Lottery of Death."

9 Whitehorse *Weekly Star*, 8 October 1915.

10 Boyd, *The Last Dance*, 8.

11 Lane, *Murder in America.*

CHAPTER TWO

1 National Archives of Canada (NA), RG13, series C1, vol. 1434.

2 Various aspects of the Nantuck case have been considered in the following articles: Cruikshank, "Oral Traditions and Written Accounts," Grove, "Where Is the Justice, Mr Mills?" and Cruikshank, *Life Lived Like a Story.* It is also briefly mentioned in Schuh, "Justice on the Northern Frontier," and in other works. The primary source for these events is the Capital Case file at NA, RG13, series C1, vol. 1434, which deals with all the Nantuck brothers.

3 Ibid.

4 From Longstreth, *The Silent Force.*

5 Cruikshank, *Life Lived Like a Story*, 166.

6 Grove, "Where Is the Justice, Mr Mills?"

7 The records do not give the date of the crime, but the autopsy on the victim occurred at the end of October 1897, when Peterson's corpse was disinterred (presumably it had been buried until a doctor could be brought to examine it). At that time, the brain was found to be partially decomposed, suggesting a date of early October or late September for the crime.

CHAPTER THREE

1 Except where otherwise noted, the source for this chapter is NA RG13, vol. 1443, file Edward Labelle.
2 An autopsy was later performed by William E. Thompson, assistant surgeon to the police in Dawson.
3 *Daily Klondike Nugget,* 17 June 1902.
4 Joseph-Édouard-Émile Léonard (1872–1933) was the Conservative member for Laval, Quebec, from 1900 to 1911.
5 Vancouver *Daily World,* 20 January 1903.
6 Ibid.
7 This account is taken from Welsh's report to the officer commanding B Division, NWMP, Dawson City, 20 September 1902.
8 Presumably not French holiday places but places where French-speaking people congregated.
9 Frederick White (1847–1918) was comptroller of the police 1880–1913 and was the equivalent of a deputy minister, reporting directly to the minister of the interior, the cabinet minister responsible for the Mounted Police.
10 Frederick Tennyson Congdon (1858–1932) was the leading Liberal politician in the Yukon in that era, but it was a Conservative stronghold, and although he was elected once, in 1908, he was defeated in 1904, 1911, 1917, 1921, and 1926.
11 Vancouver *Daily World,* 20 January 1903.

CHAPTER FOUR

1 The main source for the Elfors case is the Department of Justice Papers. See NA, RG13, series B1, vol. 1454.
2 This process is described by Stone in "Atomistic Order and Frontier Violence."
3 See Fisher, *Duff Pattullo of British Columbia.* On George Black, see Martha Black, *My Seventy Years* and *My Ninety Years.*
4 In her excellent autobiography, *I Married the Klondike,* one of the best first-person accounts of Klondike life.
5 Vidmar explains in "The Canadian Criminal Jury" how the system of triers works.
6 Whitehorse *Weekly Star,* 17 July 1908.

CHAPTER FIVE

1 The main source for the Gogoff case is the Department of Justice Papers. See NA, RG13, series B1, vol. 1469.
2 Whitehorse *Weekly Star*, 1 October 1915.
3 Ibid. The paper called him Arthur Wilkins, but his name was recorded as Wilkinson when he gave evidence in court.
4 Transcript of the trial, 15–16.
5 Strange, "The Lottery of Death," 614–15.
6 Ibid., 596.

CHAPTER SIX

1 Report of Inspector A.M. Jarvis, 1908, quoted in Morrison, *Showing the Flag*, 153. A version of this chapter was published in *Arctic* 51 (September 1998).
2 Not all the First Nations of the Yukon are Dene, though most are. The Tlingit of the southern part of the territory are related to coastal non-Dene peoples.
3 Harring, "The Rich Men of the Country," 21.
4 Grant, *Arctic Justice.*
5 Ibid., 66.
6 Harring, "the Rich Men of the Country," 7.
7 NA, RG13, Capital Case file 24861, 1923.
8 Rasmussen, *Intellectual Culture of the Copper Eskimo,* 63.
9 The July trials included those of three other Inuit, who were charged with lesser offences.
10 Harring "The Rich Men of the Country," 7.
11 Price, "The King v. Alikomiak," 317.
12 C. Starnes to W.W. Cory, Deputy Minister of the Interior, 14 August 1922, NA, NAB, RG85, vol. 607, file 2580.
13 T.L. Cory to O.S. Finnie, 12 September 1922, NA, NAB, vol. 607, file 2580.
14 Price, "The King v. Alikomiak," 226.
15 Ibid., 220.
16 See Eber, *Images of Justice.*
17 His remarks are taken from NA, RG13 Capital Case file 24861, 1923.
18 Price, "The King v. Alikomiak," 317.
19 Capital Case file 24861, 1923.
20 Ibid.

21 Letter to the Ottawa *Citizen*, 22 November 1923.

22 These letters are in Capital Case file 24861, 1923.

23 Rasmussen, *Intellectual Culture of the Copper Eskimo*, 64.

24 Harring, "Rich Men of the Country"; Price, "The King v. Alikomiak."

25 Rasmussen, *Intellectual Culture of the Copper Eskimo*, 17.

CHAPTER SEVEN

1 The main source for this case is NA, RG13, vol. 1606, Capital Case 461 (Duncan, P.), int. 81. Quotations in this chapter, except where otherwise noted, come from this file. A version of this chapter was published in the *Western Historical Quarterly*, November 1996.

2 McClellan, *My Old People Say*, 1:20.

3 Vancouver *Daily Province*, 8 July 1948.

4 Ibid.

CHAPTER EIGHT

1 *Klondike Nugget*, 25 October 1900.

2 Ibid.

3 *Klondike Nugget*, 18 November 1900.

4 *Klondike Nugget*, 22 November 1900

5 Ibid.

6 *Klondike Nugget*, 16 December 1900.

7 *Klondike Nugget*, 13 January 1901.

8 Ibid.

9 *Dawson Daily News*, 29 May 1900.

10 *Dawson Daily News*, 28 May 1900.

11 *Dawson Daily News*, 31 May 1900.

12 *Dawson Daily News*, 26 August 1900.

13 Malcolm, *Murder in the Yukon*.

14 The synopsis, and other records relating to the case are in the RCMP papers at NA, RG18, series A1, vol. 254, file 318-03. The Capital Case file for O'Brien is at NA, RG13, vol. 1440.

15 Statement of John Sarga (made through an interpreter), 30 September 1899, sworn at Nome, Alaska, before Charles S. Rosener, notary public. See NA, RG13, C1, vol. 2075, file 66. All documents relating to the Sarga case are taken from this file.

16 Statement of John Sarga.

17 Ibid.
18 See Greenhous, *Guarding the Goldfields.*
19 Frederick White, Comptroller of the NWMP, to Deputy Minister of Justice, 22 March 1900.
20 *Klondike Nugget,* 16 September 1900.
21 Records of the case are in NA, RG18, vol. 3253, file HQ-681-G-1.
22 In the records the name was spelled Casari, Caesari, and in other ways. The newspaper switched first and last names. The authorities always had trouble with non–Anglo Saxon names.
23 RNWMP crime report, Whitehorse, 1 October 1914.
24 Whitehorse *Weekly Star,* 31 July 1914.
25 Ibid.
26 In this the case the names and occupations of the six jurymen were recorded in the police crime report. They were Gordon Spragge, laundryman; Gilbert Fowler, ship carpenter; H.G. Macpherson, druggist (presumably the same H.G. McPherson who was involved in the Gogoff case the following year); J.D. Richards, sawmiller; J. Hopkins, club steward; J.H. Cole, saddler.
27 Whitehorse *Weekly Star,* 5 February 1915.
28 See *Klondike Nugget,* 31 May, 3 June, 12 July, 30 August, and 20 September 1899.
29 In the 1930s, by then a corporal, H.W. Stallworthy made some notable patrols in the High Arctic, one of which went completely around Axel Heiberg Island, covering a distance of 2,200 km. In 1935 he was made a fellow of the Royal Geographical Society.
30 The account of this case is drawn from NA, RG18, vol. 536, file 353, crime report, Rex vs. Rokuichi Yoshioka, 6 August 1917.
31 Inspector W. Moorhead to officer commanding B Division, Dawson, 21 December 1922. This document and the others dealing with this case are in the Department of Indian Affairs papers. See NA, RG10, vol. 7475, file 19166-4, pt 1.
32 Ibid.
33 The others were C.H. Johnston, a hotel keeper, A.D. McLennon, a fur dealer, H.F. Langholz, an employee of the railway, W.J. Clethero, a prospector, and J.J. Elliott, an engineer.
34 McPherson, whose name may have been spelled MacPherson (the records spell it both ways about equally), lived at 206 Hawkins Street in what is now one of the historic homes of Whitehorse. See <http://www.yukonalaska.com/yhma/houses/scott.htm>, July 2002.

35 The jurors were William Povoas, Patrick Martin, Frank Harbottle, Frederick Burnett, William Drury, and John French, occupations not given.

36 The transcript calls him Paddy Smith, but other records call him Duncan.

37 He had done the legal work for the incorporation of the Yukon Electrical Company, of which he was a major shareholder. Phelps had been in Whitehorse since at least 1906, when he was mentioned by his nickname "the Deacon" in an unpublished poem by Robert Service entitled "Bob Smart's Dream," written for a banquet. His son John Phelps and his son-in-law were the major force behind the modern electric supply to Whitehorse through the Yukon Hydro Company, incorporated in 1950. His grandson Willard Phelps was leader of the Yukon government in 1985.

38 The gold commissioner was the senior administrator in the Yukon in that period. The territorial government had been downsized by Ottawa in 1918, and the position of commissioner abolished.

39 North, *The Mad Trapper of Rat River* and *Trackdown*.

40 For instance, at Langara College in British Columbia <http://www.langara.bc.ca/library/reshelp/tempguides/engl1127h2.html>, July 2002, and the University of Saskatchewan <http://www.usask.ca/education/ideas/tplan/sslp/yukon/ratriver.htm>, July 2002.

41 Wiebe, *The Mad Trapper*.

42 *Death Hunt* (1981), with Charles Bronson, Lee Marvin, and Angie Dickinson, was apparently inspired by the case.

43 From Craig Clark in Golden Lake, Ontario. See <http://www.crow.ws/oldpages/contact.htm>, July 2002.

APPENDIX

1 D'Arcy McGee (1825–68), born in Ireland and a supporter of Irish independence, changed his mind and became its opponent and was shot dead on his doorstep, perhaps victim of a Fenian plot. Patrick James Whelan, convicted of the killing, was the last man hanged publicly in Canada.

2 Danto et al., *The Human Side of Homicide*, is a good case in point. See also Feibleman, *The Destroyers: The Underside of Human Nature*, and Malmquist, *Homicide: A Psychiatric Perspective*.

3 For a good Canadian example, see Silverman and Kennedy, *Deadly Deeds: Murder in Canada.*

4 Leyton, *Men of Blood: Murder in Everyday Life.* See also his *Hunting Humans: The Rise of the Modern Multiple Murderer.*

5 See also Hustak, *They Were Hanged.*

6 There are many good examples of this approach. One of the best is Lane, *Murder in America: A History.* See also Nash, *Murder, America: Homicide in the United States from the Revolution to the Present.* Ohio State University Press's History of Crime and Criminal Justice series provides further illustrations of this approach. For a Canadian example, with a broader coverage than the books above, see Carrigan, *Crime and Punishment in Canada: A History.* Much less historical but also useful is Hagan, *Disreputable Pleasures: Crime and Deviance in Canada.*

7 Moyles, *British Law and Arctic Men.*

8 On the role of this department in the post-Confederation era, see Swainger, *The Canadian Department of Justice and the Completion of Confederation, 1867–78.*

9 Davey, *Karla's Web: A Cultural Investigation of the Mahaffy-French Murders,* endeavours to look beyond the details of this notorious case and attempts to place it in a broader social analysis. The other books on the Bernardo-Holmolka case were potboilers.

10 Ferry and Inwood, *The Olson Murders,* and Holmes, *Where Shadows Linger: The Untold Story of the RCMP's Olson Murders Investigation.*

11 The subject of the delightfully titled *Torso,* by Marjorie Freeman Campbell.

12 See Levin and Fox, *Mass Murder: America's Growing Menace;* Kelleher, *Flash Point: The American Mass Murderer;* Hickey, *Serial Murderers and Their Victims;* Newton, *Hunting Humans: An Encyclopedia of Modern Serial Killers.*

13 The literature in this field is vast, particularly in the United States. A few Canadian examples include Starkins, *Who Killed Janet Smith? The 1924 Vancouver Killing That Remains Canada's Most Intriguing Unsolved Murder;* Simmie, *The Secret Lives of Sgt. John Wilson: A True Story of Love and Murder;* Kostelniuk, *Wolves among Sheep: The True Story of Murder in a Jehovah's Witness Community;* Siggins, *A Canadian Tragedy: JoAnn and Colin Thatcher;* Walford, *Lifers: The Stories of Eleven Women Serving Life Sentences for Murder;* Selleck and Thompson, *Dying for Gold: The True Story of the Giant Mine Murders.* See also Frasier, *Murder Cases of the Twentieth Century: Biographies and Bibliographies of 280 Convicted or*

Accused Killers. For an early variant of this theme, see Wallace, *Murders and Mysteries: A Canadian Series.*

14 See Johnson, "Homicide in Canada," and Hoffman, "Homicide: Reality and Realism." Two studies with little historical context are Gammon, *Violence in Canada,* and Ross, *Violence in Canada: Sociopolitical Perspectives.*

15 Leyton, *Hunting Humans,* argues that the incidence of serial murderers is directly related to periods of class tension and particularly involves individuals on the cusp between social groups. For a narrow view, see Schloss and Giesbrecht, *Murder in Canada: A Report on Capital and Non-Capital Murder Statistics, 1961–1970.*

16 Brown, *No Duty to Retreat: Violence and Values in American History and Society.* On the general question of American violence, see Hofstadter and Wallace, *American Violence: A Documentary History,* and Harold Hall, *Lethal Violence: A Sourcebook on Fatal Domestic, Acquaintance, and Stranger Violence.* See also Brown, *Strain of Violence: Historical Studies of American Violence.*

17 For a Canadian-American's view on this subject, see Fellman, "Violence and Crime in Nineteenth-Century America," 323–33.

18 For a very useful overview of a novelist's handling of murder, see Halttunen, *Murder Most Foul: The Killer and the American Gothic Imagination.*

19 "Who Killed William Robinson: Race, Justice and Settling the Land" <http://web.uvic.ca/history-robinson>.

20 Grant, *Arctic Justice: On Trial for Murder, Pond Inlet, 1923.*

21 For a very critical analysis of a contemporary murder involving aboriginal victims, see Goulding, *Just Another Indian: A Serial Killer and Canada's Indifference.*

22 Iacovetta, *Such Hardworking People: Italian Immigrants in Postwar Toronto,* and Dubinsky, *Improper advances: Rape and Heterosexual Conflict in Ontario, 1880–1929.*

23 See, in addition, Cameron and Frazer, *The Lust to Kill: A Feminist Investigation of Serial Murder,* and Radford and Russell, *Femicide: The Politics of Woman Killing.*

24 Rapaport, "The Death Penalty and Gender Discrimination."

25 The best overview of this issue is Strange, "Murder and Meanings in U.S. Historiography."

26 For a general review, with little historical context, see Pincus, *Base Instincts: What Makes Killers Kill?* See also Revitch and Schlesinger,

Psychopathology of Homicide, and Ross, *The Eyes of a Killer: A Psychiatrist's Journey through the Murderer's World.*

27 See, for example, Ireland, "Insanity and the Unwritten Law," and Block, "Daniel Drake and the Insanity Plea."

28 The best study of this episode is in Macleod's, *The NWMP and Law Enforcement.*

29 Much is often made of the infrequent use of capital punishment in Canada relative to the United States, particularly after the early decades of the twentieth century. See Chandler, *Capital Punishment in Canada.*

30 Pritchard, "Race, Homicide, and Newspapers." See also Bailey and Peterson, "Murder and Capital Punishment: A Monthly Time-Series Analysis of Execution Publicity," and Bailey, "Murder, Capital Punishment, and Television: Execution Publicity and Homicide Rates."

31 McLaren, "Males, Migrants, and Murder in British Columbia, 1900–1923."

32 Carlson, "The Lynching of Louie Sam."

33 For a study of violence on the American gold-mining frontier, see Rohrbough, *Days of Gold: The California Gold Rush and the American Nation,* especially chapter 14, and Brown, "Violence." For an overview that speaks directly though not exhaustively to the role of violence in murder in the American West, see White, *It's Your Misfortune and None of My Own: A New History of the American West.* See also Limerick, *The Legacy of Conquest: The Unbroken Past of the American West,* and Culberson *Vigilantism: Political History of Private Power in America.*

34 For a serious and insightful overview of the administration of justice in Canada, see Friedland, "A Century of Criminal Justice." For a critical view, see Paciocco, *Getting Away with Murder: The Canadian Criminal Justice System.*

35 See Morrison, "Canadian Sovereignty and the Inuit of the Central and Eastern Arctic."

36 For a useful example of this process, see Loo, *Making Law, Order, and Authority in British Columbia, 1821–1871.*

37 Avio, "The Quality of Mercy: Exercise of the Royal Prerogative in Canada." See also Turrell, "It's a Mystery: The Royal Prerogative of Mercy in England, Canada, and South Africa." For a critical appraissal of the courts and the treatment of the accused, see Milton, *More Than a Crime: Studies in Murder by Legal Process.* For the United States, a useful study is Monkkonen, "The American State from the

Bottom Up: Of Homicides and Courts." See also McLaren et al., *Law for the Elephant, Law for the Beaver: Essays in the Legal History of the North American West.*

38 Pate, "Indians on Trial in a White Man's Court," and McKanna Jr, "Murderers All: The Treatment of Indian Defendants in Arizona Territory, 1880–1912."

39 Weyeneth, "History, He Wrote: Murder, Politics, and the Challenges of Public History in a Community with a Secret."

40 Cruikshank's superb work can be seen in *Life Lived Like a Story* and *The Social Life of Stories: Narrative and Knowledge in the Yukon.*

41 Zaslow, *The Opening of the Canadian North* and *The Northward Expansion of Canada.*

42 Morrison, *Showing the Flag: The Mounted Police and Canadian Sovereignty in the North, 1894–1925.*

43 Diubaldo, "Canada's Inuit and Whiteman's Justice: 1900–1945: The Law Paramount," and McGrath, "Angulalik's Trial."

44 See North, *The Mad Trapper of Rat River* and *Trackdown: The Search for the Mad Trapper.* Also Malcolm, *Murder in the Yukon: The Case against George O'Brien.*

45 One of the most important contributions in this field is Hamar Foster's critical and insightful work "Sins against the Great Spirit: The Law, The Hudson's Bay Company, and the Mackenzie's River Murders, 1835–1839."

46 Bleakley, "Murder on the Koyukuk: The Hunt for the Blueberry Kid." *See also* Hunt, "Jack London's Lynching: A Murder on Lituya Bay in 1899," and Millman and Manchess, "Pursuing Justice in the Arctic."

Bibliography

PRIMARY SOURCES

National Archives of Canada (NA)
RG10, Department of Indian Affairs
RG13, Department of Justice
RG18, RCMP papers
RG85, Northern Administration Branch papers
Yukon Archives

SECONDARY SOURCES

Atwood, Margaret. *Alias Grace*. Toronto: McClelland & Stewart, 1996
Avio, Kenneth. "The Quality of Mercy: Exercise of the Royal Prerogative in Canada." *Canadian Public Policy* 13, no. 3 (1986): 366–79
Bailey, William. "Murder, Capital Punishment, and Television: Execution Publicity and Homicide Rates." *American Sociological Review* 55, no. 5 (1990): 628–33
Bailey, William, and Ruth Peterson. "Murder and Capital Punishment: A Monthly Time-Series Analysis of Execution Publicity." *American Sociological Review* 54, no. 5 (1989): 722–43
Berton, Laura. *I Married the Klondike*. New York: Little, Brown, 1954
Black, Martha. *My Ninety Years*. Anchorage: Alaska Northwest Publishing, 1976
– *My Seventy Years*. London: Thomas Nelson, 1938.

Bleakley, Geoffrey. "Murder on the Koyukuk: The Hunt for the Blueberry Kid." *Alaska History* 11, no. 1 (1996): 14–25

Block, Stanley. "Daniel Drake and the Insanity Plea." *Bulletin of the History of Medicine* 65, no. 3 (1991): 326–39

Bockstoce, J.R. *Steam Whaling in the Western Arctic.* New Bedford: Old Dartmouth Historical Society, 1977

Boyd, Neil. *The Last Dance: Murder in Canada.* Scarborough: Prentice Hall, 1986

Brown, Richard. *No Duty to Retreat: Violence and Values in American History and Society.* New York: Oxford, 1991

– *Strain of Violence: Historical Studies of American Violence.* New York: Oxford, 1977

– "Violence." In *The Oxford History of the American West*, ed. Clyde Milner II, Carol O'Connor, and Martha Sandweiss. New York: Oxford, 1994

Bugliosi, V. *Helter Skelter: The True Story of the Manson Murders.* 25th anniversary edition. New York: W.W. Norton, 1994

Cameron, Deborah, and Elizabeth Frazer. *The Lust to Kill: A Feminist Investigation of Serial Murder.* New York: New York University Press, 1987

Campbell, Marjorie Freeman. *Torso.* Toronto: Macmillan, 1974

Carlson, Keith. "The Lynching of Louie Sam." *BC Studies* 109 (spring 1996): 63–79

Carrigan, D. Owen. *Crime and Punishment in Canada: A History.* Toronto: McClelland & Stewart, 1991

Chandler, David B. *Capital Punishment in Canada: A Sociological Study of Repressive Law.* Toronto: McClelland & Stewart, 1976

Coates, Ken. *Best Left as Indians: Native-White Relations in the Yukon Territory.* Kingston: McGill-Queen's University Press, 1991

Coates, K.S., and W.R. Morrison, *Land of the Midnight Sun: A History of the Yukon.* Edmonton: Hurtig, 1988

– *The Sinking of the* Princess Sophia: *Taking the North Down with Her.* Toronto: Oxford University Press, 1990

Crosbie, Lynn. *Paul's Case: The Kingston Letters.* Toronto: Insomnia Press, 1997

Cruikshank, Julie. *Life Lived Like a Story: Life Stories of Three Native Yukon Elders.* Vancouver: University of British Columbia Press, 1990

– "Oral Traditions and Written Accounts: An Incident from the Klondike Gold Rush." *Culture* 9, no. 2 (1989): 25–34

– *The Social Life of Stories: Narrative and Knowledge in the Yukon Territory.* Vancouver: University of British Columbia Press, 1998

Culberson, William. *Vigilantism: Political History of Private Power in America*. New York: Greenwood, 1990

Daly, Martin, and Margo Wilson. *Homicide*. New York: Aldine de Gruyter, 1988

Danto, Bruce, et al., eds. *The Human Side of Homicide*. New York: Columbia University Press, 1982

Davey, Frank. *Karla's Web: A Cultural Investigation of the Mahaffy-French Murders*. Toronto: Penguin, 1995

Diubaldo, Richard. "Canada's Inuit and Whiteman's Justice, 1900–1945: The Law Paramount." *Storia Nordamericana* 5, no. 1 (1998): 125–36.

Dubinsky, Karen. *Improper Advances: Rape and Heterosexual Conflict in Ontario, 1880–1929*. Chicago: University of Chicago Press, 1993

Dykstra, Robert. "Violence, Gender, and Methodology in the 'New Western History.'" *Reviews in American History* 27, no. 1 (1999): 79–86

Eber, D.H. *Images of Justice: A Legal History of the Northwest Territories as Traced through the Yellowknife Courthouse Collection of Inuit Sculpture*. Montreal: McGill-Queen's University Press, 1997

Feibelman, James. *The Destroyers: The Underside of Human Nature*. New York: Lang, 1987

Fellman, Michael. "Violence and Crime in Nineteenth-Century America." *Canadian Review of American Studies* 12, no. 20 (1981): 323–30

Ferry, Jon, and Damian Inwood. *The Olson Murders*. Langley, BC: Cameo Books, 1982

Fisher, Robin. *Duff Pattullo of British Columbia*. Toronto: University of Toronto Press, 1991

Foster, Hamar. "Long-Distance Justice: The Criminal Jurisdiction of Canadian Courts West of the Canadas, 1763–1859." *American Journal of Legal History* 34, no. 1 (1990): 1–48

– "The Queen's Law Is Better than Yours: International Homicide in Early British Columbia." In *Essays in the History of Canadian Law*. Vol. 5: *Crime and Criminal Justice: Native Peoples and the Criminal Law*, ed. Phillips et al. Toronto: Osgoode Society, 1994

– "Sins against the Great Spirit: The Law, the Hudson's Bay Company, and the Mackenzie's River Murders, 1835–1839," *Criminal Justice History* 10 (1989): 23–76

Foster, Hamar, and John McLaren, eds. *Essays in the History of Canadian Law*. Vol. 6: *Hard Choices and Sharp Edges: The Legal History of British Columbia and the Yukon*. Toronto: University of Toronto Press and Osgoode Society, 1995

Frasier, David. *Murder Cases of the Twentieth Century: Biographies and Bibliographies of 280 Convicted or Accused Killers*. Jefferson, NC: McFarland, 1996

Friedland, M. "A Century of Criminal Justice." *Transactions of the Royal Society of Canada* 20 (1982): 285–97

Gammon, Mary Alice Bayer. *Violence in Canada*. Toronto: Methuen, 1978

Goulding, Warren. *Just Another Indian: A Serial Killer and Canada's Indifference*. Calgary: Fifth House, 2001

Grant, Shelagh. *Arctic Justice: On Trial for Murder, Pond Inlet, 1923*. Montreal: McGill-Queen's University Press, 2002

Greenhous, Brereton. *Guarding the Goldfields: The Story of the Yukon Field Force*. Toronto: Dundurn Press, 1987

Grove, Alan. "'Where Is the Justice, Mr Mills?': A Case Study of *R. v. Nantuck*." In *Essays in the History of Canadian Law*. Vol. 6: *British Columbia and the Yukon*, ed. Hamar Foster and John McLaren. Toronto: University of Toronto Press and Osgoode Society, 1995

Hagan, John. *Disreputable Pleasures: Crime and Deviance in Canada*. Toronto: McGraw-Hill Ryerson, 1977

Hall, Harold. *Lethal Violence: A Sourcebook on Fatal Domestic, Acquaintance, and Stranger Violence*. Boca Raton: CRC Press, 1999

Halttunen, Karen. *Murder Most Foul: The Killer and the American Gothic Imagination*. Cambridge: Harvard University Press, 1998

Harring, S. "The Rich Men of the Country: Canadian Law in the Land of the Copper Inuit, 1914–1930." *Canadian Law Review* 21 (1989): 1–64

Hickey, Eric. *Serial Murderers and Their Victims*. Belmont: Wadsworth, 1997

Hoffman, T. "Homicide: Reality and Realism." *Queen's Quarterly* 104, no. 2 (1997): 218–31

Hofstadter, Richard, and Michael Wallace. *American Violence: A Documentary History*. New York: Knopf, 1970

Holmes, W. Leslie. *Where Shadows Linger: The Untold Story of the RCMP's Olson Murders Investigation*. Surrey, BC: Heritage House, 2000

Hunt, William. "Jack London's Lynching: A Murder on Lituya Bay in 1899." *Alaska Journal* 15, no. 1 (1985): 20–3

Hustak, Alan. *They Were Hanged*. Toronto: James Lorimer, 1987

Iacovetta, Franca. *Such Hardworking People: Italian Immigrants in Postwar Toronto*. Montreal: McGill-Queen's University Press, 1992

Ireland, Robert. "Insanity and the Unwritten Law." *American Journal of Legal History* 32, no. 2 (1988): 157–72

Johnson, Holly. "Homicide in Canada." *Canadian Social Trends*, Winter 1987, 2–6

Kelleher, Michael. *Flash Point: The American Mass Murderer.* Westport: Praeger, 1997

Kelley, Thomas P. *Rat River Trapper: The Story of Albert Johnson, the Mad Trapper.* Don Mills, Ont.: Paperjacks, 1972

Kostelniuk, James. *Wolves among Sheep: The True Story of Murder in a Jehovah's Witness Community.* Toronto: HarperCollins, 2000

Kramer, Reinhold, and Thomas Mitchell. *Walk towards the Gallows.* Toronto: Oxford University Press, 2002

Lane, Roger. *Murder in America.* Columbus: Ohio State University Press, 1997

Levin, Jack, and James Fox. *Mass Murder: America's Growing Menace.* New York: Plenum Press, 1985

Leyton, Elliott. *Hunting Humans: The Rise of the Modern Multiple Murderer.* Toronto: McClelland & Stewart, 1995

– *Men of Blood: Murder in Everyday Life.* Toronto: McClelland & Stewart, 1997

Limerick, Patricia. *The Legacy of Conquest: The Unbroken Past of the American West.* New York: Norton, 1987

Longstreth, T. Morris. *The Silent Force: Scenes from the Life of the Mounted Police of Canada.* New York and London: Century Company, 1927

Loo, Tina. *Making Law, Order, and Authority in British Columbia, 1821–1871.* Toronto: University of Toronto Press, 1994

McClellan, Catherine. *My Old People Say: An Ethnographic Survey of Southern Yukon Territory.* 2 vols. Ottawa: National Museums of Canada, 1975

McGrath, Robin. "Angulalik's Trial." *Beaver* 79, no. 2 (1999): 2–29

McKanna, Clare, Jr. "Alcohol, Handguns, and Homicide in the American West: A Tale of Three Counties, 1880-1920." *Western Historical Quarterly* 26, no. 4 (1995): 455–82

– *Homicide, Race, and Justice in the American West, 1880-1920.* Tuscon: University of Arizona Press, 1997

– "Murderers All: The Treatment of Indian Defendants in Arizona Territory, 1880–1912." *American Indian Quarterly* 17, no. 3 (1993): 359–69

– *The Trial of "Indian Joe": Race and Justice in the Nineteenth-Century West.* Lincoln: University of Nebraska Press, 2003

McLaren, Angus. "Males, Migrants, and Murder in British Columbia, 1900–1923." In *On the Case: Explorations in Social History*, ed. Franca Iacovetta and Wendy Mitchinson. Toronto: University of Toronto Press, 1998

McLaren, John, et al., eds. *Law for the Elephant, Law for the Beaver: Essays in the Legal History of the North American West*. Regina: Canadian Plains Research Centre, 1992

Macleod, R. *The NWMP and Law Enforcement*. Toronto: University of Toronto Press, 1976

Malcolm, M.J. *Murder in the Yukon: The Case against George O'Brien*. Saskatoon: Western Producer Prairie Books, 1982

Malmquist, Carl. *Homicide: A Psychiatric Perspective*. Washington: American Psychiatric Press, 1996

Milgaard, Joyce, with Peter Edwards. *A Mother's Story: The Fight to Free My Son David*. Toronto: Doubleday Canada, 1999

Millman, Lawrence, and Gregory Manchess. "Pursuing Justice in the Arctic." *Smithsonian* 29, no. 2 (1998): 74–8

Milton, Frank. *More Than a Crime: Studies in Murder by Legal Process*. London: Pall Mall, 1962

Mocho, Jill. *Murder and Justice in Frontier New Mexico, 1821–1846*. Albuquerque: University of New Mexico Press, 1997

Monkkonen, Eric. "The American State from the Bottom Up: Of Homicides and Courts." *Law and Society Review* 24, no. 2 (1990): 521–33

Morrison, W.R. "Canadian Sovereignty and the Inuit of the Central and Eastern Arctic." *Études/Inuit/Studies* 10, nos. 1–2 (1986): 245–59

– "Eagle over the Arctic: Americans in the Canadian North, 1867–1985." *Canadian Review of American Studies* 18 (spring 1987): 61–75

– "Imposing the British Way: The Mounted Police and the Klondike Gold Rush." In *Policing the Empire: Government, Authority, and Control, 1830–1940*, ed. D. Killingray. Manchester: Manchester University Press, 1991

– "Policing the Boomtown: The Mounted Police as a Social Force on the Klondike," *Northern Review* 6 (winter 1990): 81–97

– *Showing the Flag: The Mounted Police and Canadian Sovereignty in the North, 1894–1925*. Vancouver: University of British Columbia Press, 1985

Moyles, R.G. *British Law and Arctic Men*. Saskatoon: Western Producer Prairie Books, 1979

Nash, Jay. *Murder, America: Homicide in the United States from the Revolution to the Present*. New York: Simon and Schuster, 1980

Newton, Michael. *Hunting Humans: An Encyclopedia of Modern Serial Killers*. Port Townsend: Loompanics, 1990

North, Dick. *The Mad Trapper of Rat River*. Toronto: Macmillan, 1972

– *Trackdown: The Search for the Mad Trapper*. Toronto: Macmillan, 1989

Paciocco, David. *Getting Away with Murder: The Canadian Criminal Justice System.* Toronto: Irwin, 1999

Pate, J. "Indians on Trial in a White Man's Court." *Great Plains Journal* 14, no. 1 (1974): 56–71

Pincus, Jonathan. *Base Instincts: What Makes Killers Kill?* New York: W.W. Norton, 2001

Price, G. "The King v. Alikomiak." In *Glimpses of Canadian Legal History,* ed. D. Gibson and W.W. Pue. Winnipeg: Legal Research Institute of the University of Manitoba, 1991

Pritchard, David. "Race, Homicide, and Newspapers." *Journalism Quarterly* 62, no. 3 (1985): 500–7

Radford, Jill, and Dianna Russell, eds. *Femicide: The Politics of Woman Killing.* Toronto: Maxwell Macmillan, 1992

Rapaport, Elizabeth. "The Death Penalty and Gender Discrimination." *Law and Society* 25, no. 2 (1991): 367–83.

Rasmussen, Knud. *Intellectual Culture of the Copper Eskimo.* Copenhagen: Gyldendalske Boghandel, 1932

Reid, John Phillip. "Certainty of Vengeance: The Hudson's Bay Company and Retaliation in Kind against Indian Offenders in New Caledonia." *Magazine of Western History* 34, no. 1 (1993): 4–17

– *Patterns of Vengeance: Cross-Cultural Homicide in the North American Fur Trade.* Pasadena: Ninth Judicial Historical Society, 1999

– "Principles of Vengeance: Fur Trappers, Indians, and Retaliation for Homicide in the Transboundary North American West." *Western Historical Quarterly* 24, no. 1 (1993) 21–43

Revitch, Eugene, and Louis Schlesinger. *Psychopathology of Homicide.* Springfield: Charles Thomas, 1981

Rohrbough, Malcolm. *Days of Gold: The California Gold Rush and the American Nation.* Los Angeles: University of California Press, 1997

Ross, Drew. *The Eyes of a Killer: A Psychiatrist's Journey through the Murderer's World.* New York: Plenum, 1998

Ross, Jeffrey Ian, ed. *Violence in Canada: Sociopolitical Perspectives.* Don Mills: Oxford, 1995

Schloss, Barbara, and N.A.Giesbrecht. *Murder in Canada: A Report on Capital and Non-Capital Murder Statistics, 1961–1970.* Toronto: University of Toronto Centre of Criminology, 1972

Schuh, Cornelia. "Justice on the Northern Frontier: Early Murder Trials of Native Accused." *Criminal Law Quarterly* 74 (1979–80)

Selleck, Lee, and Francis Thompson. *Dying for Gold: The True Story of the Giant Mine Murders.* Toronto: Harper Perennial, 1998

Siggins, Maggie. *A Canadian Tragedy: JoAnn and Colin Thatcher, a Story of Love and Hate.* Toronto: Macmillan, 1985

Silverman, Robert, and Leslie Kennedy. *Deadly Deeds: Murder in Canada.* Scarborough: Nelson, 1993

Simmie, Lois. *The Secret Lives of Sgt. John Wilson: A True Story of Love and Murder.* Vancouver: Greystone Books, 1995

Starkins, Edward. *Who Killed Janet Smith? The 1924 Vancouver Killing That Remains Canada's Most Intriguing Unsolved Murder.* Toronto: Macmillan, 1984

Statistics Canada, *Canadian Crime Statistics.* Ottawa: The Centre/Le Centre, 1985

– *Homicide in Canada: A Statistical Synopsis.* Ottawa: Ministry of Industry, Trade, and Commerce, 1976

Steele, S.B. *Forty Years in Canada.* London: H. Jenkins, 1915

Stone, Thomas. "Atomistic Order and Frontier Violence: Miners and Whalemen in the Nineteenth-Century Yukon." *Ethonology* 22 (October 1983): 327–39

Strange, Carolyn. "The Lottery of Death: Capital Punishment, 1867–1976. *Manitoba Law Journal* 23, no. 3 (1996): 594–619

– "Murder and Meanings in U.S. Historiography." *Feminist Studies* 25, no. 3 (1999): 679–97

Swainger, J.S. *The Canadian Department of Justice and the Completion of Confederation, 1867–78.* Vancouver: University of British Columbia Press, 2000

Turrell, Rob. "It's a Mystery: The Royal Prerogative of Mercy in England, Canada, and South Africa." *Crime, Histoire, et Sociétés* (Switzerland), 4, no. 1 (2000): 83–101

Vidmar, Neil. "The Canadian Criminal Jury: Searching for a Middle Ground." *Law and Contemporary Problems* 62 (spring 1999): 141–72

Walford, Bonny. *Lifers: The Stories of Eleven Women Serving Life Sentences for Murder.* Montreal: Eden, 1987

Wallace, W. Stewart. *Murders and Mysteries: A Canadian Series.* Toronto: Macmillan, 1931

Weyeneth, Robert. "History, He Wrote: Murder, Politics, and the Challenges of Public History in a Community with a Secret." *Public Historian* 16, no. 2 (1994): 51–73

White, Richard. *It's Your Misfortune and None of My Own: A New History of the American West*. Norman: University of Oklahoma Press, 1991

Wiebe, Rudy. *The Mad Trapper: A Novel* (school edition). Toronto: McClelland & Stewart, 1987

Williams, Stephen. *Invisible Darkness: The Strange Case of Paul Bernardo and Karla Homolka*. Toronto: Little, Brown, 1996

Wilson, Colin. *A Criminal History of Mankind*. London: Granada, 1984

Zaslow, Morris. *The Northward Expansion of Canada*. Toronto: McClelland & Stewart, 1988

– *The Opening of the Canadian North*. Toronto: McClelland & Stewart, 1971

Index